The

GREAT CHESS
TOURNAMENTS

and

Their Stories

.

Also by Andy Soltis

THE BEST GAMES OF BORIS SPASSKY

MORPHY CHESS MASTERPIECES
(With Fred Reinfeld)

AMERICAN CHESS CHAMPIONS:
FROM MORPHY TO FISCHER
(With Arthur Bisguier)

The

GREAT CHESS
TOURNAMENTS
and
Their Stories

■

ANDY SOLTIS

CHILTON BOOK COMPANY
Radnor, Pennsylvania

Copyright © 1975 by Andrew Soltis

First Edition   *All Rights Reserved*

Published in Radnor, Pa., by Chilton Book Company
and simultaneously in Don Mills, Ontario, Canada
by Thomas Nelson & Sons, Ltd.

Manufactured in the United States of America

Designed by Anne Churchman

LIBRARY OF CONGRESS CATALOGING IN PUBLICATION DATA

Soltis, Andrew.
    The great chess tournaments and their stories.

    Includes indexes.
    1. Chess—Tournaments.   2. Chess—Biography.
I. Title.
GV1455.S67   794.1'57   75–1202
ISBN 0–8019–6138–6

Preface

The great tournaments you'll find described in these pages are not always the strongest contests ever held. AVRO 1938 is left out, as is Carlsbad 1929, St. Petersburg 1895–1896, Moscow 1935, and several others. In selecting the tournaments and games to highlight, I've avoided those that are too close to one another in time and physical location, while seeking the occasions of the best stories, the most interesting games, and the most remarkable personalities.

I want to thank *The British Chess Magazine* for allowing me to quote from their reprint of the London 1883 tournament book. Other excellent paperbacks that were helpful and that belong in the library of any chess fan are *BCM*'s St. Petersburg 1914, Dover Publications' Hastings 1895, New York 1924, and Nottingham 1936, and RHM Chess Publishing's San Antonio 1972. Valuable background information was gleaned from articles by Irving Chernev and Paul H. Little in *Chess Review*, Anthony Saidy in *Chess Life and Review*, Harold Lommer in *American Chess Bulletin*, and from Dr. J. Hannak's fine biography, *Emanuel Lasker: The Life of a Chess Master*.

ANDY SOLTIS

Contents

The
GREAT CHESS TOURNAMENTS
and
Their Stories

■

Introduction

What?
A Chess Tournament?

Like all new ideas, it did seem a bit bizarre. A chess tournament? Why a chess tournament? How would it work? Who would watch it? Who would care?

There were a great many new ideas on display at the Crystal Palace in the Victorian London of 1851. But the chess tournament being organized so conscientiously by St. George's Chess Club appeared a bit odd.

After all, wasn't chess basically an entertainment and not a sport? And even if it could be considered a sport, didn't it involve only two people at a time? A tournament meant several competitors. If there were spectators—that is, if anyone came—how could the players concentrate? And wouldn't the whole thing just drag on and on and on?

No one really knew if the idea would work—if an international tournament could be organized and be of interest to anyone besides the players—simply because no one had ever done it before.

The game itself was several centuries old, but chess or-

1

ganization was just beginning to accelerate in the nineteenth century. The first correspondence match of consequence, between players from London and Edinburgh, had taken place twenty-five years before the London tournament. The first chess magazine, *Le Palamède*, had appeared in France ten years after the match and the first newspaper columns were just appearing.

The increasing tempo was clearer to any fan of over-the-board play. During the previous century there had been fewer than half a dozen serious matches, chiefly those of François André Danican Philidor (1726–95) of Paris. The first half of the nineteenth century had already seen the marathon eighty-five-game match between the French and British stars, Louis Charles Mahe de LaBourdonnais and Alexander McDonnell, the several matches of the Frenchman's successor, Pierre Saint Amant, and the latter's loss of the unofficial world championship to Howard Staunton of London.

But instead of individual matches, how much better it would be to stage a general tournament with sixteen of the best players in the world. No one, for example, knew how really good the players of Budapest, Josef Szen and Johann Löwenthal, were except that they had beaten the best of the Parisians in a postal match. The strength of the seven German masters, the "Berlin Pleiades," was also something between a legend and a mystery. And it was said that in the Russia of Czar Nicholas I a passion for chess was taken for granted. But no one knew for certain.

So in the winter of 1850–1851 letters went out to beckon the world's masters to convene in London during the Great Exposition for what was clearly the most challenging chess competition ever devised. The letters went to four German masters including Adolf Anderssen, a Breslau mathematics teacher known for composing problems, and three of the famous Pleiades themselves—Carl Mayet, Bernhard Horwitz, and Baron Tassilo von Heydebrand und der Lasa. The letters also summoned Alexander Petrov, Carl Jaenisch, and I. C. Shumov of St. Petersburg and Szen and Löwenthal of Hungary. The leading Parisian, Lionel Kieseritsky, a native of Livonia, was considered one of the favorites. Saint Amant was sought, but he was off in California serving as French consul. And from the better British clubs there were places for Howard Staunton, H. E. Bird, Elijah Williams, Marmaduke Wyvill, and others.

The London tournament, despite the worries that accompany the execution of every new enterprise, was expected to be a landmark. And no one in chess has ever been disappointed.

The sport that is tournament chess has changed considerably in the past 120 years. Some 800 or so international events have been played, and prizes have grown larger, rules more complex, preparations for play more involved, and the level of play, inevitably, greatly improved. But there are elements of drama and skill that unite all tournaments.

So, for the perhaps 90 percent of the chess audience who have never witnessed an international tournament, a few explanations are in order.

Every tournament begins with people who want to organize and finance it. This is no small detail. An event of twelve players, a third of them from foreign countries, can cost as little as $2,000 and require the part-time help of three people. Or it can be a prestigious sixteen- to twenty-player event with more than half the competitors from abroad. The expense then runs as high as $100,000 and requires a cast of dozens.

The 1851 tournament had a prize fund of £355, but there were few other expenses. It was expected that players would pay their own transportation and living expenses and even come up with a £5 entry fee. Today you can win $1,000 from the brilliancy prize alone at a tournament such as Manila 1973. And the tournament committee usually meets all the players' costs while they play.

The 1851 organizers were mainly officials and members of the St. George's Club who were interested in holding an historic event to determine the best players in the world. Since then we have seen other men and motives at work. In 1925 the first tournament entirely paid for by a government was held in Moscow. Government funding is common in Communist nations today. In the business world there are four major corporations in Holland alone that finance tournaments. British newspapers, Dutch steel mills, American fast-food entrepreneurs, as well as noncommercial figures as diverse as the Prince of Monaco, the wife of cellist Gregor Piatigorsky, and the entertainer Bobby Darin have offered to be patrons in recent years.

Today a tournament will have a staff separate from the fund-raising committee. The staff is headed by a director who may also be called judge, referee, or arbiter. He tries to keep both the tournament committee – the organizers – and the players happy while enforcing the rules of the game. The title of International Judge is currently awarded by the international chess federation (FIDE, or Fédération Internationale Des Échecs). A FIDE-certified judge has to be experienced in national events, have a solid knowledge of international rules, and be understandable in two of the FIDE languages (French, Russian, English, German, and Spanish).

The tournament director will have several assistants who record the moves of each game so that the number of moves played is known and so that the position on the board is supported by hard evidence. Behind this staff there may be several unknown faces – "go-fers," who bring snacks and soft drinks to players during rounds; wallboard helpers, the ballboys of chess, who keep the larger audience informed of the games' progress by moving giant wood, metal, or plastic cutout pieces on five-to-twenty-five-foot tall wallboards; office personnel, who type tournament bulletins, notify news media of round-by-round results, arrange trips and excursions for the players for the days when no round is scheduled, make sure that players get their daily spending allowance and that their hotel and return trip arrangements are in order, set up the traditional awards banquet, and in general, act as troubleshooters.

The opening event of a tournament is the rules meeting — a preliminary get-together at which the players discuss the rules of play. Nowadays this is usually a formality, and most of the attention is directed toward the drawing of lots. In London, however, the rules meeting was a key part of the first tournament because when the invitees sat down on May 26, 1851, they had no precedent to follow. They decided among other things to allow unlimited time for thought and for the so-called knockout system of pairings. This is the system we see today in America only in contests such as professional football, hockey, and basketball eliminations. The players are randomly paired in the first round, and losers are eliminated from further play. The winners keep meeting winners until there is only one survivor. The problems of this arrangement quickly became apparent in 1851, but more of that later.

Even as late as the 1920s the rules meeting was an important event because new regulations were frequently being pushed into acceptance by some of the more powerful players. At New York 1927, for example, José Capablanca insisted on a rule that draw offers be communicated through tournament officials. The comic results of this can be found in Chapter Five.

At the rules meeting the players are also notified of the tournament schedule. Some tournaments, like St. Petersburg 1909, are planned so that each game can be completed in one day. The first move may come at 10 or 11 A.M. Today it is more popular to begin rounds in the late afternoon or evening and then adjourn them after five hours of play. The adjournments are finished the following morning or, in the more leisurely programmed tournaments, on an "Adjournment Day" in the following week. There are also at least one or two "Free Days" on the calendar with nothing scheduled. It is not unusual in very strong tournaments and matches to find players at work only three days a week unless they "blunder" into an adjournment.

The drawing of lots is the feature attraction of the rules meeting. In 1851 the tournament committee placed eight white and eight yellow numbered tickets in a ballot box.

The recipient of white ticket #1 had the white pieces in the first game against the player who drew yellow ticket #1.

After the round-robin system — in which each player plays everyone else in the event — came into vogue following the London 1862 tournament, the initial drawing held even greater weight. It told a player not only whom he met in the first round but in what sequence he would face the rest of the field and whether he would have white or black in the first game against each of them. (At Hastings 1895 and New York 1924 it was thought that this gave too much of an advantage to players who prepare openings in advance. Accordingly, a modified system was used.)

The actual drawing has remained very much the same since 1851. The players in turn draw slips of paper from a box or a hat.* After the numbers are recorded by the director, the pairings for each round can be deduced by checking a standard pairing chart. (Sample: For eleven or twelve players — Round One: 1 vs. 12, 11 vs. 2, 3 vs. 10, 9 vs. 4, 5 vs. 8, 7 vs. 6.) As any experienced round-robin player knows, it's best to draw a low number because in a tournament with an even number of contestants, the low digits will have White more often than Black.

Finally, the tournament begins. In 1851 the action took place in the main room of the St. George's Club at 5 Cavendish Square. Hotel ballrooms, civic auditoriums, and university assembly halls have been popular sites over the years. Nowadays the playing tables are usually roped off from the spectators' chairs or set above them on a platform. Wallboards stand on the far side of the players, facing the audience.

As the playing hour arrives, stewards begin the clocks of the players who have White. A gong signals the beginning of play; in a modern tournament it is heard five hours later to signal the end of the session. Or at least it should be.

---

* Some ceremonies are more exotic. For instance, at the eleventh Capablanca Memorial tournament in Camaguey, Cuba, in March 1974 each player chose a local schoolchild to dive into a swimming pool near the tournament site. The children each plucked a conch shell from the pool's bottom. Inside the conch was the player's pairing number.

When, as at Nottingham 1936, a player is not notified by a gong or other device that he must seal a move to adjourn the game, another great tournament argument is sure to break out.

Arguments are almost a staple of big-league play. There are always complaints about pairing improprieties, adjournment snafus, the quality of lighting, size of pieces, or whether a draw was offered or a piece was touched. As incidents described later will show, Robert J. Fischer is not unique. Réti and Alekhine argued for the better part of an hour over a simple point of rules that every tournament player should know. Euwe and Capablanca exchanged harsh words during a critical game at Nottingham and the Cuban blamed a key loss to Flohr on it. Nimzovich ran to tournament director Maroczy about Vidmar's "threat" to smoke a cigarette. Browne blew up because Mecking made time pressure moves with one hand and punched his clock with another. Temperament is nothing new.

Meanwhile, the opening moves are usually played quickly. The rhythm of play is not established until the second half-hour of the round; when each player finds a pattern of thought. Every few moves he may take fifteen or twenty minutes for a "big think." Most other moves are played after three or four minutes of thought.

During the session of play the contestants sustain their nervous energy with little habits. Alekhine loved to curl wisps of his hair. Richard Teichmann twirled his moustache. Lasker puffed on his ration of five cigars. Robert Byrne chain-smokes cigarettes. Petrosian is one of the great pacers today. When Fischer was thinking about his moves during their 1971 Candidates match in Buenos Aires, the Armenian would stride back and forth on a side of the playing stage. After Fischer objected that it was annoying him, the officials arranged for a special offstage pacing court for Petrosian. Other players sway their legs at the board, bob their heads up and down, grimace at the position—even when it looks good—or shoot dark glances at the opponent. Some hum tunes to themselves.

There was no time pressure in 1851, and so one of the

great elements of chess drama was missing. Some players took up to two and a half hours for a single move, according to Staunton. "When a player, *upon system*, consumes hours over moves when minutes might suffice and depends, not upon out-maneuvering, but out-sitting his antagonist, patience ceases to be a virtue." The target of these remarks was Elijah Williams, who defeated Staunton for third place.

The audience is the last actor in the tournament drama— and, hopefully, a silent one. They analyze the positions to themselves, turning now from the Rook endgame on board two to examine the possible Knight sacrifice on board seven. The audience is a catalyst. How many speculative offers of material have been made to please an appreciative gallery! Most grandmasters would never acknowledge such influence: They play the board, not the man or the gallery. But secretly, they can't always ignore it.

The opening round at Cavendish Square was something of a letdown. Petrov, "The Northern Philidor," sent word that he couldn't make the historic event. Major Jaenisch, an officer in the Czar's army, and Shumov, who served in the admiralty, were reported on their way but hadn't shown up yet. Two reserve players, E. S. Kennedy and Brodie, were added to fill up the sixteen-player lineup. Von der Lasa, like his fellow diplomat Saint Amant, is also tied up by national concerns.

At the rules meeting it was agreed that each pairing would consist of a match of the best-of-three games with draws not counting. Some invitees preferred best-of-five, but in a long and sometimes heated exchange of views, the shorter schedule was voted.

The first cycle created four sensations. It was no surprise when Szen and Staunton rolled over their unheralded opponents, Newham and Brodie. And Horwitz, ostensibly representing Germany but actually a London resident, came back as expected to eliminate Bird after losing the second game. Bird, a twenty-one-year-old accountant who was to become one of the world's experts on railway finance, had more than a half-century of tournament play ahead of him.

But three of the highly touted foreigners were upset. First to go down was Johann Jakob Löwenthal, a Budapest merchant just returning from America, where he had taken refuge after the Hungarian rebellion of 1848 fizzled. After touring the States, "discovering" Paul Morphy, the 12-year-old prodigy of New Orleans, and beginning negotiations for opening a "smoking and chess divan" in Cincinnati, Löwenthal accepted the London invitation.

Unfortunately, he was worn out by the transatlantic trip and lost the first and third games to Williams. This was the only major tournament in which Williams ever played. But consider his skill. The 1850s were a period of "close openings," as Morphy noted with disdain, and Williams anticipated the theoretical revolution of the Hypermoderns by some sixty years.

DUTCH DEFENSE

J. J. Löwenthal	*E. Williams*
1 P–Q4	P–K3
2 P–K3	P–KB4
3 P–QB4	N–KB3
4 N–KB3	B–N5ch
5 N–B3	BxNch!
6 PxB	P–B4

This is actually an improvement over 6 . . . O–O; 7 B–Q3, P–QN3; 8 O–O, B–N2; 9 Q–B2, B–K5 as played by Reshevsky and Alekhine in 1938! Black will set up a pawn structure with blocks at QB4, Q3, K3, and KB4. This formation is attributed by the late Hans Kmoch to Williams's colleague, Marmaduke Wyvill.

7	B–Q3	Q–K2
8	O–O	O–O
9	P–QR4?	. . .

This kind of transparent tactics thrived in the early days of tournament play. White plans for 10 PxP, QxP; 11 B–R3 winning the Exchange. However, 10 PxP would probably be met by 10 . . . N–R3! and 11 . . . NxP.

9	. . .	P–Q3
10	Q–B2	N–B3
11	B–R3	P–QN3
12	KR–K1	B–R3?

Here is exceptionally modern play. Black intends 13 . . . QR–B1 and 14 . . . N–QR4 to restrain and cripple White's Queenside. But the idea gets Black into big trouble tactically.

13	P–K4!	PxKP
14	BxKP	B–N2
15	BxN!	BxB
16	P–Q5	B–Q2
17	PxP	B–B3

Black's last series was forced. On 14 . . . NxB he would lose the KP and 17 . . . BxP would drop a piece to 18 N–N5.

White is a pawn ahead but faces threats of ... BxN, ... N–N5 and ... N–R4–B5. He can try one of four possibilities:

(1) 18 Q–Q3 or 18 Q–K2 or 18 R–K3, each of which are met by 18 ... N–N5. On 18 Q–Q3, N–N5, for example, Black threatens 19 ... BxN and 20 ... N–K4.

(2) 18 Q–B5, P–N3, and White does not have a convenient square for the Queen.

(3) 18 N–Q2, N–N5; 19 P–B3, Q–R5!; 20 N–B1, BxP?; 21 P–K7! would win, but 20 ... N–K4! is difficult for White.

(4) 18 B–B1! (best), BxN; 19 PxB, N–R4; 20 Q–K4! with advantage to Löwenthal now that his Bishop is back in the game, his Queen is centralized, and his Pawn secure. No better would be 19 ... QR–K1; 20 B–N5, P–KR3; 21 B–R4, P–KN4; 22 Q–N6ch.

18	N–N5?	P–KR3
19	N–R3	N–N5!
20	Q–K2	N–K4
21	P–B4	N–N3

White is about to lose his extra Pawn to 22 ... R–B3, e.g., 22 Q–N4, R–B3; 23 P–B5, N–K4; 24 Q–R5, QR–KB1; 25 R–KB1, B–K5. White cannot support his KBP with P–N4 in this line without facing ... N–B6ch.

22	P–N3?	R–B3
23	Q–R5?	RxP!
24	RxR	QxR

Now Black can meet 25 P–B5 with 25 ... Q–K6ch; 26
N–B2, N–K4, or 26 K–B1, B–B6!
Löwenthal played 25 N–B2 and after 25 ... R–K1
(threatening 26 ... Q–K8ch) 26 P–R3, Q–K6! saw that
27 QxN allows 27 ... Q–B6 and mates. So he chose the
hopeless ending with 27 Q–N4, QxQBP; 28 R–KB1, QxB;
29 K–R2, Q–KB6 and resigned on the thirty-eighth move.
Wyvill, who was more at home in Parliament than at
the chessboard, pulled the second upset by winning two
straight from Lowe of Germany. Another German, Mayet,
prepared for a quick voyage home by losing to Captain H. A.
Kennedy.
The German colors, however, were salvaged by Adolf
Anderssen, one of the nicest men ever to rise in the chess
world. He had spent the early years of his life acquiring the
skills to teach mathematics and only entered competitive
chess at the late age of 30. A contemporary, the Irish player
and columnist Rev. George Alcock MacDonnell, described
him as "massive in figure, with an honest voice, a sweet
smile, and a countenance as pleasing as it was expressive."
A potbelly and whiskers were to come in Anderssen's
later years.
When Anderssen was paired with Lionel Kieseritsky in
the very first round, the flaws of the knockout system were
revealed. Kieseritsky was Saint Amant's successor, and the
first of a long line of Eastern Europeans to dominate
Parisian chess. (His successors included Daniel Harrwitz,
a native of Anderssen's Breslau; Samuel Rosenthal, Jean
Taubenhaus, and David Janowski of Poland; and Savielly
Tartakover and Nicholas Rossolimo of Russia.)
Although Kieseritsky had lost a short match three years
before to the historian Henry Buckle, the Livonian's club
play had established him as one of the tournament favorites.

But his pairing with Anderssen in the first round made it instantly clear that one of the strongest players had to be eliminated at the outset. It was Kieseritsky who drew one and lost two.

The first-round surprises chastened the tournament organizers, who then decided that the remaining matches should be best-of-seven-games to ensure that accidental losses would not further depopulate the tournament of strong players.

The second cycle saw only one easy victory—Williams winning four straight games from the unknown Mucklow, who was even slower than Williams. According to Staunton, Mucklow avoided elimination in the first cycle only by lulling his opponent, E. S. Kennedy, to sleep. After his humiliating loss to Williams, Mucklow disappeared. He forefeited his remaining games but still ended up with eighth prize.

Wyvill eliminated Captain Kennedy in a seesaw match, and Staunton beat Horwitz four games to two. Today Staunton is remembered largely as the man who did everything he could to deny Paul Morphy an unmuddied reputation as the world's best player. But in his day Staunton was a titan and one of the most progressive forces in the game's history. Besides organizing this tournament, the Englishman wrote both the most influential chess column of the era in the *Illustrated London News* and perhaps the most important chess book of the nineteenth century, *The Chess Players Handbook*. He also approved the pattern of chess pieces that is considered standard today—the Staunton pattern. As a player Staunton defeated Saint Amant, Horwitz, Harrwitz, and Williams in their prime. Bobby Fischer, a century later, listed him as one of the ten greatest players in history and called him the most profound opening analyst ever.

As is the case with so many players, Staunton's enormous energy and combativeness in personal confrontations belied his agonizingly slow-paced, trench-warfarelike style of play at the board. If an opponent didn't have the

positional equipment to outplay him, Staunton could turn
a solid position into a devastating one:

STAUNTON–HORWITZ: *1 P–QB4, P–K3; 2 N–QB3, P–KB4;
3 P–KN3!, N–KB3; 4 B–N2, P–B3; 5 P–Q3, N–R3; 6
P–QR3, B–K2; 7 P–K3, O–O; 8 KN–K2, N–B2; 9 O–O,
P–Q4; 10 P–N3, Q–K1; 11 B–N2, Q–B2; 12 R–B1, B–Q2;
13 P–K4!, BPxP?; 14 PxKP, QR–Q1; 15 P–K5!, KN–K1;
16 P–B4, QPxP?; 17 PxP, B–B4ch; 18 K–R1, B–K6; 19
R–N1, P–KN3?; 20 Q–N3, B–B1; 21 N–K4!, B–N3; 22
QR–Q1, N–R3; 23 Q–B3, RxR; 24 RxR, N–B4; 25 N–Q6,
Q–QB2; 26 Q–B2, N–N2; 27 P–N4!, Q–K2; 28 B–Q4,
Q–QB2; 29 P–QR4, N–R3; 30 P–QB5!, B–R4; 31 Q–N3,
P–N3; 32 N–K4!, PxP; 33 N–B6ch, K–R1; 34 Q–KR3,
N–K1; 35 B–R1, NxN?; 36 PxN, K–N1; 37 B–K5, Q–QN2;
38 B–K4, Q–KB2; 39 N–N1!, B–Q1; 40 P–N5, B–N2;
41 N–B3, R–K1; 42 B–Q6, BxP; 43 PxB, QxP; 44 N–N5,
Q–N2; 45 B–K5, Q–K2; 46 BxNP! Resigns.*

To tell the truth, most of the eighty-five games contested
at Cavendish Square are forgettable, and Staunton's winning technique here was one of the brighter spots.

Anderssen's second-round opponent was Szen, the
founder of the Budapest Chess Club and, at 46, one of
the oldest in the tournament. While his match with the
Breslau professor was still in doubt, they agreed that if
either one took the £183 first prize, he would give one-third
to the other. "Unbecoming arrangement," snorted Staunton
of the first tournament chess deal, albeit a comparatively
honest one.

Szen's eventual defeat left four finalists: Wyvill, Williams,
Staunton, and Anderssen. With three Englishmen among
the survivors, it seemed certain that the home crowd
would be pleased with the final rounds.

Both semifinal matches appeared to be runaways as
Williams and Anderssen won three straight. But Wyvill
made a fine recovery and allowed Williams only a draw in
the next five games. Staunton was less fortunate. He rallied

for one game and then succumbed to another furious Anderssen broadside. In contrast to Staunton's intricate maneuvers, Anderssen jumped in with both feet. Punch, punch, punch, and Staunton went down.

With his defeat came an explanation from Staunton that he was weakened by poor health, weak heart, overtaxed brain, and so on. He exercised the same excuse to explain his loss in a playoff match to Williams with third place at stake. However, Staunton did credit Williams's "great judgment" in this fine game. With White, Staunton began: *1 P–QB4, P–K3; 2 P–K3, P–KB4; 3 P–KN3, N–KB3; 4 B–N2, B–K2; 5 N–QB3, O–O; 6 KN–K2, B–N5?; 7 O–O, P–Q3; 8 P–Q4, BxN; 9 PxB?, Q–K2; 10 B–QR3, P–B4.*

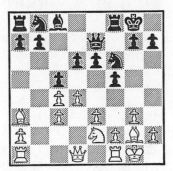

After a silly opening, Williams again has the Wyvill formation. Staunton, like Löwenthal, has misplaced his QB and proceeds to waste whatever initiative he has.

11	R–N1	P–K4
12	R–N5?!	P–QR3
13	R–N6?	QN–Q2
14	R–N1	P–K5!

In four moves Black's game has blossomed with Nimzo-vichian subtlety. He prepares to attack and win the QBP

with 15 . . . Q–B2; 16 P–Q5, N–K4. Now 15 Q–R4 makes
sense.

15	Q–Q2?	Q–B2
16	P–B3	QxP
17	PxKP	PxKP
18	B–R3	P–QN4!
19	N–B4	N–N3
20	B–KN2	Q–B2!

Another fine move, which leads to a positional rout of
Staunton's pieces within ten moves. This Williams was a
real player!

21	PxP	N–B5
22	Q–B1	Q–R2!

White's last chance to relieve pressure here is 23 PxP,
NxKP: 24 K–R1 sacrificing the Exchange.

23	R–K1	PxP
24	B–N2	P–N4
25	N–K2	B–N5
26	P–KR3	B–B6!
27	K–R2	QR–Q1
28	B–QR1	R–Q7
29	R–N2	KR–Q1

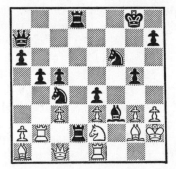

By protecting his advanced rook, Black threatens 30 . . . NxR and 31 . . . BxN. On 30 RxR, RxR; 31 B–B1 Black can penetrate for the kill with either . . . Q–Q2–Q6 or . . . Q–KN2–R3. The cutest line is 30 R–B2, BxN; 31 RxB, R–Q8!!

Staunton played 30 N–Q4 and resigned in seven moves: *30 . . . RxR; 31 BxR, PxN; 32 BPxP, BxB; 33 KxB, N–Q4; 34 K–R2, R–KB1; 35 Q–B2, Q–KB2; 36 R–K2, Q–B8; 37 B–B1, N–N5!.*

There were only two survivors left—the parliamentarian and the professor. Wyvill made a gallant fight. He lost the first game, drew the second, and carefully scored in the third. The next two games were tough battles, filled with errors. Anderssen took both and was one game from the top prize.

In the sixth game, Wyvill turned the tables in what the annotators like to call "a game of many vicissitudes." The seventh game gave Wyvill Black and he tried "The Sicilian Game," an opening with a bad reputation.* Played the way Wyvill does, the opening deserves that opinion: *1 P–K4, P–QB4; 2 B–B4?!, P–QR3; 3 P–QR4, N–QB3; 4 N–QB3, P–K3; 5 P–Q3, P–KN3; 6 KN–K2, B–N2; 7 O–O, KN–K2; 8 P–B4, O–O; 9 B–Q2, P–Q4; 10 B–N3, N–Q5; 11 NxN.*

---

* The first game of this last match illustrated the "latest" theory in the opening. Anderssen, with White, won quickly: 1 P–K4, P–QB4; 2 B–B4, N–QB3; 3 N–QB3, P–K3; 4 P–Q3, N–K4? 5 B–B4!, NxB; 6 PxN, P–QR3; 7 Q–K2, N–K2; 8 O–O–O, N–N3; 9 B–N3, B–K2; 10 P–B4, O–O; 11 P–B5, B–N4ch; 12 K–N1 PxP?; 13 PxP, R–K1; 14 Q–N4, N–B1; 15 N–B3, B–B3; 16 N–K4, P–QN4?; 17 B–B7!, Q–K2; 18 NxBch, QxN; 19 R–Q6!, N–K3; 20 PxN, QPxP; 21 KR–Q1, B–N2; 22 R–Q7, B–B3; 23 B–K5, BxN; 24 Q–N3, Q–N3; 25 QxB, PxP? 26 QxR Resigns.

Incidentally, one of the curious rules agreed upon at the players' meeting stipulated that the player who made the first move in a game could choose between the White and Black pieces. In the second Wyvill-Anderssen game, for example, the Englishman made the first move even though he marshalled the Black forces.

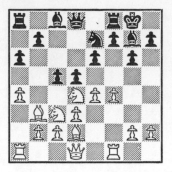

Now 11 . . . PxN! is thematic since the advanced QP will interfere with White's pieces while granting Black chances on the half-open QB-file. Perhaps Wyvill feared 11 . . . PxN; 12 N–K2, PxP; 13 PxP, P–Q6; 14 PxP, QxP; 15 B–N4! with clear advantage. However, 12 . . . B–Q2! is much safer. He played:

11	...	BxNch
12	K–R1	B–Q2?

What Black does to his game with this and the next two moves is criminal. Apparently it was just an oversight.

13	PxP	BxN?

Seeing that he could lose a Pawn, Black gives up the only defensive piece on the Kingside.

14	BxB	PxP?
15	B–B6!	

And White's game is won due to the threat of P–B5 and Q–Q2–R6. The decisive game of the world's first international tournament ended with *15 . . . B–K3; 16 P–B5!, BxP; 17 RxB!, PxR; 18 Q–R5, Q–Q3; 19 Q–R6, QxB; 20 QxQ Resigns.*

SCORETABLE

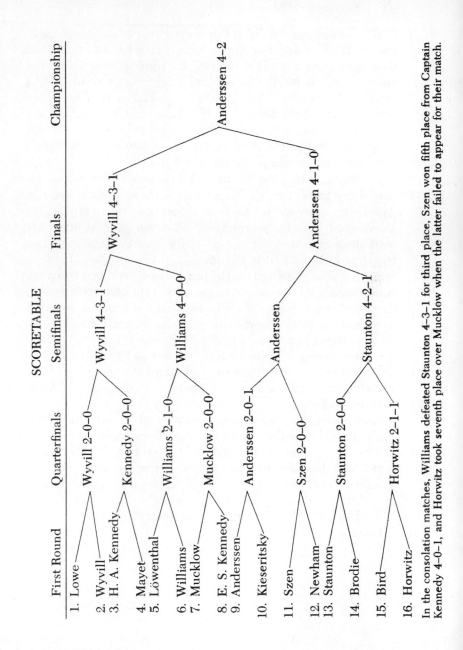

First Round   Quarterfinals   Semifinals   Finals   Championship

1. Lowe
Wyvill 2–0–0
2. Wyvill
Wyvill 4–3–1
3. H. A. Kennedy
Kennedy 2–0–0

4. Mayet
Williams 2–1–0
5. Löwenthal
Williams 4–0–0
6. Williams
Mucklow 2–0–0
7. Mucklow

Wyvill 4–3–1

8. E. S. Kennedy
Anderssen 2–0–1
9. Anderssen
Anderssen
10. Kieseritsky
Szen 2–0–0
11. Szen

Anderssen 4–1–0

12. Newham
Staunton 2–0–0
13. Staunton
Staunton 4–2–1
14. Brodie
Horwitz 2–1–1
15. Bird
16. Horwitz

Anderssen 4–2

In the consolation matches, Williams defeated Staunton 4–3–1 for third place, Szen won fifth place from Captain Kennedy 4–0–1, and Horwitz took seventh place over Mucklow when the latter failed to appear for their match.

What were the results of this weird idea of a chess tournament? Well, those directly involved liked it so much that they proceeded to the nearby London Chess Club for another tournament. The second event was a round robin starring Löwenthal, Kieseritsky, and Harrwitz. The latter was the club professional at the London Chess Club and had refused an invitation to the first tournament because it was organized by the rival St. George's Club. And with this the future of tournaments was established.

Löwenthal decided to make London his home, and he was there to renew his friendship with Morphy when the American arrived to take Europe by storm in 1858. Löwenthal became secretary of St. George's, founded his own magazine and club, and served as columnist of the *Illustrated News of the World.*

Szen, who finished fifth (and received one-third of Anderssen's first prize), disappeared from competition and died six years later. Wyvill and Williams never became involved in international play again. A pity. Kieseritsky was confined to a mental home in Paris within two years of the tournament and died without a sou shortly after. Staunton went into semiretirement and spent the rest of his time working on a new edition of Shakespeare's plays and belittling Anderssen.

Anderssen, of course, was recognized by all but Staunton's disciples as the unofficial champion of the world. But not being independently endowed, he returned to the math texts and blackboard, venturing abroad occasionally to produce great games like "The Evergreen" and eventually to hand the world title to Paul Morphy.

And, finally, Major Jaenisch arrived from Petrograd—a bit late.

I

Will the Real World
Champion Please Stand Up?

As a matter of fact there *was* a banquet at which a toast to the World Champion was raised, and both Wilhelm Steinitz and Johannes Zukertort stood up. But that was after London 1883, and that's getting ahead of the story.

Today chess enthusiasts tend to regard the last half of the nineteenth century as a fairly barren period for tournament chess — with one landmark at London 1851 and, at the other end, Hastings 1895. It is true that much of the historic chess of the period was played in man-to-man matches or in casual games. Paul Morphy, for example, played fewer than seventy-five serious games and only eighteen of them in tournament competition.

But there were at least a dozen powerful and exciting events over the half-century, and a majority of them — London 1851, London 1862, Dundee 1867, Hastings 1895, London 1883 and 1899 — were organized by the leading British clubs. This was no accident. Britain was where competitive chess could be found. It was the center of the chess world. To begin with, there were some fine English, Irish, and Scottish talents to play for the home colors. Bird, who we met briefly in 1851, Thomas Wilson Barnes, who had the best score against Morphy of anyone (eight wins, nineteen losses!), Samuel Standidge Boden, the coauthor with Kieseritsky of a now-defunct gambit, and, of course, John Henry "Black Death" Blackburne, were among the keenest playing minds of their day.

But London was also the center of chess organization, the capital of patronage and prestige. When Morphy wanted to prove that the players of the New World were as good as those of the Old, he went straight to Simpson's Divan in the Strand, to the Westminster Chess Club, and to St. George's. Both the Prague-born Steinitz and Riga-born Zukertort were professionals at these clubs in the 1870s and '80s. Emanuel Lasker spent a good part of the '90s in London, where he first gave the series of lectures that became *Common Sense in Chess* at the time of Hastings 1895.

We could also mention the earlier London club habitué, Ernest Falkbeer, an Austrian known for the famous counter-gambit that bears his name. And add Richard Teichmann and Bernhard Horwitz, who emigrated from Germany, or Isidor Gunsberg, who came from Hungary. There was even room for minor emigrant masters such as Rudolf Loman and Louis Van Vliet, both native sons of Amsterdam who later became the stars of the Divan.

So with no real national, not to mention international, chess bureaucracy, the British clubs, led by those of London, filled the void. It should be no surprise, then, that the first actor in the story of London 1883 was Löwenthal's successor as secretary of St. George's, James Innes Minchin.

In May of 1882 the most powerful of the Wiener Schach-kongresses was held in the Austrian capital with virtually every master in Europe attending. A record prize fund even lured Steinitz out of his nine-year hibernation. He promptly tied for first with Winawer ahead of Mason, Mackenzie, Zukertort, Tchigorin, Blackburne, Paulsen, and others.

The English, who had started it all in 1851, felt upstaged.

The leading organizer of the most active of British clubs, Minchin, summoned a meeting of club representatives in October. He prepared a circular that went to every gathering place for chess in the Empire asking for a subscription, or contribution. It read in part:

From that period [1862] such Tournaments have repeatedly taken place on the Continent, and on each occasion the interest of the Chess community in all countries has been increasingly stimulated by the closeness of the contests. . . . No master has yet made a monopoly of the chief prize. . . .

True enough. Everyone who aspired to the then-unofficial world title had scored first in at least one major tournament: Steinitz at Vienna 1873, Louis Paulsen in Leipzig 1877, Zukertort at Paris 1878, Russia's Simon Winawer at the recent Vienna congress, and Blackburne at Berlin 1881.

There were other leading figures: Berthold Englisch of Austria had shown himself to be the number-two player of the Dual Monarchy after Steinitz; George Henry Mackenzie had dominated the American contests so easily that he was spoken of as another Morphy; Mikhail Tchigorin closely followed Winawer's lead as the best Czarist representative; and Samuel Rosenthal was clearly the finest French master since Kieseritsky's heyday.

The problem for those seeking to establish a hierarchy of players—in the days before Elo points (see Chapter Nine)—was that since Anderssen's decline began in 1873, everyone had a claim to the world championship. Anderssen had lost matches to Steinitz, Zukertort, and Paulsen before his death in 1879. Steinitz hadn't lost in match play since then, but he had only ventured into one tournament in ten years. There were other claimants, and it was all very confusing.

The secretary of St. George's, James Minchin, concluded that by holding a great event in the spring of 1883 the British would be helping solve the mystery of the chess world—the identity of the best player. The subscription

lists filled up quickly. More than £600 were contributed
by St. George's Club members alone — including Marmaduke Wyvill, now retired from tournament play, and his
parliamentary colleague, Lord Randolph Churchill.* From
Bristol and Liverpool, Newcastle and Oxford University
subscriptions poured in. During military service in India
Minchin had struck up an acquaintance with the Maharaja
of Vizayanagaram. The Maharaja's son sent in a £200
contribution, and a minor tournament played concurrently
with the master section was organized with the funds.

The tournament, scheduled to begin on April 26th,
loomed as the most exciting chess event since 1851. If
Steinitz could win again, his title would be confirmed as
unofficial champion. If someone else took first place, a
match with Steinitz was virtually assured.

One player who wasn't at Victoria Hall for the first
round was Paulsen, one of the world's best players in
Anderssen's day. The German-born Paulsen was a blindfold master, an opening theoretician who was decades
ahead of his time, but he was notoriously slow.

An hour's thought over one move was common for him.
On one occasion he studied the position for considerably
longer than that and then moved his Queen one square.
"Such a long thought, such a short move," an onlooker
derisively noted. On another occasion he forfeited a game
for excessive thought in a hopelessly drawn position. What
was he thinking about? Well, Paulsen explained, if he
offered a draw, he would have to play the same player again,
and he was wondering what opening he would choose in
the second game.

---

* Lord Churchill was an avid player from his student days at Oxford on.
"It puts my thoughts into other channels, and I can free myself entirely
from all political cares when I play the game," he remarked to Steinitz,
who visited the Churchill mansion on several occasions. He appeared
only once during the tournament, to watch the first Steinitz–Zukertort
game for about three hours — *sitting on my side of the board,* Steinitz
added with pride.

Because of the excesses of men like Paulsen, organizers and other masters had begun in the 1850s to introduce timing devices. First, they tried hourglasses and then various kinds of clocks. It would be impossible, everyone agreed, to insist that each move be played within a period of, say, ten to fifteen minutes. Some moves take longer. But a blanket rule that allowed players to take twenty minutes for any move would mean that two players could drag out the first thirty-five moves of a game to more than twenty hours.

Thomas Bright Wilson of the Manchester Chess Club had the latest wrinkle. Wilson connected two clocks so that while one clock ran, the other rested. To complete a move you only had to push the button on top of the clock at your side. This stopped your side and started your opponent's. Thus, London 1883 became the scene of the first use of the tournament clock now standardized in international play. And it may have been the reason Paulsen declined an invitation to play.

In any event, the first round began on the 26th with a rousing victory by Dr. Zukertort over young Tchigorin. The Russian's inexperience was apparent when he handed over the advantage of the two Bishops without compensation on the seventh move. Black's Pawn mass was preserved with 8 . . . P-B3! and later activated with 11 . . . N-B2! Finally it tore White's Kingside apart with 15 . . . P-B6.

TCHIGORIN–ZUKERTORT: *1 P-K4, P-K4; 2 N-KB3, N-QB3; 3 B-N5, N-B3; 4 O-O, NxP; 5 P-Q4, B-K2; 6 P-Q5?, N-Q3! 7 BxN?, QPxB; 8 PxP, P-B3!; 9 PxP, BxP; 10 B-K3, O-O; 11 QN-Q2, N-B2!; 12 Q-K2, P-KB4; 13 N-N3, P-B5; 14 B-B5, P-K5; 15 KN-Q4, P-B6; 16 Q-N5, Q-B1!; 17 KR-Q1, B-R3; 18 Q-R4, N-N4!; 19 NxP!, PxN; 20 R-Q7, PxP! 21 RxB, N-R6ch; 22 KxP, N-B5ch; 23 K-B3, Q-R6ch; 24 K-K4, B-N2ch; 25 K-Q4, N-K3ch; 26 K-B4, R-B5ch; 27 N-Q4, NxB; 28 KxN, Q-R4ch; 29 K-B4, RxNch; 30 Resigns.*

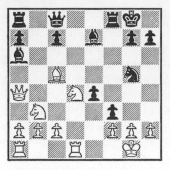

Position after 18 . . . N–N4

Zukertort's fine 18th move threatens 19 . . . N–R6ch! with a quick mate. Later on 21 BxB, N–R6ch; 22 KxP, Q–N2ch!; 23 KxN, Q–B6ch White's K is sentenced to death on KR4. So Tchigorin ran it to the Queenside, where he lost the Q. (Note that 28 R–K8ch is met by 28 . . . K–B2!) Tchigorin was then just beginning his international travels. A low-level clerk in a St. Petersburg government office, he learned the moves at the age of 16. This is quite a late stage for a budding master today, but it was quite common then. Zukertort and James Mason played their first games at age 18 and Blackburne began at 19.

But Mikhail Ivanovich Tchigorin progressed slowly and was still receiving odds of a knight from Petrograd masters when he was 24. Nevertheless, he became the first Russian to essentially spend his life on chess organization. Surprisingly, this speeded rather than stultified his growth as a player, and by 1881 he had tied for third place with countryman Winawer, behind Blackburne and Zukertort, at his first international event.

Meanwhile, back at Victoria Hall, Blackburne couldn't budge Alexander G. Sellman, and they drew in 29 moves. Sellman, the 27-year-old champion of Baltimore, was one of four "rabbits" in the tournament. A rabbit is a rank outsider who, for various reasons, is invited to the tournament. This position is treasured by every woodpusher who dreams of a chance to sit down against a grandmaster and watch his own moves, however poorly coordinated and tactically weak, being relayed to a huge wallboard where hundreds of eyes can consider them.

The rabbits are the meat of the tournament favorites. If one of the superplayers is in contention for a prize, he must beat every rabbit. Otherwise, he loses ground, since his rivals are likely to win their rabbit games. On the other hand, if the master is doing badly, the only way he is going to recoup is to beat the rabbits.

The rabbits at London 1883 were Sellman, Dr. Josef Noa of Budapest, Rev. Arthur Bolland Skipworth, and James Mortimer of Richmond, Va. Noa had beaten Blackburne, Mason, and Tchigorin at the preceding Vienna tournament. Skipworth was the worthy editor of *The Chess Player's Chronicle*, a successor of Staunton's original journal. And Mortimer was a multifaceted playwright, editor, diplomat, a friend of Morphy's and a regular at Simpson's.

Ah, but there was good news for Blackburne. The tournament committee led by Minchin strongly disapproved of the innovation of Dundee 1867, where for the first time players received a half point for each drawn game. Instead, the committee insisted that all draws be played over at least twice. The third game after two draws would count whatever the result. The explanation from Minchin was clearly antirabbit:

> As regards drawn games it was felt by all the members of the Sub-Committee who drew up the rules that the previous practice . . . was most unfair to the strongest players, as it compelled them in effect to give the odds of the drawn games to the weaker competitors. . . .

So Blackburne got another shot at Sellman later on and naturally used it well. Also in the first round, James Mason derailed the third American, Captain Mackenzie. Actually Mason, who was born in Kilkenny, had spent nearly as much time in America as Mackenzie, a Scottish-born professional soldier who served in the Union Army during the Civil War and then settled down as a New York club professional. Bird and Rosenthal also drew on the first day, and Steinitz defeated Winawer. But therein lay trouble for the world champion.

Steinitz scored his first victory with the Steinitz Gambit (*1 P-K4, P-K4; 2 N-QB3, N-QB3; 3 P-B4, PxP; 4 P-Q4!?, Q-R5ch; 5 K-K2*) and this reinforced the notion in the mind of the already-stubborn Austrian that this was the last word in scientific chess. "The main object of this gambit," he explained, "is to make the King available for both wings in the ending." Whether it is also available for checkmate in the middlegame is up to Black.

Winawer responded *5 ... P-Q3; 6 N-B3, B-N5; 7 BxP* and now, when he had the opportunity to crack open the center with *7 ... P-B4!*, Black played *7 ... O-O-O*. White answered with *8 K-K3!* and soon had a huge edge after *8 ... BxN; 9 QxB, P-B4; 10 P-Q5, QN-K2; 11 K-Q2, PxP?; 12 NxP, N-KB3; 13 N-N5!* "My King goes for a walk," Steinitz liked to say.

But the following day Englisch the opportunist was ready. He was willing to enter the same opening with the Black pieces so that he could try out an idea of Rev. George A. MacDonell: *5 ... P-Q4 6 PxP, Q-K2ch*. After *7 K-B2* (not *7 K-Q2???, Q-K6 mate*) *Q-R5ch* Black is eager to accept a draw and get the White pieces in the second game.

This is, in fact, what happened five days later between Winawer and Rosenthal. Since it was a reasonable perpetual check, it didn't qualify as one of the shadow-boxing grandmaster draws that began to dissipate tournament excitement after 1910. But Blackburne, a classic fighter, wrote a formal protest to the tournament committee about the game's shortness anyway.

Steinitz, hated draws, and he played a further gambit— 8 P-N3!?, PxPch; 9 K-N2. (Later it was pointed out that 9 PxP! leads to a clear advantage for White after either 9 . . . QxR; 10 B-N2, Q-R7; 11 PxN or 9 . . . QxQPch; 10 B-K3, QxQ; 11 RxQ, N-K4; 12 B-KB4.)

Englisch's 9 . . . B-Q3! is a good reply, especially since Steinitz came back with the weak 10 PxN?, PxRP; 11 Q-B3, PxN(Q)ch; 12 KxQ, QxPch; 13 B-K3, Q-B3; 14 Q-K2? N-K2; Black's two pawns were enough to force resignation on move 33.

To make matters worse, the hardheaded champion exposed his gambit to a third straight test in the next round against Tchigorin. This time Steinitz had an improvement over the Englisch game: 10 Q-K1ch!, QN-K2; 11 PxP. The Russian played 11 . . . QxQP, and now White could have seized superiority with 12 N-B3! e.g., 12 . . . Q-B3; 13 B-K3, B-KN5; 14 N-KR4, B-K4; 15 N-K4, or 12 . . . Q-N3; 13 B-N5ch, P-B3; 14 B-K3.

But Steinitz missed this, played 12 R-R4?, Q-B3; 13 N-K4, Q-N3; 14 B-Q3, B-KB4; 15 NxBch, PxN; 16 B-N5ch, K-B1, and conceded his lack of material on the 31st move. Two full points were lost by this opening, and on April 30th the world champion was in tenth place.

On that same day Zukertort made it three in a row with a nine-hour grind against Mason. Blackburne was off to a miserable start in comparison. He drew with Mackenzie on the second day, lost to him in the rematch and then drew a game with Rosenthal, normally one of his regular customers. But the most entertaining game of the 30th was Bird–Englisch.

Bird had completely outplayed the Austrian throughout the middlegame but weakened just before trading Queens. Now his eyes lit up as he played *39 RxN, R–R4ch; 40 K–N1, RxR; 41 NxP.* Black was expected to resign in face of the unstoppable "Arabian mate" or loss of a Rook.

But Englisch, ever ready to take advantage of slim resources, found a grand stalemate with *41 . . . R–R8ch!!; 42 KxR, R–K8ch; 43 K–R2, R–R8ch!;*

In the next week, the first of May, Zukertort scored wins over Mackenzie and Skipworth without trouble. Due to the odd pairing arrangement, the doctor had Black for the first six games while Steinitz, for example, had four Whites in a row. Somehow the Black pieces were a good tonic for Steinitz because he won four games straight when his colors changed. Zukertort was clearly in first place at this point, followed by Steinitz and Tchigorin two points behind. Clearly the week's highlight was Zukertort–Blackburne.

QUEEN'S GAMBIT DECLINED

J. H. Zukertort	J. H. Blackburne
1 P–QB4	P–K3
2 P–K3	. . .

This was not a terribly ambitious beginning, but Zukertort preferred to enter the Queen's Gambit in such a manner. The fact that 2 P-K3 blocks in White's QB was not considered a handicap. Until the rise of Pillsbury it was agreed by all right-thinking masters that the QB was needed on the Queenside, not on KB4 or KN5. Here are later examples from the tournament of Zukertort's handling of the opening:

1. May 14 vs. Rosenthal — 1 N-KB3, P-Q4; 2 P-Q4, P-K3; 3 P-K3, N-KB3; 4 P-B4, B-K2; 5 N-B3, O-O; 6 B-K2, P-B4; 7 O-O, N-B3; 8 P-QN3, N-K5?; 9 B-N2, BPxP?; 10 NxN!, PxN; 11 NxP, P-B3?; 12 NxN, PxN; 13 Q-B2, P-KB4; 14 P-B5!, Q-B2; 15 P-QN4 with a big Queenside edge. 1–0 in 32 moves.

2. May 21 vs. Englisch (same opening as vs. Rosenthal except that White has played B-N2 instead of N-QB3) — 8 . . . BPxP; 9 KPxP, P-QN3; 10 QN-Q2, B-N2; 11 R-B1, R-B1; 12 B-Q3, B-R3; 13 R-K1, N-QR4; 14 Q-K2, B-N5?; 15 P-QR3, B-Q3; 16 P-B5!, and 1–0 in 68 moves.

3. June 9 vs. Winawer — 1 P-Q4, P-Q4; 2 P-K3, B-B4; 3 N-KB3, P-K3; 4 B-K2, B-Q3; 5 O-O, N-KB3; 6 P-B4, P-B3; 7 N-B3, QN-Q2; 8 P-B5?!, B-B2; 9 P-QN4, P-QR3; 10 P-QR4, N-N5?; 11 P-KR3, P-KR4 (artificial — there is no attack unless White accepts the piece sacrifice); 12 B-N2, B-K5; 13 P-N5!, BxN?!; 14 BxB, Q-N4; 15 P-N6!, B-Q1; 16 PxN, PxP; 17 BxP, and 1–0 in 79 moves.

4. June 11 vs. Blackburne — 1 P-Q4, P-Q4; 2 N-KB3, N-KB3; 3 P-K3, P-K3; 4 B-Q3, B-K2; 5 O-O, O-O; 6 P-QN3, P-B4; 7 B-N2, N-B3; 8 QN-Q2, PxP; 9 PxP, P-QN3; 10 P-B4, B-R3; 11 R-K1, R-B1; 12 R-QB1, N-QR4; 13 N-K5, B-N5?; 14 P-B5! and 1–0 in 41 moves.

2	. . .	N-KB3
3	N-KB3	P-QN3
4	B-K2	. . .

Zukertort felt that B-Q3 was better only when Black had played . . P-Q4. When Black developed with . . . P-QN3, he reasoned that White needed a more conservative plan, perhaps involving P-Q3.

4	. . .	B–N2
5	O–O	P–Q4
6	P–Q4	B–Q3
7	N–B3	O–O
8	P–QN3	QN–Q2
9	B–N2	Q–K2?!

A very normal and untheoretical position, the kind Zukertort liked. He could play his pieces to these squares virtually without interference from his opponent, as evidenced by the other games cited from this tournament. Blackburne saw that with 10 N–QN5 Zukertort could now win the "minor Exchange." But he thought that the resulting pawn on Q3 and half-open QB-file would be just compensation.

In any event, 8 . . . P–QR3 or 8 . . . P–B4; 9 N–QN5, B–K2 would confer only a slight advantage to White. Now he gets more.

10	N–QN5!	N–K5
11	NxB	PxN
12	N–Q2	QN–B3
13	P–B3	NxN
14	QxN	PxP

White was about to play 15 PxP anyway so that he could follow with P–K4. Zukertort already has a fine game.

15 BxP	P-Q4?

This ugly move was not immediately necessary. Years later the Hypermoderns would argue that in such positions Black must strike back in the center, but only when there was a target. Best here was 15 . . . QR-B1!, so that on 16 P-K4 Black could break open the center with 16 . . . P-Q4!. And on 16 B-Q3, R-B2; 17 P-K4 Black had the effective 17 . . . P-K4!

16 B-Q3	KR-B1
17 QR-K1!	. . .

Typical Zukertort. He anticipated Black's plan of exchanging off the heaviest wood along the only open line, the QB-file. Instead of 17 QR-B1, White strove for P-K4-5 with a violent attacking wedge. Black also conveniently used the wrong Rook to occupy the open file and removed a Kingside defender. Blackburne's idea was to play . . . N-Q2-KB1 for defense. But three moves later he changed plans.

17 . . .	R-B2
18 P-K4	QR-QB1

It may be desirable to play 18 . . . PxP; 19 PxP, QR-QB1 so that he can bring his N to Q4 after P-K5. But White would jump at the opportunity to open his favorite diagonal with 20 P-Q5! (20 . . . PxP; 21 BxN, or 20 . . . P-K4; 21 Q-N5, R-K1; 22 R-B5).

19 P-K5	N-K1
20 P-B4	P-N3

Zukertort suggested 20 . . . P-B4 as a better defense but gave no analysis. It still looked bad after 21 PxP e.p. and 22 P-B5. The . . . P-B4 idea might have worked better with the KR at KB1.

21 R–K3!   . . .

"When Zukertort made this move, he had in his mind's eye the whole combination that follows, down to Black's 28th move," wrote Minchin in the tournament book.

It may seem singular that his opponent should have played the next seven moves exactly as anticipated but it must be remembered that Mr. Blackburne doubled his R's with the intention of playing to B7 as soon as he got rid of the White KB, and played for that purpose expecting to win a piece. The real beauty of Zukertort's play is that he led his opponent into this trap, correctly calculating its real results.

The idea of 21 R–K3 is simply 22 R–R3 followed by P–KN4 and P–B5 in preparation for a decisive Q–R6.

21 . . .   P–B4

Blackburne was annoyed that he could never play, for example, 21 . . . B–R3; 22 BxB, R–B7; 23 Q–Q1, RxB because the other R is hanging. He should restrain the P–B5 with the idea of 21 . . . N–N2; 22 P–KN4, P–B4; 23 PxP e.p., QxP, but Blackburne wants to put his N to better use.

22	PxP e.p.	NxP
23	P–B5!	N–K5
24	BxN	PxB

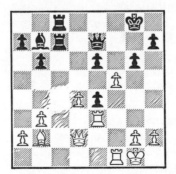

25 PxNP!! R–B7

"The excited spectators naturally thought that Zukertort had here lost a piece and the game, but one confident believer in his skill at this point bet a shilling he would win the game, not having the slightest conception of the manner in which he could escape from the apparently impending loss," Minchin reported.

There was no stepping back for Black. On 25 . . . PxP; 26 R–N3 he loses after (*a*) 26 . . . Q–R2; 27 R–B6!, R–N2; 28 R–R3!; (*b*) 26 . . . Q–K1; 27 Q–R6, R–N2; 28 R–R3, or finally (*c*) 26 . . . Q–N2; 27 P–Q5, P–K4; 28 Q–N5, R–K1; 29 R–B6. He burned his bridges, but 25 . . . B–Q4 was best.

26 PxPch K–R1

It didn't take much calculation to see that 26 . . . QxP; 27 R–N3ch, K–R1; 28 P–Q5ch *or* 26 . . . KxP; 27 R–R3ch, K–N1; 28 Q–R6 led to mate.

27 P–Q5ch P–K4
28 Q–N4!! . . .

Without a doubt, this was a great move, one that ranks in fame with Lasker's 35 P–K5!! against Capablanca at St. Petersburg (see Chapter Three) or Marshall's 23 . . . Q–KN6!! against Levitsky at Breslau 1912 (in which the American forced mate by placing his Queen on a square on which it could be captured by either of two enemy Pawns).

Black, presumably, was floored by this move. He was astounded and shocked to find variations such as 28 . . . QxQ; 29 BxPch, KxP; 30 R–R3ch, K–N3; 31 R–N3ch, K–R3; 32 R–B6ch, K–R4; 33 R–B5ch, K–R3; 34 B–B4ch; and 35 R–R5ch mates — correct? Not at all.

"An enthusiastic critic, who by-the-bye, was not present, says this literally electrified the lookers-on," Black Death noted drily. However, the Englishman wrote, he had expected it all along because anything else would cost White the game. Of course, 28 Q–N4. Naturally.

28   ...   QR–B4

"At this stage, walking round to see how the other games were going," Blackburne recalled, "one of the players said to me, 'You've got the little man.' 'I don't know,' I replied, 'It's tremendously difficult.'

On returning, Zukertort had not yet made his move, but it dawned on me that the sacrifice of the Rook was fatal and the only question was whether he would find it. This did not long remain doubtful.

Returning to the other boards I presently heard a crash as though a piece were being slapped down with all the emphasis a man's muscles could give it, and presently there came a tap to my shoulder. 'Your clock is going, I have made my move,' he said, and from the expression of his face and the manner in which he drew himself up to his full height I felt that I might remark as the writer did when the audience damned his play, 'he has found it out, has he?'"

29   R–B8ch!!   KxP

Again, if Black accepts the offered material, White's B enters the game decisively: 29 ... QxR; 30 BxPch, KxP; 31 QxPch and mates.

30	QxPch	K–N2
31	BxPch!	KxR
32	B–N7ch!	K–N1
33	QxQ	Resigns

Even Steinitz, no friend of anyone's, called this "one of the most brilliant games on record." It was perhaps the first great Queen's Gambit.

Johannes Hermann Zukertort, 41, became 7–0 two days

later and suddenly in early May was running off with a
tournament that was predicted to be a tough battle between
five or six equals.

He was a remarkable man. Like Aron Nimzovich, born
three years after this tournament, and Mikhail Tal, born a
half-century after that, Zukertort was a native of the Latvian
capital, Riga. But his Prussian-Polish parents moved to
Breslau when he was 13 and Zukertort grew up a German.

As a young man he showed proficiency at everything—
fencing, music criticism, marksmanship, foreign languages
(he spoke eleven fluently and in addition could carry on a
conversation in Arabic, Sanskrit, and Turkish), piano playing, journalism, and medicine. Concerning the latter, he
became a battlefield medic during the Danish War and was
decorated for bravery.

In chess Zukertort became a major figure after defeating
Anderssen in 1871. His mental powers were enormous. It
was said that he committed every game he ever played to
memory. He held the record temporarily of playing sixteen
games simultaneously without sight of the boards.

There was one doubt about Zukertort in 1883. Despite
all his physical vigor and cerebral accomplishments, he was
not a well man. Apparently it was no particular ailment,
just a recurring weakness of the constitution. Minchin
reports that his health was so doubtful that there was fear
he couldn't enter the tournament at all. Zukertort's personal
physician told him to give up the strain of four hours of
intense concentration for periods of two months or more.
But he played. At any given moment, his many fans feared,
Zukertort would collapse and undo all the work of the early
rounds. Everyone knew he would eventually fall apart—
and they were right. The only question was when.

On May 8 Zukertort's string of victories was broken by his
old nemesis, Steinitz. "If a man has been twenty years in a
country, and has succeeded like Mr. Steinitz, in alienating
his friends and well-wishers, is the whole of the chess community wrong and is he right?" Zukertort once asked. The
answer was that almost the entire master membership of

the London clubs was not on speaking terms with the un-official champion. Blackburne, so the story goes, once threw Steinitz out of a window: The defenestration of Prague's famous citizen.

Zukertort's health may have been an issue here because he failed to increase his large edge even more with 29 R–KN1, e.g. 29 . . . QxP; 30 R–R8, N–B3; 31 R–K1ch, N–K5; (31 . . . R–K5; 32 R–K8ch!); 32 P–N3, Q–B6; 33 RxNch, RxR; 34 Q–K8ch and 35 QxR.

But White played 29 R–K1ch? and, after 29 . . . R–K5, compounded his error with 30 RxRch?? after which 30 . . . QxR; 31 QxRP, P–N3 forced his immediate resigna-tion. A "harikarizug," as Tarrasch would later say.

Steinitz then had a score of 6–2 compared with Zukertort's 7–1, Blackburne's 4–2, Tchigorin's 5–3, and Mason's 5½–2½. (Because of the replaying of draws, some players had finished more games than others.) The closeness was shortlived: May 10 – Zukertort over Bird in 34 moves; May 11 – Zukertort over Sellman in 55; May 14 – Zukertort sacrificing his Queen to beat Rosenthal in 32. Then a draw with Winawer and two with Englisch before he took their points. The last of these was pretty:

Having muffed earlier chances at converting a crushing Queenside initiative, the Prussian kept a clear edge in the Q–and–N ending. To answer the threat of 47 N–B4, Englisch could try 46 . . . P–N4, but Zukertort had planned on 47 Q–Q3, K–N2; 48 N–K7, QxP; 49 Q–N6ch, K–B1; 50 QxBPch, K–K1; 51 N–B5! winning all the Kingside pawns.

So Englisch played *46 . . . K–K1* and White unleashed *47 Q–N5!!, QxQ; 48 P–B8(Q)ch, K–B2; 49 QxNch!, KxQ; 50 N–B7ch* and *51 NxQ* to win quickly.

Meanwhile the hometown fans finally had something to cheer about with Blackburne's return to form. Describing the players at Vienna 1873, the tournament book says: "The pale, lean, muscular young man opposite is the iron Blackburne, the Black Death of chess players. But very seldom there falls from his moustache-covered lips a laconic English word. He surveys the game with the eye of a hawk; even now he is tearing to bits a snare laid for him by his unsuccessful opponent, and a demure smile steals over his face."

Steinitz fumbled about in the opening with his 10th, 13th, and 15th moves. Later, with 22 . . . N–N3 or 23 . . . P–KR3, he might have held the game. But as played, Blackburne had his chance to smile.

BLACKBURNE–STEINITZ: *1 P–K4, P–K4; 2 N–KB3, N–QB3; 3 N–B3, P–KN3; 4 P–Q4, PxP; 5 NxP, B–N2;*

6 B–K3, N–B3; 7 B–K2, O–O; 8 O–O, N–K2!?; 9 B–B3,
P–Q3; 10 Q–Q2, N–Q2?; 11 B–R6, N–K4; 12 BxB, KxB;
13 B–K2, P–KB3; 14 P–B4, N–B2; 15 QR–Q1, P–B3?; 16
B–B4, B–Q2; 17 BxN!, RxB; 18 P–B5, N–B1; 19 P–K5!,
BPxP; 20 N–K6ch, BxN; 21 PxB, R–K2; 22 Q–N5, Q–K1?;
23 R–Q3!, RxP?; 24 R–R3, Q–K2; 25 Q–R6ch, K–N1; 26
R–B8ch! Resigns.

Position after 18 . . . N–B1

At the halfway mark everyone had a week's rest, greatly
appreciated by the tournament leader. The scoretable read:
Zukertort 12–1, Mason 9½–3½, Tchigorin and Steinitz 9–4,
Blackburne 8½–4½, Englisch, Rosenthal, Winawer, and
Bird 7–6, and the rabbits trailed—Noa and Sellman 3½,
Skipworth 3, and Mortimer 0.

With the first cycle of play over—this was a double-round
event—a great banquet was held with seventy guests including all contestants. The tournament patron, the Duke
of Albany, didn't attend, but the Earl of Dartrey, president
of the tournament committee, presided in his place. They
all enjoyed a sumptuous nine-course meal ("Noisettes de
Mouton a la Chasseur, Filet Pique a la Portuguese . . .")
with seven wines and eleven toasts ("To the Queen," "The
Royal Family and Duke of Albany," "The Continental
Competitors in the Major Tournament," "The American

Competitors . . .*"*). A few days later during the rest week most of the masters rode by carriage to Epsom for Derby Day. Baron Kolisch (a title he acquired after he gained his fortune and long after retiring from play as one of Anderssen's chief rivals) had no difficulty beating Winawer in a blindfold game played to pass the time en route.

On the 28th of May play resumed at Victoria Hall. As so often happened in the later stages of tournaments, James Mason immediately fell apart. He was a sharp attacking master, a chronic alcoholic, and a prolific writer whose books are still sold today. Finding himself in the dizzying heights of second place, he promptly lost four straight games and fell to sixth. Noa became the leading rabbit (Rev. Skipworth having dropped out of the event on grounds of ill health) by upsetting Tchigorin. Tchigorin then lost two more, to Winawer and Blackburne. Thus Zukertort's rivals fell off the furious pace one by one.

Winawer had unique good fortune against Mason on May 31, when this position occurred:

The Russian (Black) played *43 . . . N–QB4!* – certainly a devastating move. It forced resignation in a few moves. But how was it possible to make a diagonal jump with the N? Minchin's explanation is that during the process of adjournment and resumption of play, the N must have been moved from K2 to Q2. No one has come up with a better explanation to this day.

Simon Winawer played his favorite 3 . . . B–N5 in the French Defense (after 1 P–K4, P–K3; 2 P–Q4, P–Q4; 3 N–QB3) three times in London, winning two and losing one. Only Mortimer ventured 4 P–K5, for which he was condemned for misunderstanding "the principles of the close game."

Winawer was born in Warsaw in 1838 and frequently traveled to Western Europe on business. On one occasion he was in Paris while an international tournament was about to begin. He found some of the competitors in a local café and surprised them by winning game after offhand game. The competitors told the tournament officials and in this manner a Russian citizen was invited to a foreign master tournament for the first time. Winawer finished in a tie for second with Steinitz in the event (Paris 1867) behind Kolisch.

Tchigorin returned to the fold and damaged another rival of Zukertort's on June 1.

TCHIGORIN–STEINITZ: *1 P–K4, P–K4; 2 N–KB3, N–QB3; 3 B–B4, B–B4; 4 P–QN4, BxP; 5 P–B3, B–B4; 6 O–O, P–Q3; 7 P–Q4, PxP; 8 PxP, B–N3; 9 N–B3, N–R4; 10 B–KN5!, P–KB3; 11 B–B4, NxB; 12 Q–R4ch, Q–Q2; 13 QxN, Q–B2; 14 N–Q5, P–N4?* (White is also better after 14 . . . B–K3; 15 Q–R4ch, B–Q2; 16 Q–B2!); *15 B–N3, B–K3; 16 Q–R4ch, B–Q2; 17 Q–R3, R–B1; 18 KR–K1, P–N5; 19 NxB, RPxN; 20 N–Q2, B–K3?* (Better is 20 . . . P–KR4.) *21 P–B4!, PxP e.p.; 22 NxP, N–K2; 23 P–K5, BPxP; 24 PxP, P–Q4; 25 R–KB1, N–B4?; 26 N–Q4, Q–N3; 27 NxN, BxN; 28 B–R4!, P–B4; 29 R–N3, K–Q2; 30 QR–KB1, KR–B1; 31 R–KN3, Q–R3; 32 B–B6, B–K3; 33 Q–R7!, K–B2?* (Black was also lost after 33 . . . K–B3; 34 R–QN3, P–N4; 35 RxP, KxR; 36 R–N1ch, K–B5; 37 Q–R4ch, K–Q6; 38 Q–N3ch followed by R–K1 or Q1 with check); *34 R–QN3, K–Q2; 35 QxP(6), R–B3; 36 QxPch,*

R–B2; 37 Q–N5ch, R–B3; 38 Q–N7ch, R–B2; 39 Q–R6!
Resigns.

Position after 27 . . . BxN

At this point Zukertort was flying high, having won eight
games and drawn four since his loss to Steinitz. His score
of 15–1 was four points ahead of anyone else in the minus
column. The minus column was important because the
clumsy pairings made it possible for Zukertort to have ten
games left while Englisch and Rosenthal, the drawing
masters, had fourteen. A contender with a score of 3–1
could conceivably equal Zukertort's 15–1, but a player with
13–2 could not match it.

Here again the fans asked: How long would it last? The
good-natured doctor had not only taken the lead in the
strongest tournament of his life but was putting together
an almost superhuman streak of wins.

The best answer to the fans was Zukertort's play with
Black on June 6 versus Tchigorin's Evans Gambit (*1 P–K4,
P–K4; 2 N–KB3, N–QB3; 3 B–B4, B–B4; 4 P–QN4, B–N3;
5 O–O, P–Q3; 6 P–QR4, P–QR3; 7 P–B3, B–N5; 8 P–Q3,
Q–B3!; 9 B–K3, KN–K2; 10 QN–Q2*):

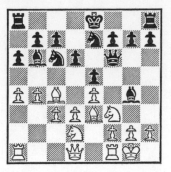

Zukertort played 10 . . . N–N3! intending to increase pressure on the Kingside with 11 . . . N–B5 or 11 . . . N–R5. Tchigorin realized he couldn't trap Black's Q but thought 11 B–KN5 would win a pawn after 11 . . . QxB; 12 NxQ, BxQ; 13 BxPch, K–K2; 14 BxN. The alternative of 14 QRxB, N–B5 (threatens 15 . . . P–R3)–15 B–B4, N–K7ch–was no better.

Now Zukertort regained his pawn with 14 . . . B–K7!; 15 KR–K1, BxP, and after Tchigorin's 16 NxP he seized a large endgame superiority with 16 . . . P–Q4!; 17 P–R4, P–Q5!; 18 P–QR5, PxP!; 19 PxB, PxN; 20 KR–Q1, PxP; 21 RxP, KR–Q1; 22 R–N2, P–N4 (stops P–N5 and fixes the weak QNP); 23 R–K1, R–Q5, winning a pawn. Zukertort scored the point in fifty-two moves.

In fact Zukertort's tremendous pace picked up in the beginning of the fourth quarter of the tournament. June 7 saw Steinitz with the White pieces in his last chance to gain ground on his rival. Zukertort let him throw all of his Kingside pawns forward and then picked them off one at a time in an ending that lasted eighty-nine moves. Zukertort drew with Winawer on the 8th but won the rematch the following day with White. On the 11th and 12th Blackburne and Rosenthal fell victim. Zukertort's score was twenty-two wins, seven draws that didn't count, and that one loss to Steinitz. By comparison, the World Champion was a very distant second place with 15–6. No one has ever achieved such a rout in a tournament of comparable strength.

Steinitz's last chance was burned out on June 13:

He was White and had just played *28 N–B5*, a positional crusher in a game already materially superior. The French champion had banked on *28 . . . NxP?!; 29 NxR, RxN.* But the sacrifice only looked strong, for White could simply play 30 PxN!, BxP; 31 Q–N2, B–R7ch; 32 K–B1! remaining a full R ahead.

Yet White, the defensive master of his age, played *30 B–B4??* and was surprised by *30 . . . N–K5!* Now 31 PxN, R–N3ch would be crushing. But he could have tried 31 Q–N2, R–N3; 32 B–N3, QxQch; 33 KxQ, BxB; 34 PxB, RxPch. Steinitz chose a third course— *31 RxN, PxR; 32 BxB, PxP; 33 R–K1* and was mated via *33 . . . R–N3ch; 34 B–N3, RxBch!; 35 PxR, P–B7ch!*

Now it was Steinitz on the defensive. First place was out of the question, but he had to finish at least in a tie for second to preserve his reputation. He had placed among the top two positions in every one of his tournaments since Paris 1867. Against this same Zukertort he easily won a match in 1872 with seven wins to one. But now at 47 his name was being challenged.

Steinitz was no longer the Romantic attacker who tried to fill the void created by Morphy's retirement. He was a deep strategic planner who believed he could defend any position. An angry, irascible man, he was described by a contemporary:

Every thing about him denoted power rather than grace, strength rather than beauty . . . features were rugged in outline . . . the face of a man of action rather than a man of thought . . . with bright tawny locks, round face, a crushed-up nose . . . broad forehead, deepset eyes and shaggy beard . . . and a short massive body supported by short legs–with feet planted firmly on the ground.

Now in a bitter fight for second place with Tchigorin, Blackburne, Englisch, and Rosenthal, he came out in his best form. On June 6 he had demonstrated his patented Fianchetto Defense to the Ruy Lopez (*1 P-K4, P-K4; 2 N-KB3, N-QB3; 3 B-N5, P-KN3*) and Englisch played the natural *4 P-Q4, PxP; 5 NxP, B-N2; 6 B-K3, N-B3; 7 N-B3, O-O; 8 O-O.* Here Steinitz discovered *8 . . . N-K2!*, a regrouping maneuver so typical of him.

Earlier in the event Mackenzie had tried *9 P-KR3?* and obtained an awful position after *9 . . . P-B3!; 10 B-Q3, P-Q4; 11 PxP?, QNxP; 12 NxN, NxN; 13 P-QB3, NxB; 14 PxN, Q-N4.* Englisch failed to improve when he played *9 Q-Q2, P-Q4; 10 PxP, QNxP; 11 NxN, QxN; 12 B-K2, N-N5!; 13 BxN, BxB; 14 N-N3* after which Black won a fine ending. Black's winning plan consisted of restricting White's minor pieces with his mobile Pawns and creating a passed Pawn. The technique was beautiful:

*14 ... QxQ; 15 NxQ, QR–Q1; 16 P–QB3, KR–K1; 17
N–N3, P–QN3; 18 P–KR3, B–K3; 19 KR–Q1, P–QB4;
20 B–N5, P–B3; 21 B–B4, K–B2; 22 P–B3, P–KN4!;
23 RxR?, RxR; 24 B–K3, P–KR3!; 25 R–K1, P–B4; 26
P–KB4, B–B3; 27 P–N3, P–QR4!; 28 N–B1, P–R5; 29
P–R3, B–B5; 30 K–B2, PxP!; 31 BxKBP, B–KN4!; 32 BxB,
PxB; 33 K–K3, K–B3; 34 P–R4, PxP; 35 PxP, R–K1ch;
36 K–B2, RxR; 37 KxR, K–K4; 38 N–K2, BxN!; 39 KxB,
K–B5; 40 P–B4, K–N5; 41 K–K3, P–B5ch; 42 K–K4, P–B6;
43 K–K3, K–N6 and White Resigns.*

The following day Sellman played *9 B–QB4* (*9 B–KB4!* is
best) against the same variation, and once again Steinitz
obtained a superior ending, this time winning in thirty-two
moves after *9 ... P–Q4; 10 PxP, QNxP; 11 NxN, NxN;
12 BxN?, QxB; 13 P–QB3, P–QN3; 14 Q–B3, QxQ; 15 NxQ,
P–QB4; 16 P–KR3, B–K3; 17 KR–Q1, KR–Q1; 18 P–QR3,
B–N6; 19 RxR, RxR.*

Steinitz finished off with four wins in a row and overtook
his rivals for the £150 second-place money. He was almost
as far ahead of Blackburne and Tchigorin as he was behind
Zukertort.

This was because it finally happened – Zukertort's health
cracked. Minchin reported:

It was well known to his friends for the last ten days, while he
had been completing the toll of the successive victories with
which his second round had opened, that he had been compelled
to drench himself nightly with a most virulent poison to keep up
his failing energies to the mark. But Nature would not submit to
any such dictation, and at last the long threatened breakdown
occurred.

Zukertort fell to the three Americans in a succession of
blunder-filled games, his last three in the event. Clearly by
losing to Sellman and Mortimer, two of the weakest players
in the event, Zukertort was a sick man.

SCORETABLE

	Z	St	Bl	T	E	Mac	Mas	R	W	Bi	N	Se	Mo	Sk	Total
1. Zukertort	X	01	11	11	11	10	11	11	11	11	11	10	10	11	22–4
2. Steinitz	10	X	10	00	01	11	11	00	11	11	11	11	11	11	19–7
3. Blackburne	00	01	X	01	10	00	11	1–	½1	01	11	11	11	11	16½–8½
4. Tchigorin	00	11	10	X	01	11	01	01	10	10	10	11	10	11	16–10
5–7. Englisch	00	10	01	10	X	½½	00	½1	01	01	11	11	11	11	15½–10½
5–7. Mackenzie	01	00	11	00	½½	X	01	01	01	01	11	½1	11	11	15½–10½
5–7. Mason	00	00	0–	10	10	10	X	10	10	11	½1	11	11	11	15½–10½
8. Rosenthal	00	11	0–	10	10	01	01	X	½1	10	01	01	11	11	14–11
9. Winawer	00	00	½0	01	10	10	01	½0	X	01	10	11	11	11	13–13
10. Bird	00	00	10	01	10	10	00	01	10	X	00	11	11	11	12–14
11. Noa	00	00	00	01	00	00	½1	10	01	11	X	01	11	01	9½–16½
12. Sellman	01	00	00	00	00	½0	00	10	00	00	10	X	11	01	6½–19½
13–14. Mortimer	01	00	00	01	00	00	00	00	00	00	00	00	X	01	3–23
13–14. Skipworth	00	00	00	00	00	00	00	00	00	00	10	10	10	X	3–23

(The second Blackburne–Rosenthal game was never completed because it had no bearing on the final order of prizewinners.)

Dr. Zukertort at present holds the honoured post of champion," Minchin argued in the tournament book. "But only a match can settle the position of these rival monarchs of the Chess realm." There were as many after London 1883 who strongly felt that Zukertort was the true champion as there were supporters of Steinitz.

And Minchin was right, a match had to be held. It began on January 11, 1886, in New York City and was recognized as the first official World Championship contest—if for no other reason than both contestants said it was.

Zukertort led in games played in New York but collapsed when the match moved to St. Louis and New Orleans. Steinitz won ten, lost five, and drew five to keep the now official championship title. Two years later Zukertort was dead of a cerebral hemorrhage after a game at Simpson's.

Mackenzie died penniless of a heart attack in a New York hotel in 1891. Mason played only briefly after 1883. Englisch continued on the Continent and achieved his greatest success by drawing a five-game match with Harry Nelson Pillsbury, then at the height of his powers, in 1896.

Tchigorin continued to improve and nearly defeated Steinitz in 1892. Blackburne and Bird lived long lives and played in other great tournaments as we will see.

And at Ostend 1907 20-year-old Russian master Savielly Tartavover, a highly acclaimed new talent, was upset in the first round of his first international event by the oldest player invited, that veteran rabbit, 74-year-old James Mortimer.

II

Dark Horse

There are tournaments and there are tournaments. Some are runaways, such as London 1883, where one player wins virtually every game and dominates a field of supposed equals. Some tournaments are come-from-behind chases, such as St. Petersburg 1914, where even the near-last may come first. And some tournaments are musical-chairs events with a different player in first place each round. Such was Hastings 1895.

But there are other dimensions and sidelights to these competitions. Hastings had two special features: the dark horse and the changing of the guard.

The dark horse is the rabbit who makes good. He can be an unknown like Pillsbury in 1895 or Capablanca in 1911 who does violence to the handicappers by winning. Perhaps the first notable example of this was the upset victory of Hungarian-born Isidor Gunsberg in the Hamburg 1885 tournament, ahead of names like Blackburne, Englisch, Mason, Mackenzie, and Bird. Gunsberg's only previous

50

result in a master event was a relatively dismal fourth in the Vizayanagaram tournament, the minor section of London 1883.

The Dark Horse can also be an established master who has put in creditable showings before (e.g., von Bardeleben in 1895) but suddenly exceeds them 400 percent. A recent example is Milko Bobotsov, a Bulgarian grandmaster who came out of nowhere to place second in the Moscow 1967 tournament, which celebrated the October Revolution's 50th birthday. Bobotsov had won his national championship and a few minor events before. But to finish ahead of Spassky, Portisch, Geller, Keres, Petrosian, and Najdorf was something else. He has yet to repeat this success.

Besides the surprise of von Bardeleben's rise and fall and of Pillsbury's victory, the first Hastings owes much of its fame to the clash of generations it brought about. On one hand were Bird, Blackburne, Steinitz, Mason, and Tchigorin. All but Tchigorin had played Anderssen in the early days of tournament chess. Together these five masters accounted for 141 years of international experience.

On the other hand was a highly promising but inexperienced new generation. Emanuel Lasker was World Champion at the age of 26 but had never played in a major tournament outside of his native Germany. His countryman, a 33-year-old physician named Siegbert Tarrasch, had registered his first success just five years before at Manchester. Carl Schlechter, playing in his first foreign event, was, at 21, the youngest at Hastings. David Janowski, the 27-year-old French champion, had entered his first international competition a year before, a less-than-exciting tie for sixth at Nuremberg. And there was Harry Nelson Pillsbury.

Hastings is an English Channel port in Sussex, not far from the beaches of Brighton in the west and the Straits of Dover to the northeast. Before the 22 masters gathered there on August 5, the big-league tournaments had always been held in large cities — London, Paris, Berlin, Leipzig,

Hamburg, Vienna, Breslau, and Frankfurt. Chess associations and clubs flourished in urban surroundings and naturally they chose major cities as the venue of each event. Hastings, however, was the predecessor of all the charming resortlike sites that have followed—San Remo, Margate, Palma de Mallorca, Marienbad, and Santa Monica. When word went out about the attractive event—highest quality players, £1,000 in prizes, excellent Queen's Hotel accommodations—thirty-eight masters suggested their names as invitees. This was in the days when players volunteered themselves to tournament committees. One potential invitee withheld his name—he wanted to enter as "Anonymous." But, as the tournament book noted," the condition was declined and entry lost." There were enough entries to make up a strong minor event, which was won by a 25-year-old engineering student from Hungary named Geza Maroczy who was destined to become one of the strongest players in the world during the next twenty years. Finally, there was poor N. W. Van Lennep of Holland, whose entry was placed in limbo. He was to be the reserve master in case one of the important names failed to show up. But they didn't fail, and Van Lennep disappeared from the pages of chess history.

When the Hastings Congress became an annual event at Christmastime beginning in 1920, play was held in a succession of local sites including the Town Hall, the Waverley Hotel, and the Sun Lounge at nearby St. Leonard's-on-Sea. But the original event began in one of the largest rooms of the Brassey Institute and the lesser competitions took place in other rooms.

The British love to accompany their major tournaments with subsidiary events. Besides the master event, the first Hastings Congress also included the first international women's tournament (won by the mother of Sir George A. Thomas, a future British chess and badminton champion), the four eight-man preliminary sections of the British Amateur championship and its finals. Today it's not uncommon to find more than 300 players competing in the non-master events of an English congress or in imitators like the magnificent Wijk-an-Zee tournaments in Holland each spring. Play began at 1 P.M. on August 5 in "a very large room covered with red baize and with walls hung with pictures by the best artists; eleven tables in two rows of four and one of three, whilst rows of chairs cause about 100 spectators to keep a sufficient distance from the players," according to the book of the tournament.

The new World Champion, Lasker, won quickly, and most of the other favorites followed suit except Tarrasch. In a vastly superior position against Mason, the doctor ran short of time (the limit was thirty moves for the first two hours). When Mason brought this to Tarrasch's attention—chessplayers were chivalrous in those days—the doctor ignored him, incorrectly thinking he'd made thirty moves. But Tarrasch had written his name where the first move should have been recorded and thus lost a game carelessly on that rare instance, a time forefeiture.*

Also in the opening round, Harry Bird, the oldest player (65) at Hastings, spun his way out of a loss to the Rumanian-American business speculator, Adolph Albin, by sacrificing his Q impressively. "Russia's Chess Teacher," Emmanuel Schiffers, had an easy time with Gunsberg because his opponent tried one of his typically bizarre defenses: 1 P–K4, P–K4; 2 N–KB3, N–QB3; 3 N–B3, P–QR3?. Richard Teichmann, blind in one eye, was cleverly outplayed by Walbrodt's two Bishops. Von Bardeleben manhandled Amos Burn's Queen's Gambit.

But the most interesting and, as it turned out, significant contest was a meeting of attacking generations.

---

* About 1.2 percent of decisive master games end in time forfeiture, according to a study of 1,005 games played between 1895 and 1970. The study, by Ernest Rubin and published in the June 1973 issue of *The American Statistician*, found that of the 658 games ending in victory, 95 percent concluded with resignation, 3 percent by mate, and less than 1 percent by one player's failure to show up for play. Of the 347 draws, 83 percent came about by agreement, 10.7 percent by perpetual check, 4.6 percent by repetition of moves, 1.2 percent by stalemate, and .5 percent by insufficient mating material.

KING'S GAMBIT DECLINED

	M. I. Tchigorin	*H. N. Pillsbury*
1	P-K4	P-K4
2	P-KB4	B-B4
3	N-KB3	P-Q3
4	B-B4	N-QB3
5	N-B3	N-B3
6	P-Q3	B-KN5
7	P-KR3	BxN
8	QxB	N-Q5
9	Q-N3!	. . .

This position (with the slight difference that both sides had pushed their QRP one square) first occurred during a key game late in the great Vienna Schachkongress of 1873, when Blackburne held the White pieces against Anderssen. Blackburne won after 9 . . . Q-K2; 10 K-Q1, P-B3; 11 PxP, PxP; 12 R-B1, and the Monday-morning annotators took Anderssen to task for not grabbing White's QR.

The variation gained considerable fame after the current game, and some critics suggested that even 8 . . . N-Q5 was an error. They proposed 8 . . . PxP; 9 BxP, N-Q5; 10 Q-N3, N-R4 or 9 QxBP, N-K4 as better. But twenty years later Akiba Rubinstein observed that simply 9 B-N5!, O-O; 10 BxN! and 11 BxP gave White the edge in the center and kingside.

9 ...   NxPch

But here 9 . . . PxP! is safe and sound as the Russian
analyst Ilya Rabinovich discovered, e.g. 10 QxNP, R–KB1;
11 K–Q1, Q–K2; 12 R–B1, R–KN1!;

10 K–Q1   NxR
11 QxP   K–Q2!

It's just paralysis after 11 . . . R–KB1; 12 PxP, PxP;
13 R–B1, B–K2; 14 B–KN5 and now: (*a*) 14 . . . P–B3;
15 RxN!, BxR; 16 BxB, Q–Q3; 17 N–N5!, or (*b*) 14 . . .
N–R4; 15 BxPch, K–Q2; 16 QxKP. But in the Blackburne–
Anderssen game, with the subtle addition of P–QR3 and
. . . P–QR3, Black would have 14 (15) . . . P–QN4! and win.

12 PxP   PxP
13 R–B1   B–K2
14 QxBP!   . . .

The right move? This has been an issue of debate for
decades. First we look to Emanuel Lasker, who argued in
favor of 14 B–KN5. The World Champion gave, for example,
14 B–KN5, R–KN1; 15 QxBP, RxB; 16 Q–K6ch, K–K1;
17 RxN, R–N2; 18 N–Q5, P–B3 ("or 18 . . . Q–Q3; 19
NxPch, QxN; 20 B–N5ch, K–Q1; 21 R–B8ch, BxR; 22
Q–K8 mate") 19 QxKP, R–B1; 20 NxB, RxN; 21 R–B8ch.
"But it appears to us," wrote Tchigorin, "that Lasker
has erred in analysis." He picked up the key parenthetical
line, 18 . . . Q–Q3, gave it two exclamation points, and
suggested that 19 NxPch be met by 19 . . . K–Q1! 20 QxQ,
BxQ; 21 NxR and now 21 . . . B–B4; 22 P–KN4, P–KR4!;
23 R–B7 ("or . . . ?"), RxR; 24 BxR, PxP; 25 PxP, B–K6;
26 B–K6, B–N4.
Ten years after the game an 18-year-old master from
Rostov-on-Don wrote to Tchigorin suggesting there was
even a second defense. He recalled Lasker's main line and
then said that 19 . . . Q–N1! was better than the champion's

19 ... R–B1?–then 20 Q–R5ch, (20 N–B7ch, QxN!) K–Q1; 21 NxB, Q–R7!!. And rubbing in the point that Lasker spent three quarters of a page of the tournament book on his comment, young Savielly Tartakover added that the world champion still hadn't found the best line of defense.

14 ...   K–B1

The next series of moves were fairly simple: *15 B–KN5, R–B1; 16 Q–K6ch, K–N1; 17 B–KR6!* (17 QxP, N–N1!) *R–K1; 18 QxP, N–Q2; 19 Q–KR5!, N–N3; 20 B–Q5, P–QR3;*

Deutsche Schachzeitung, already in 1895 *the* German chess magazine (founded by one of the Pleiades, L. E. Bledow, in 1846) suggested 20 ... NxB; 21 NxN, P–QR4 to activate the QR via QR3. But Tchigorin pointed out that Black's position was so impotent that White could exchange Q's: 21 QxN!, QxQ; 22 NxQ, P–R4; 23 B–B4, B–Q3; 24 P–K5, B–B4; 25 P–K6, B–Q3; 26 BxB, PxB; 27 P–K7, K–R2; 28 R–B7 and Black, a R ahead, must struggle for a half-point.

The game actually continued: *21 K–Q2, NxB; 22 NxN, R–N1; 23 P–KN4* and now, seeing that 23 ... B–N4ch;

24 BxB, QxBch; 25 QxQ, N–N6ch; 26 PxN, RxQ; favors White after 27 R–B7, and that 23 . . . B–B4; 24 RxN, P–B3; 25 B–B4ch, K–R2; 26 N–B7, Q–Q5 (Lasker's suggestion) is not unfavorable after 27 QxBch, QxQ; 28 B–K3, QxBch; 29 KxQ, QR–KB1; 30 N–K6, R–B3; 31 N–Q4 and 32 N–B5, Pillsbury played:

23 . . . B–N5ch!; 24 NxB, Q–Q5! White still had a choice of strong moves. He could have continued 25 B–B8!, QxNPch; 26 K–K3, N–B7ch; 27 NxN, QxN; 28 QxRP, QxP; 29 R–B7, R–N4; 30 RxP, R–N4; 31 B–Q6! but Black could improve with 25 . . . RxB! to obtain drawing chances. Tchigorin found:

25 N–B2!, NxN; 26 KxN, R–N3 (better was 26 . . . K–R2; 27 R–B3, P–B4, says recent Russian analysis) *27 B–Q2, R–Q3; 28 R–B3, Q–R5ch; 29 K–B1, QxRP; 30 B–B3, R–QB3; 31 QxP, P–N4; 32 Q–K7, Q–N6; 33 K–Q2, P–R4; 34 R–B5!* (to meet 34 . . . P–N5 with 35 R–N5ch, K–R2; 36 B–Q4ch, K–R3; 37 R–QB5 and wins) *K–N2; 35 R–B5, QR–R3; 36 P–N5, RxR; 37 QxR, R–B3; 38 Q–Q5!, Q–R5; 39 P–N6!, P–N5; 40 P–N7, PxBch; 41 PxP,* and after White made a second Queen, Black had only another ten moves of life. A momentous fight. But its significance was overlooked until much later. After all, who was Pillsbury?

The second round brought another startling success for the older generation as Tchigorin's two N's triumph over Lasker's two B's:

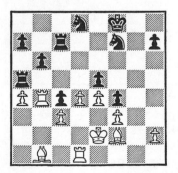

Black's threat of 47 . . . N–B3 can be met in several ways. 47 P–Q5? allows the Black N's to find dominating squares at Q3 and QB4. But 47 B–R2! forces a liquidation such as 47 . . . P–N4; 48 RxNP, RxP; 49 R–N2, which may hold for White.

Lasker, still recuperating from illness incurred during his championship match in America, played *47 R–Q2?* and after *47 . . . N–B3; 48 R–N5, RxP; 49 PxP, N(2)xP; 50 B–R4, R–KN2; 51 K–B2, R–N3; 52 R(2)–Q5* the Black R's finished off the game with *52 . . . R–R8; 53 B–Q8, N–Q6ch!; 54 BxN, PxB; 55 RxQP, QR–KN8!; 56 R–B5ch, K–K1; 57 B–N5, R(3)xB* and White Resigned.

This put Tchigorin in a first place tie with Jacques Mieses of Leipzig, who lived long enough to win a brilliancy prize at another Hastings some fifty years later. Almost overlooked in the second round was Pillsbury's victory over the highly touted Tarrasch. The American chose a novel plan in the Queen's Gambit Declined involving B–KN5. After a long struggle in which each side attacked on one side of the board, White (Pillsbury) held the decisive momentum:

He found *44 Q–N3ch!* and after *44 . . . KxN* (44 . . . K–B1 hangs a R to 45 Q–KN8ch) played the subtle *45 K–R1!!*. Incredibly, Black has no answer to 46 R–KN1. The best Tarrasch could come up with was *45 . . . Q–Q4; 46 R–KN1,*

QxBP; 47 Q-R4ch, Q-R4; 48 Q-B4ch and White won in a few moves.

Tchigorin was 3-0 after defeating Mason on August 7. It was a round distinguished only by young Janowski's loss to the 48-year-old London *Times* correspondent, Samuel Tinsley. So far the younger generation hadn't been impressive, considering Tchigorin's wins over Lasker and Pillsbury, the Tarrasch–Mason fluke, Blackburne's and Tinsley's successes over Janowski, and other surprises.

The 8th was a rest day with a trip to Battle Abbey and Normanhurst Court on the schedule. For the evening's entertainment there was a concert on Hastings pier and, at Gaiety Theatre, a performance of *Charley's Aunt*. The masters had a choice and they all took the music.

The fourth round featured another setback for the World Champion. Curt von Bardeleben marshaled his White forces and threatened 18 NxP. Rather than defend, Lasker played:

17 . . . Q-KR3? White replied *18 P-KR3, N-B3; 19 BxN!, BxB; 20 NxP* and now instead of taking the QNP, Lasker tried *20 . . . BxRP?* This overlooked *21 NxBch, QxN; 22 Q-R5* with dual threats. Black was forced into an inferior ending after *22 . . . Q-KR3; 23 QxQ, PxQ,* and White slowly consolidated his chances with *24 KR-Q1, QR-B1; 25 R-B3, KR-Q1; 26 KR-QB1, R-B3; 27 B-K4,*

R–R3; 28 RxP, RxP; 29 R–QN5!, B–K3; 30 R–B7, P–QR4; 31 B–B5. He won in fifty-eight moves.

But this round finally allowed Tarrasch to demonstrate his ability in one of the greatest combinations ever played. With a crushing opening advantage, the 23-year-old Dutchman, Carl Walbrodt, carelessly chose 33 . . . N–R4? when he could have safely won the Exchange by putting the N on K3. The difference is . . .

34 RxP!! Black loses the Q on the newly opened diagonal after 34 . . . PxR; 35 BxP. His best try is 34 . . . B–KB3 (not 34 . . . N–B3; 35 RxB, QxB; 36 RxB); 35 RxB, QxB; 36 N–K4! with obvious compensation.

But Walbrodt had not overlooked 34 RxP; he had expected it. His prepared answer was *34 . . . NxP; 35 NxN, RxNch; 36 PxR, RxPch,* winning White's Q and N for two R's.

However, Tarrasch calmly answered *37 K–B1!, RxQ; 38 R–N4!!,* a line that delightfully allows no reply. Walbrodt didn't try. He resigned.

Again almost unnoticed during the afternoon of play was young Pillsbury's fine endgame against W. H. Pollock, an English-born Canadian master.

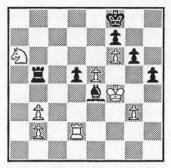

Black was a P behind, but 42 . . . RxP cannot be prevented. On 42 N–B7, RxP; 43 NxP, BxN; 44 RxB White had winning chances, but 42 . . . R–B4! would repeat the position.

Pillsbury played *42 K–K3!!, RxPch; 43 K–Q4,* and after *43 . . . RxKNP?* (better 43 . . . P–N4) he had winning chances a P behind. The right method was *44 N–B5!* (not 44 P–N4, R–N6!), *P–R5; 45 P–N4, P–R6?* (45 . . . R–QR6); *46 R–QR2!!*. The threat of mate and the inability of Black's pieces to control events in the path of White's passed P sealed Pollock's fate. The game went *46 . . . K–N1; 47 R–R8ch, K–R2; 48 P–K6!* and Black saw that he lost the foot-race after 48 . . . P–R7; 49 PxP, P–R8(Q); 50 R–R8ch!. Pollock played *48 . . . PxP* and resigned soon after *49 NxB, PxN; 50 P–B7.*

The fifth round saw von Bardeleben, Tchigorin (over Tarrasch), Pillsbury, and Lasker win, but the tournament leader was none other than 59-year-old Wilhelm Steinitz, who had beaten Blackburne, Mason, Gunsberg, and the Italian champion, Benjamin Vergani. By this time the old man had mellowed. "Why don't you retire? You've had enough glory for one man," a fan said to Steinitz. "The glory I can spare," he replied. "But I need the prize money."

But he was an old man, and the sixth round brought him the first of four straight losses. His tormentor turned out to be Pollock. Already this was a tournament of upsets.

Meanwhile, Steinitz's greatest student, Harry Pillsbury, was winning his fourth straight.

MIESES–PILLSBURY: *1 P–K4, P–K4; 2 N–QB3, N–KB3;
3 B–B4, B–N5; 4 P–B4, P–Q3; 5 N–B3, O–O; 6 N–Q5?,
NxN; 7 BxN, N–B3; 8 P–B3, B–QB4; 9 P–B5, N–K2; 10
B–N3, P–Q4!; 11 P–Q4, KPxP; 12 P–B6?, NPxP; 13
NxQP, QPxP; 14 B–R6, N–N3!; 15 BxR, QxB; 16 R–KB1,
Q–R3!; 17 Q–K2, BxN; 18 PxB, P–KB4; 19 P–KN4, N–B5;
20 Q–B4, N–Q6ch; 21 K–K2, QxRPch; 22 K–K3, P–B5ch;
and White Resigned.*

To keep two streaks going, Pillsbury met Steinitz in the
following round, August 13. Again the American developed
his QB on KN5 in the Queen's Gambit—1 P–Q4, P–Q4;
2 P–QB4, P–K3; 3 N–QB3, N–KB3; 4 B–N5. But then
Steinitz played 4 . . . P–B4, a move Gunsberg called a simple oversight. The speculative qualities of 5 BPxP, Q–N3!?
or 5 . . . BPxP were unknown in 1895. So on 5 BPxP Steinitz
played 5 . . . KPxP?; 6 BxN, PxB and arrived in the middlegame with this inferior Pawn structure:

Pillsbury found an ingenious plan of redevelopment. He
closed up the Queenside so that he can bring two N's to
bear on the QP: *23 P–N6!, P–QR3; 24 N(2)–B3, R–B3; 25
B–B1, R–Q1; 26 N–R2!, B–Q2; 27 N–N4, R(3)–B1; 28
N–B3!* and now 28 . . . BxN; 29 PxB, QxP(3) would have
allowed White to open up for an attack with 30 P–N5!,
PxP; 31 N–R4 and 32 N–B5.

So Steinitz threw his own hopes on an attack with 28 . . . R–N1; 29 K–B2, P–KR4?; 30 P–KR4, BxN; 31 PxB, QxP(3). Here White decided that Black's P's were sufficiently vulnerable that he could play 32 NxP and win one after another of them until interrupted on the fifty-third move by Black's resignation.

The eighth round continued the pattern with another Pillsbury win, another Steinitz loss, and another Tchigorin win. This put the Russian in clear first because his coleader from the previous two rounds had not been able to win against the Viennese drawing master.

SCHLECHTER–VON BARDELEBEN: 1 P–K4, P–K4; 2 N–KB3, N–QB3; 3 B–N5, P–QR3; 4 B–R4, N–B3; 5 N–B3, B–B4; 6 NxP!?, NxN; 7 P–Q4, B–Q3; 8 O–O, O–O; 9 P–B4?!, N–B5; 10 P–K5, B–K2; 11 PxN, BxP; 12 P–Q5!, P–B4!; 13 N–K4!, BxP; 14 BxB, NxB; 15 Q–R5, NxB; 16 P–B5, P–B3; 17 R–B4, Q–K1; 18 NxPch!, PxN; 19 Q–N4ch, K–R1; 20 R–K4, Q–B2; 21 QR–K1, P–Q3; 22 R–K7, B–Q2??; 23 RxQ, RxR; 24 R–K6!, R–N2; 25 Q–R4, BxR; 26 QPxB, N–N3; 27 QxP, N–Q4; 28 Q–N2, K–N1; 29 P–B6, NxP; 30 QxN and drew in four moves.

Quite incomprehensible, said Lasker, about Black's twenty-second move. Why give up the Q when he could have consolidated with 22 . . . Q–N1; 23 QxN, BxP; 24 RxP, QR–K1? But White had scored another draw. He eventually drew eleven of his first thirteen games.

In the ninth round the World Championship was fought all over again—with the same result. Steinitz anticipated the Hypermoderns in his treatment of the Black side of a Ruy Lopez. Don't advance your pieces and you won't have any weaknesses, he seemed to say: 1 P–K4, P–K4; 2 N–KB3, N–QB3; 3 B–N5, P–QR3; 4 B–R4, P–Q3; 5 O–O, KN–K2; 6 P–B3, B–Q2; 7 P–Q4, N–N3; 8 R–K1, B–K2; 9 QN–Q2, O–O; 10 N–B1, Q–K1; 11 B–B2, K–R1; 12 N–N3, B–N5; 13 P–Q5, N–N1; 14 P–KR3, B–B1?!; 15 N–B5, B–Q1; 16 P–KN4, N–K2; 17 N–N3, N–N1!? and now, with all of

Black's pieces resting on the first rank, one would expect an act of violence from White. But White was the cautious Lasker. He was methodical, played 18 K–N2 *in preparation* for violence, and was rewarded with victory in forty moves.

This was Steinitz's fourth consecutive loss. In the following round he met von Bardeleben, who had not lost once — three draws and six wins. Curt von Bardeleben was an imposing Berliner with a slight smile, an enormous forehead, and a distinguished name. Late, in the pre-World War years of Germany, von Bardeleben was earning a living from small prizes in chess tournament and from marrying rich women who wanted to acquire the "von" for their names. A witty conversationalist, von Bardeleben could not make a living from either divorce or chess and in 1924 he threw himself out of a window.

After winning the Vizayanagāram tournament in 1883, his best showing was a fourth place at Frankfurt, an event remembered largely for being Mackenzie's best result (first place) and Zukertort's worst (fourteenth-sixteenth in a field of twenty-one). Hastings was von Bardeleben's greatest success — so far. Now against Steinitz he met an old idea of the seventeenth-century master Gioachimo Greco — *1 P–K4, P–K4; 2 N–KB3, N–QB3; 3 B–B4, B–B4; 4 P–B3, N–B3; 5 P–Q4, PxP; 6 PxP, B–N5ch; 7 N–B3!?*

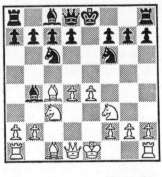

7 . . .   P–Q4?!

Schlechter in a later round played 7 . . . NxKP!; 8 O–O, BxN; 9 PxB, P–Q4, which is still considered safe enough for equality. The next few moves look convincing, but Black has considerable resources that only modern research has unearthed.

8	PxP	KNxP
9	O–O!	B–K3!

Black was too good a tactician to miss seeing that a double capture on QB6 would allow 11 BxPch and 12 Q–N3ch.

10	B–KN5	B–K2
11	BxN!	QBxB
12	NxB	. . .

Good enough, considering the result. But, asked Soviet master Igor Zaitsev in 1973, why not the simple 12 BxB, NxB 13 R–K1? Black can't castle because of 14 RxN. Therefore, Zaitsev said, 13 . . . P–QB3; 14 NxB, PxN; 15 Q–R4ch, Q–Q2; 16 QxQch, KxQ; 17 N–K5ch, K–K1; 18 QR–QB1, P–B3; 19 R–B7! or 14 . . . QxN; 15 Q–K2, Q–Q3; 16 QR–Q1, K–B1; 17 N–N5 must be considered despite White's clear edge. Zaitsev also analyzed 13 . . . P–KB3; 14 Q–K2, P–B3; 15 NxB, PxN; 16 QR–B1, Q–Q2; 17 N–K5!? as favoring White.

The only problem with this analysis is 13 . . . O–O, which is perfectly playable since 14 RxN can be met by 14 . . . BxN!

12	. . .	QxN
13	BxB	NxB
14	R–K1	P–KB3
15	Q–K2	. . .

Second try, Gospodin Zaitsev. He suggests 15 Q–R4ch followed by Q–N4! giving as the key line 15 . . . K–B2; 16 QR–B1, P–B3; 17 RxNch!, KxR; 18 Q–N4ch, K–B2; 19 QxPch, K–N3; 20 RxP. White, he wrote, is better, and there-

fore Black must look for a better defense in 16 . . . Q–Q3.
That move may be excellent, but in the line he cited Black
is still very much alive after 20 . . . KR–QB1!

15 . . .   Q–Q2
16 QR–B1   . . .

This, as it turns out, is the key point in the course of the
game and a redeeming feature of Zaitsev's analysis.
Steinitz's last move can be quite handily met by 16 . . .
K–B2! since 17 QxNch is not sound. Nor is 17 N–K5ch,
PxN; 18 PxP, Q–K3; 19 RxP, KR–Q1; or 17 N–N5ch, PxN;
18 Q–B3ch, N–B4!; 19 P–KN4, KR–K1.
The right move, as the Russian analyst pointed out in
"64," is 16 QR–Q1!. For example, (a) 16 . . . K–B2; 17
Q–B4ch, N–Q4; 18 N–K5ch!, PxN; 19 PxP with threats of
P–K6ch and RxN; (b) 16 . . . R–Q1; 17 Q–B4, K–B1; 18
Q–N4, P–B3; 19 P–Q5!, PxP; 20 N–Q4, K–B2; 21 N–K6,
QR–K1; 22 Q–N4, N–B4; 23 NxP or 17 . . . P–B3; 18 R–Q3,
K–B1; 19 N–N5!, PxN; 20 R–B3ch, N–B4; 21 Q–B5ch; and
finally, (c) 16 . . . K–B1; 17 P–Q5!, NxP; 18 N–N5!, R–K1
(18 . . . PxN; 19 Q–B3ch); 19 Q–B3!, P–B3; 20 Q–R3ch,
K–N1; 21 N–K4, P–QN3 (else N–B5); 22 P–QN4!, P–N3;
23 Q–N3 (23 RxN, RxN!), K–N2; 24 P–N5.

Zaitsev's analysis is actually more extensive, but this should give the reader a hint of the complexity of White's chances and Black's resources. The game continues to be something of a mystery after eighty years.

16	. . .	P–B3?
17	P–Q5!!	PxP
18	N–Q4	K–B2
19	N–K6	KR–QB1
20	Q–N4	P–KN3
21	N–N5ch	K–K1
22	RxNch!!	

There were many critics of Steinitz who said he played penny-pinching chess. But if that were true, he would have played 22 NxP!, which wins a Pawn and probably the endgame. But he has more.

Von Bardeleben couldn't take the R with his K because of 23 R–K1ch, K–Q3; 24 Q–N4ch, K–B2; 25 N–K6ch, K–N1; 26 Q–B4ch and wins. He couldn't take the R with his Q because of 23 RxR with check. The same goes for 22 . . . K–Q1; 23 QxQ, except that it is not just check.

So Black nonchalantly played 22 . . . *K–B1* and was met by 23 *R–B7ch!*, *K–N1*; 24 *R–N7ch!*, *K–R1*; 25 *RxPch*, and here resignation was in order because of the great variation —25 . . . K–N1; 26 R–N7ch, K–R1; 27 Q–R4ch (the point— there is no KRP any more), KxR; 28 Q–R7ch, K–B1; 29 Q–R8ch, K–K2; 30 Q–N7ch, K–K1; 31 Q–N8ch, K–K2; 32 Q–B7ch, K–Q1; 33 Q–B8ch, Q–K1; 34 N–B7ch and 35 Q–Q6. The "Pearl of Hastings."

But Bardeleben didn't resign. He stared at 25 RxPch, shot a glance at Steinitz, and without a word got up from his chair and left the room. He didn't come back. Tournament officials searched and found Bardeleben pacing angrily. No, he wouldn't return to the board so that that outrageous Austrian could mate him.

So Steinitz had to wait for Bardeleben's time to run out before he could claim the win. Not only claim it—he demonstrated the final ten-move mate and the crowd cheered.

John Henry Blackburne, who occasionally called Hastings home, had gotten off to a bad start (3–6) but fought back and in the eleventh round became the second player to defeat the German upstart.

BLACKBURNE–VON BARDELEBEN: *1 P–Q4, P–Q4; 2 P–QB4, P–K3; 3 N–QB3, P–QB3; 4 P–K3, B–Q3; 5 N–B3, N–B3; 6 B–K2, O–O; 7 O–O, QN–Q2; 8 Q–B2, PxP; 9 BxP, P–K4; 10 R–Q1, PxP; 11 NxP, N–K4; 12 B–K2, Q–B2; 13 P–KR3, N–N3; 14 B–Q2, Q–K2; 15 B–K1, N–R5; 16 N–B3, B–KB4; 17 Q–R4, NxNch; 18 BxN, Q–K4; 19 P–KN3, BxP?; 20 N–K2, B–QB4; 21 Q–R4, B–K3; 22 B–B3, Q–B4; 23 K–N2!, B–Q4; 24 RxB!, PxR; 25 P–KN4, Q–K3; 26 N–B4, Q–Q3; 27 R–R1, KR–Q1; 28 P–N5, P–Q5; 29 PxN, P–KR3; 30 PxQP, BxP and Resigned.*

The eleventh round also signified the midway point in the tournament with the standing: Tchigorin and Pillsbury 9½; Lasker 8½; von Bardeleben 7½; Bird, Schiffers, Steinitz, and Walbrodt 6; Teichmann and Tarrasch 5½; and on down to the 2 draws for Vergani, the principal rabbit.

One of the peculiar rules at Hastings was the random selection of pairings for each round. After the players had drawn numbers on the first day, it was explained that for each day of play a round number would be drawn. This additional number would tell which of the twenty-one different pairing schedules for the twenty-one playing days would be used for that session. In this manner the organizers prevented players from preparing openings for the next day's opponent. The masters had no idea who their next opponent was.

The fans, of course, couldn't plan either. And on August 20 those who arrived early were happy to see a match between two of the leaders, Lasker and Pillsbury. The younger players were expected to make up for their early failures by taking advantage of their elders' physical tired-

ness in the closing rounds of the long event. The fans saw
Pillsbury try Steinitz's 3 . . . P–KN3 against the Ruy Lopez
and develop an excellent game. In a rush to exchange off-
pieces Lasker blundered away a P on the eighteenth move.
He faced this phalanx of Black P's just before the first time
control.

To get the Pawns moving, Pillsbury should have played
29 . . . R–K1 and 30 . . . P–Q4. Instead, *29 . . . R–N5?; 30
Q–K1, P–K5; 31 P–R5!, P–Q4; 32 P–R6* forced him to worry
about White's passed P.

Now Black *had* to pull back his R to protect the first rank.
But he played *32 . . . Q–K2?; 33 Q–N3!, P–K6; 34 R–R1,
Q–B3; 35 R–K1, P–Q5* to preserve all his children. The
roof fell in with *36 P–R7, Q–Q1; 37 R–R1, Q–R1; 38 Q–Q6!,*
and Pillsbury had to *resign* after *38 . . . R–N2; 39 QxP(6),
P–K7; 40 QxR!.*

This was the American's second crisis, the first being his
loss to Tchigorin. In between, Pillsbury had won nine
games in a row! But Tchigorin was in first place at the start
of the thirteenth round. Not for long, however.

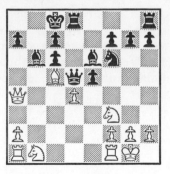

Steinitz's latest attempt at refutation of the Evans Gambit had fallen on its face. With 15 NxP, N–Q2; 16 NxQBP! or 15 . . . N–K5; 16 BxB, White (Tchigorin) would have gained the upper hand.

However, Tchigorin's penchant for long, involved variations took hold of him and he played *15 Q–R6ch?, K–N1; 16 NxP, N–Q2; 17 N–QB3, NxB; 18 Q–K2!, Q–Q3; 19 PxN, QxP; 20 N–R4, Q–QN4* followed by *21 QxQ, 22 NxB* and *23 N–B6ch.* The only problem is that when it was all over, Steinitz's two Queenside pawns proved much more valuable than the Exchange White had won. Steinitz scored in twenty more moves.

Therefore, Lasker's victory over Tinsley on the 21st gave him the lead. Pillsbury could only draw with "Black Death" but moved into a second-place tie with Tchigorin. Von Bardeleben, fading fast, lost to Walbrodt in twenty-three moves and was never again a major figure in the event. He couldn't lose in the first nine rounds and couldn't win in the next nine.

The following day, the 22nd, was a rest day, and some of the players took part in a problem-solving tournament. Each contestant was given a red-and-gold-edged program with three problems that turned out to be toughies. Mieses offered the first solutions, but it was discovered that he'd made mistakes. So Georg Marco won by returning with the right answers after an hour and thirty-five minutes. At the grand banquet afterward, Lasker announced that he would make England his home. And Tchigorin added that a magnificent tournament was being organized for the end of the year in St. Petersburg. It would be the first major Russian tournament.

The fourteenth round was unspectacular as all three leaders — Lasker, Pillsbury, and Tchigorin — won to pull ahead of the field. The following day allowed Tchigorin to gain ground with a win over Tinsley while his rivals drew. And in the sixteenth round all three won, but Pillsbury's strangulation of Amos Burn, the best new English player since Blackburne, was the best. Black never got around to playing . . . P–QB4 until too late.

PILLSBURY-BURN: *1 P–Q4, P–Q4; 2 P–QB4, P–K3; 3 N–QB3, N–KB3; 4 B–KN5, B–K2; 5 P–K3, O–O; 6 N–B3, P–QN3; 7 R–B1, B–N2; 8 PxP, NxP; 9 BxB, QxB; 10 NxN, BxN?; 11 B–Q3, R–QB1; 12 P–K4, B–N2; 13 O–O, N–Q2; 14 Q–K2, P–QR3?; 15 R–B3, P–QB3; 16 KR–B1, P–QN4?; 17 Q–K3!, R–B2; 18 Q–B4, QR–B1; 19 P–K5!, P–QB4; 20 BxPch!, KxB; 21 N–N5ch, K–N1; 22 R–R3, Q–K1; 23 Q–R4, K–B1; 24 N–R7ch, K–N1; 25 N–B6ch, K–B1; 26 NxQ, KxN; 27 Q–N5, PxP; 28 R–R8ch Resigns.*

And who was this remarkable cigar-puffing American from Somerville, Massachusetts, who was holding his own with the world's best? As a matter of fact, Harry Pillsbury hadn't learned the moves until seven years before, and was known only to fellow Boston club players until 1892. He made a marginal living on the fringes of big tournaments for a while. He reported the goings-on of the Steinitz–Lasker match for American newspapers in 1894, for example. But he never exercised much enthusiasm for the American championship, which had been held by three different men in the few years since Mackenzie's death. Pillsbury's interest was in Europe.

His main adversary, Lasker, was four years older. The German shared a distinctive name. There had been a town called Lask where in the eighteenth century the founder of his family lived. His three sons moved to other parts of Germany and began three branches of Laskers. Emanuel, born in Berlinchen in 1868, represented one branch. A seventh cousin, Edward, was born in Berlin and came from the second branch. He and Emanuel became lifetime friends later through chess. The third branch of the family produced Albert B. Lasker, founder of the American advertising empire.

Lasker had planned a career in mathematics and philosophy, but as so often happened, his part-time preoccupation grew into a full-time profession. By 1889 he was a master and defeated several German colleagues in matches—von Bardeleben in 1889, Mieses in 1890. Tarrasch considered him an unworthy opponent and refused to play. Lasker played some more matches and then challenged Steinitz while Tarrasch was reluctant to play the Austrian. Lasker won, and Tarrasch missed a golden opportunity to be champion.

The seventeenth round brought the three leaders into a triple tie as Lasker couldn't make any progress against Mason in eighty-two moves and Tchigorin couldn't do any better against Albin in fifty-eight. Pillsbury received a full point when von Bardeleben failed to show up to answer 1 P–Q4. That left three men with 13½ points and four rounds to go.

Just when the American's fortunes appeared to be on the rise, however, he collapsed against the youngster from Vienna.

White had a Pawn, but Schlechter's R served the double function of attack and defense. The real problem was Black's Queenside majority, a natural outgrowth of Pillsbury's favorite line in the Queen's Gambit. Play continued with *33 Q–B3, P–B6; 34 PxP, PxP; 35 R–B8ch, K–N2; 36 R–N8, Q–K2!; 37 Q–B4, P–KR4.* Black was primed for 38 . . . R–N5. Now Pillsbury had a hallucination.

The safe 39 R–QB8!, R–N5; 40 Q–B6ch would trade off so many Pawns that a draw would be automatic. But White saw a chance of more and played *39 P–K6??, RxP; 40 R–QB8*, thinking that 41 R–B7 could not be answered. Perhaps he thought that *40 . . . R–K5; 41 R–B7, RxQ; 42 RxQch* would win a Rook but overlooked *42 . . . R–B2.* As it turned out, White had to resign because of the pregnant Black P after *43 R–K5, P–B7; 44 R–N5ch, K–R3; 45 R–N1, R–QN2!*

Lasker took solid possession of the top place without much struggle because he was paired with Vergani. Tchigorin grabbed an opening P from Mieses but had too many difficulties making it count: Lasker 14½, Tchigorin 14, Pillsbury 13¾.

But the nineteenth round had more surprises. It followed another rest day and a trip to the sideshows during Carnival Week. While Tchigorin was accepting Pollock's unsound offer of a piece and Pillsbury downed Tinsley, Lasker was missing a chance to put the tournament on ice:

Tarrasch (White) had been fighting for a draw for ten moves and now overlooked 41 NxP!, KxN; 42 K–B5, which would have split the point. He played *42 K–B5?*, after which Lasker could have made *two* Q's instead of one following 41 . . . P–B7!; 42 P–N5, BxP!; 43 KxB, K–Q6; 44 N–B1ch,

K–Q7; 45 N–N3ch, K–Q8; 46 K–B5, P–R4!; 47 P–QR4,
P–N4!; 48 PxP, P–R5.

But Lasker, obviously tiring from the length of the event,
played *41 . . . K–Q6??*, and then *42 NxP, KxN; 43 P–N5* left
him trying to promote his unmoved P's before White's
advanced soldiers. Black resigned in six moves.

So it was Tchigorin 15, Lasker and Pillsbury 14½; the
Russian was two rounds away from the most impressive
success of his life. However, the eighteenth and nineteenth
rounds had only been previews of the twentieth. "Everyone is in fever heat," noted the tournament book descrip-
tion. Pillsbury had no problems against Vergani, but
Lasker ran into immediate problems with Blackburne. On
the twentieth move Lasker was faced with a forced loss;
but Blackburne missed it. On the twenty-second move
Blackburne again had his chance with a brilliant piece
sacrifice to start a six-move combination. He missed it.
Finally, after Lasker's twenty-third move Blackburne let a
third opportunity for the brilliancy prize pass through his
fingers. He only won a Pawn. But it was enough.

That left Tchigorin alone to butcher his own game. His
play was unbelievably wretched:

TCHIGORIN–JANOWSKI: *1 P–K4, P–K4; 2 N–QB3, N–KB3;
3 P–Q3?!, P–Q4!; 4 PxP, NxP; 5 Q–K2?, N–QB3; 6 B–Q2,
B–K2; 7 O–O–O, O–O; 8 Q–B3?, B–K3; 9 KN–K2, P–B4!;
10 Q–R3, Q–Q3; 11 NxN, QxN; 12 N–B3, Q–R4; 13
P–QR3??, BxP; 14 N–N1, BxPch!; 15 KxB, Q–R7ch; 16
K–B1, N–Q5, and White Resigns.*

This fantastic double-shock catapulted Pillsbury into first place with 15½ points, half a point ahead of Tchigorin and a full point before Lasker. That meant with only a round to go the American needed only to win against the declining Gunsberg.

Isidor Gunsberg had won one major tournament, and his reputation rested on a won match (over Blackburne, 1886), a drawn match (with Tchigorin, 1890), and a narrowly lost match (to Steinitz, 1891). But at Hastings he was fumbling around tenth place with only 9 points.

Pillsbury sat down with amazing self-assuredness. He showed little aggressive nature with the White pieces in the first fifteen moves while Lasker was crushing Burn. And he entered a drawish endgame with minor pieces while Tchigorin was grabbing a decisive P from Schlechter. Thus, Tchigorin ended the tournament with 16 points, Lasker with 15½. First place depended on White's chances in this ending:

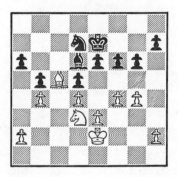

Despite the slightly bad Bishop, White had something of an advantage because of Black's Queenside Pawn weaknesses. But 25 ... N–N1!; 26 BxBch, KxB; 27 N–B5, P–K4! —or 25 ... NxB; 26 NPxN, B–B2; 27 P–KR3, P–QR4! should draw. Gunsberg seemed oblivious and played 25 ... *BxB?!; 26 NPxB, N–N1?*. Even here he could have held with 26 ... P–QR4; 27 P–B5!, P–N4!; 28 P–B6, N–N3; 29 N–B5, PxP; 30 PxP, K–Q3.

SCORETABLE

	Pi	Tc	L	Ta	St	Sc	Ba	Te	Sc	Bl	W	Bu	J	M	Bi	G	A	Mar	Po	Mi	Ti	V	Total
1. Pillsbury	X	0	0	1	1	1	1	1	0	½	½	1	1	1	1	1	1	½	1	1	1	1	16½–4½
2. Tchigorin	1	X	1	1	0	0	1	1	1	1	½	1	0	1	½	1	½	1	1	½	1	1	16–4
3. Lasker	1	0	X	0	1	1	0	1	1	0	1	1	1	½	1	1	½	1	1	½	1	1	15½–5½
4. Tarrasch	0	0	1	X	1	1	½	0	½	1	1	1	1	0	1	½	1	1	0	½	1	1	14–7
5. Steinitz	0	1	0	0	X	1	1	½	½	1	1	½	0	1	0	1	1	1	0	½	1	1	13–8
6. Schiffers	0	1	0	0	0	X	½	½	0	1	1	½	1	½	1	1	0	½	1	½	1	1	12–9
7–8. Bardeleben	0	0	1	½	0	½	X	½	½	0	0	1	½	1	½	1	½	1	1	1	0	1	11½–9½
7–8. Teichmann	0	0	0	1	½	½	½	X	½	0	0	1	½	1	1	0	½	1	½	1	1	1	11½–9½
9. Schlechter	1	0	0	½	½	1	½	½	X	½	½	1	0	1	½	½	½	½	½	½	1	0	11–10
10. Blackburne	½	0	1	0	0	0	1	1	½	X	0	1	1	0	½	0	1	0	1	0	1	1	10½–10½
11. Walbrodt	½	½	0	0	0	0	1	1	½	1	X	0	0	½	½	½	0	½	½	1	1	1	10–11
12–14. Burn	0	0	0	0	½	½	0	0	0	0	1	X	1	0	½	0	1	1	1	1	1	1	9½–11½
12–14. Janowski	0	1	0	0	1	0	½	½	1	0	1	0	X	½	½	0	0	1	½	1	0	1	9½–11½
12–14. Mason	0	0	½	1	0	½	0	0	0	1	½	1	½	X	1	0	½	0	1	1	0	1	9½–11½
15–16. Bird	0	½	0	0	1	0	½	0	½	½	½	½	½	0	X	1	1	½	0	½	½	1	9–12
15–16. Gunsberg	0	0	0	½	0	0	0	1	½	1	½	1	1	1	0	X	1	½	0	1	0	0	9–12
17–18. Albin	0	½	½	0	0	1	½	½	½	0	1	0	1	½	0	0	X	0	0	1	1	½	8½–12½
17–18. Marco	½	0	0	0	0	½	0	0	½	1	½	0	0	1	½	½	1	X	1	1	0	½	8½–12½
19. Pollock	0	0	0	1	1	0	0	½	½	0	½	0	½	0	1	1	1	0	X	0	0	1	8–13
20–21. Mieses	0	½	½	½	½	½	0	0	½	1	0	0	0	0	½	0	0	0	1	X	1	1	7½–13½
20–21. Tinsley	0	0	0	0	0	0	1	0	0	0	0	0	1	1	½	1	0	1	1	0	X	1	7½–13½
22. Vergani	0	0	0	0	0	0	0	0	1	0	0	0	0	0	0	1	½	½	0	0	0	X	3–18

Now, before Black played 27 . . . N–B3, Pillsbury demonstrated a forced win with 27 *P–B5!!, P–N4* (27 . . . KPxP; 28 PxP, PxP; 29 N–B4); 28 *N–N4!, P–QR4; 29 P–B6!, K–Q3; 30 PxP!, NxP; 31 NxN, KxN;* and now 32 *P–K4!!.* Although better defenses were found for Black after this brilliant method, it was agreed that he was inevitably lost. The game ended with *32 . . . PxP; 33 P–Q5ch, K–Q3* (33 . . . KxP allows a Pawn to Queen); *34 K–K3, P–N5; 35 KxP, P–R5; 36 K–Q4, P–R4?; 37 PxP, P–R6; 38 K–B4, P–B4; 39 P–R6, P–B5; 40 P–R7 Resigns.*

The virtually unknown dark horse from Massachusetts had won the strongest tournament in history. Tchigorin would win the special prizes – a ring and a copy of Salvioli's *The Theory and Practice of Chess* for winning the most Evans Gambits, and a framed photograph for being the first to win seven games. But Pillsbury took home all the glory.

Hastings marked the end of British domination of chess. Great tournaments were soon to be found throughout Europe, especially at cities like St. Petersburg, Carlsbad, and Amsterdam. There were few English stars to replace the aging Blackburne and Bird. Many of the foreign masters drifted away. Steinitz moved on to America, and Lasker followed him.

And Pillsbury? He went on to St. Petersburg for the great quadrangular tournament with Lasker, Steinitz, and Tchigorin. This was the scene of Lasker's first major tournament success. He could beat Steinitz (4–2) in his six games with the old man, but Pillsbury (1–5) couldn't.

And it was at St. Petersburg, the story goes, that Pillsbury contracted syphillis, the disease that slowly weakened his mind until he was overtaken by death at the age of 33 in 1906. He never won a clear first place again after Hastings.

III

Profession: Grandmaster

(Excerpted from the memoirs of J. O. Sossnitsky,
vice-president of the St. Petersburg Chess Club,
1906–1914)

"I, Julius Sossnitsky, do hereby set down for future generations of chess lovers an account of the great international
tournament held here in Petrograd during the April and
May months of 1914, in the twentieth year of the reign of
our beloved Czar, Nicholas II.

"As is generally conceded even throughout the Western
part of Europe, the Petrograd Masters' tournament was the
most successful meeting of champions since the gathering
at Hastings, England in 1895. The years have been many,
the changes have been many. Only one thing has remained
constant in the chess world. Dr. Lasker is still the champion.

"Since the immortal English tournament nineteen years
ago we friends of the Royal Game have suffered many
losses. The years have seen the passing of old Steinitz,
Pillsbury, Harry Bird, the Irishman Mason, and of course,
Mikhail Ivanovich Tchigorin of our own Gatchina. But we
should add that at the time of Hastings, our Alexander
Alekhine was only 3 years old, Señor Capablanca was 7,

78

Aron Nimzovich was 9, and Akiba Rubinstein was only 13. It is said that the American, Paul Morphy, progressed to masterdom while reading the games of the historic tournament in London in 1851. It is well known that our new generation grew up on the games of Hastings.

"In recounting the changes of these many years it should be said that the nature of tournament chess has been transformed drastically. The players of 1851 were amateurs — Staunton the Shakespearean critic, Anderssen the mathematics professor, Wyvill the parliamentarian. I reluctantly add that professionalism began to creep into Our Game when Herr Steinitz gave up mathematics and Zukertort, the pride of Russian Riga, limited his many talents to the one of chess-play. Today the majority of the masters spend most of their time in study of the game. At the Petrograd tournament the few exceptions included our Dr. Bernstein, the lawyer, and Tarrasch of Germany, the doctor. Capablanca, they say, contributes some of his hours to diplomacy for the Cuban government. And how can we ignore Dr. Lasker?

"While this professional revolution has been going on, Herr Lasker has been in, if not retirement, at least sabbatical leave from chess. Since the magnificent Tchigorin memorial event which graced our Petrograd quarters five years ago he has not accepted an overture to compete in a tournament. He did play that match in 1910 with Schlechter of Vienna, that memorable encounter which ended with Lasker's come-from-behind seventy-one-move victory in the tenth game after dangling most of the game and the match on the verge of defeat. And there were two easy meetings with the 'Polish Morphy,' David Janowski, which ended 7–1 and 8–0 in Lasker's favor during 1909 and 1910.

"We have learned that the world champion has used his time away from the board to think, to get married and, alas, to lose his money. The doctor has finished his *Das Begriefen der Welt*, which is to say, *The Comprehension of the World*, during his grand tours of the chess clubs of the Americas. Three years ago he became one of the few Kings of the

Chess World to take a wife. She is Martha Kohn Bamberger, the daughter of a banker.

"And as if to cut himself off completely from the game, Lasker bought a patch of farm acreage outside of Berlin hoping to set off on an idyllic life as a gentleman farmer. But, as with his other financial plans, the farm idea was a disaster for our urbanized champion. The players at Petrograd described with glee how Herr Lasker capped this agricultural disaster by trying for months to mate two pigeons so that their offspring would take a top prize in the Berlin poultry show. Both pigeons, however, were male.

"Yet the lure of competition—or, as I suspect, the lure of the 4,000 rubles we offered as honorarium and the chance to take the lion's share of the 6,000-ruble prize fund—brought Emanuel and Martha to Petrograd in April 1914. The champion may have reminded himself that in these same rooms five years ago he lost to young Rubinstein in the third round and had to overcome that beautiful positional disaster in the later rounds to score an equal-first with the Pole.

"Akiba Rubinstein appeared at the apogee of his talent when our play started on April 21. He was born, as the chroniclers have noted, in an obscure Polish village in 1882. Rubinstein grew up the youngest of twelve children in an impoverished family and in a world sheltered from the outside life of cities and fortunes, and, yes of chess. The only languages he knew as a teenager, I am told, were Hebrew and Yiddish. When he caught the chess bug at age 16, Rubinstein was fortunate to find a copy of the only Hebrew chess book, *Chess, Checkmate*, by Sossnitz.

"The story has been told many times since those days of how 19-year-old Akiba struggled to the nearest city, Lodz, to play the great George Salwe, one of the best players in Poland. Rubinstein was disappointed to find that ordinary club players who received Rook odds from Salwe could defeat him. But when he returned to Lodz after a few months' mysterious disappearance, Akiba approached Salwe and challenged him. To the astonishment of the club players—and the reader must know, chess club members are among the most cynical and blasé of city dwellers— Rubinstein won.

"He proceeded to win a serious, clocked match with Salwe and that set him off on a tour of distant resorts like Ostend (1907), Carlsbad (1907), San Sebastian (1912), and Bad Pistyan (1912). In fact, Rubinstein won all four of the major tournaments of 1912. By the time of the Petrograd tournament he had finished first or second in eighteen of his twenty-two competitions. It is no wonder that with Dr. Tarrasch returned to medicine and Lasker to his philosophy, when Señor Capablanca was asked in my presence who he thought would win the Petrograd event, he said simply, Rubinstein.

"Lasker had played once—and lost—to Rubinstein, but the only regrettable contacts he had with Capablanca before this year were exchanges of vitriol in newspaper interviews. Despite all the talk of Rubinstein as Dr. Lasker's next challenger, Capablanca has been the fastest rising star. In less than three years of international play Capa has earned Dr. Lasker's animosity. It took Dr. Tarrasch a decade!

"If the Lodz club members were shocked in 1900, the Havana enthusiasts one year later were astounded. At 12 Capablanca was the champion of Cuba, with his defeat of J. Corzo. By 21 he was the finest master of the Western Hemisphere after defeating Marshall in the 1909 match. Then in 1911 he was admitted to his first foreign event, the San Sebastian tournament, over the objections of Nimzovich and Dr. Bernstein. It should be added that Capablanca took great pleasure in defeating them both and winning the highest prize.

"The convergence of these three stars—Lasker, Rubinstein, and Capablanca—is exactly what the Chess Society of Petrograd had hoped for. Lasker and Capablanca were not speaking to one another before our tournament because of the bitterness of negotiating a title match. 'He overrated himself,' Herr Lasker has been quoted as saying of his

Cuban rival. 'His record is a match won and one first prize. I have stood for twenty years before the chess world and have won many matches and first prizes.' It would be better, he and we urged, to have a match with Rubinstein. But when we pressed our case, Dr. Lasker lost interest.

"The tournament we designed was a perfect test for the threesome. There was to be a preliminary event of eleven players, of whom the top five scorers would advance to the finals. The preliminaries would be an obstacle course but the finals would be the supreme test. If we could not bring Lasker to meet his two rivals in matches, we would induce him into a match-tournament similar to the great 1895–1896 event in this city which gave our German guest Lasker his first great victory. That was what he hoped for, but as the record shows Caissa, the goddess of chess, was not entirely kind to us.

"Since there were to be five finalists altogether, and we assumed the identity of three of them to be a foregone conclusion, our other hopes lay in the qualification of one of our own Russian masters as fellow competitors in the finals. Our troika of new talent included the remarkable Ukrainian lawyer, Dr. Ossip Samoilovich Bernstein; his junior of four years, the Latvian, Nimzovich; and the latter's cowinner in the just-completed Championship-of-All-the-Russias, 22-year-old Alexander Alekhine.

"Our foreign guests included Dr. Tarrasch of Germany, Frank Marshall from America, Janowski who now regrettably makes his home in France, and, as a gesture to the Anderssen generation, 72-year-old J. H. Blackburne and 60-year-old I. Gunsberg of England. Tarrasch was not speaking to Lasker as usual. All followers of their match six years ago recall the good doctor's declaration that he would only speak three words to Lasker—check and mate. Since the score was 8–3 with five draws in the World Champion's favor, I'm afraid the occasion to speak did not arise often.

"Not so with Mr. Marshall, who is one of the most amiable of masters, the typical American. Everybody likes him. It is perhaps the only thing that Capablanca, Tarrasch, and Lasker can agree with. A gregarious, outgoing, bowtied gentleman, Marshall enjoys a cigar as much as poor Pillsbury, but unfortunately for his game, he also seems to enjoy a good drink as much as Blackburne. Yet he has been the only man in recent years to finish ahead of Lasker or Capablanca in a tournament.

"But where, the reader may rightfully ask, was Schlechter, so close to the world title just four short years ago? Or Maroczy of Budapest? Or the young sacrificial genius of Vienna, Rudolf Spielmann? Or that familiar face from all recent tournaments, Oldrich Duras of Prague?

"I'm afraid, dear reader, that we live in turbulent times, and even chess has had to suffer. You may recall how the great Baden-Baden tournament of 1870 was interrupted by the opening blast of the Franco-Prussian War. And how our good friend Blackburne was arrested by the suspicious Germans as a French spy.

"Now we are in another Time of Troubles. Our ally, little Serbia, has been making futile attempts to preserve her dignity against the brutal government of the Austro-Hungarian Empire. It is no secret that plans are already drawn up by the military for the next great war. And so, with reluctance, the Chess Society of Petrograd had to recognize Schlechter, Maroczy, Spielmann, and Duras as citizens of an enemy power and thus, persona non grata. . . .

"The first round on April 21 revealed the new scientific approach to the Royal Game that is often spoken of by our younger players. Black scored 4½ points out of five games. The age of Grand Attack is passing before us. The young law student, Alekhine, accepted a speculative sacrifice of the Exchange from Gunsberg and consolidated easily to win in thirty moves. Lasker took two ripe pawns from Blackburne, who never got in a check for his investment until the sixty-first move. Janowski, true to his form, took a solid positional game and transformed it into an unsound attacking one. He lost to Bernstein. Marshall and Rubinstein sparred for thirty-four moves, made a draw, and called it peace.

"The highlight of the round was the turnabout in Nimzovich's contest with Capablanca. 'Nimzo,' as his friends have begun to call him, began with a theoretical improvement on the sixth and seventh moves of the Ruy Lopez, an idea attributed to J. Showalter of America: *1 P-K4, P-K4; 2 N-KB3, N-QB3; 3 N-B3, N-B3; 4 B-N5, P-Q3; 5 P-Q4, B-Q2; 6 BxN!, BxB; 7 Q-Q3!, PxP; 8 NxP, P-KN3; 9 NxB, PxN; 10 Q-R6, Q-Q2; 11 Q-N7, R-B1; 12 QxRP, B-N2; 13 O-O, O-O; 14 Q-R6, KR-K1.*

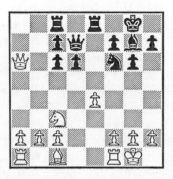

"All the spectators thought that with his extra pawn, Nimzovich would consolidate easily, as he should have after *15 Q-B4, R-N1; 16 R-N1, P-B4; 17 P-QR3, N-N5; 18 B-Q2.* But White began to lose the thread with *15 Q-Q3?, Q-K3!; 16 P-B3, N-Q2; 17 B-Q2?!, N-K4; 18 Q-K2, N-B5; 19 QR-N1, R-R1; 20 P-QR4?* Later, during the post-mortem analysis, Señor Capablanca said that White's last chance for equality (!) lay in 20 P-QN3. But after Nimzovich's move the Black heavy pieces invaded with *20 . . . NxB; 21 QxN, Q-B5!; 22 KR-Q1, KR-N1; 23 Q-K3, R-N5!; 24 Q-N5, B-Q5ch; 25 K-R1, QR-N1.* In this position White faced the loss of all his Queenside pawns, so he played *26 RxB* and struggled on for fifteen moves before surrender.

"The second round was more of a feast for the many spectators. Our inexperienced Alekhine lost a Bishop in the opening against Blackburne's wily Bird's Defense (*1 P-K4, P-K4; 2 N-KB3, N-QB3; 3 B-N5, N-Q5?!; 4 NxN,*

PxN; 5 O-O, P-KN3; 6 P-Q3, B-N2; 7 P-KB4?!, P-QB3; 8 B-B4, P-Q4; 9 PxP, PxP; 10 B-N5ch, K-B1!; 11 N-Q2??, Q-R4; 12 P-QR4, P-QR3). But White valiantly hung on until the ending and made things so difficult that Blackburne conceded a draw on the forty-fourth move.

"Lasker seemed to be off on another of his bad tournament starts as he lost two Pawns quickly to Nimzovich. But he found just the right strategy—to wit, doing nothing. Nimzo was encouraged into a shaky continuation which allowed the champion to sacrifice a Rook for perpetual check.

"Tarrasch-Janowski was an odd contest. From a bad opening with White, Tarrasch blocked the center and gave up a Bishop for a Knight. Both sides doubled Rooks on the KR-file before Janowski closed it. Finally the Queenside became Armageddon. After thirty moves of maneuver, Janowski's Queen and Bishop cracked through. The spectators then gleefully pointed out that Black could have won fifteen moves earlier when both players had overlooked a Tarrasch blunder.

"Two other old rivals met in the final game of the round. Capablanca-Marshall began: *1 P-K4, P-K4; 2 N-KB3, N-KB3; 3 NxP, P-Q3; 4 N-KB3, NxP; 5 P-Q4, P-Q4; 6 B-Q3, B-Q3; 7 P-B4, B-N5ch?!; 8 QN-Q2, O-O; 9 O-O, NxN; 10 BxN, BxB; 11 QxB, N-B3; 12 KR-K1, B-N5; 13 N-K5, NxN; 14 RxN, PxP; 15 BxBP, Q-B3; 16 QR-K1, QR-Q1.*

"White seemed to have a crushing advantage in space—just the kind of simplified middlegame that Capa is known to love. He played *17 R–K7!?* which prevented 17 . . . RxP; 18 RxKBP! or 17 . . . QxP; 18 QxQ, PxQ; 19 RxQBP.

"It also appeared to deter *17 . . . B–K3* because of *18 R(7)xB, PxR; 19 RxKP,* but Marshall allowed the combination: *19 . . . QxQP!.* Our fans thought the deadly discovered check would spell Marshall's doom. But a surprised Capablanca searched vainly and could only find *20 R–Q6ch, QxB; 21 RxR, RxR; 22 QxRch, K–B2* with a certain draw.

"The best news was Bernstein's second victory (over Gunsberg), which put him in first place. He drew with Blackburne in the third round and could have been tied with Lasker if the champion hadn't made yet another error which permitted Marshall to draw. Two Lasker errors in a row is never a good sign early in a tournament. But the big story of the day was the spectacle of Rubinstein botching an endgame just when he had Capablanca in his net.

"The Polish master, so eerily quiet as to unnerve even the spectators, only had to defuse the Cuban's Queenside majority of Pawns. Black's 27 . . . P–N5! is a good try to obtain activity for his Queen. If all the Queenside pawns are liquidated, White would still have winning chances on the Kingside. But they were acknowledgably slim.

"However, 28 P-QB4! would have kept the Queen bottled up. For example, 28 . . . Q-K5; 29 QxBP, Q-N8ch: 30 K-R2, QxP; 31 QxP, QxKBP; 32 Q-K7! with the winning advance of the Bishop's Pawn.

"Yet, inexplicably, Rubinstein played *28 QxBP?*, and the draw was obvious after *28 . . . PxP; 29 QxP, Q-N8ch; 30 K-R2, QxP.*

"In the fourth round Alekhine won a fine ending from Marshall to move up into a tie for first place. It might have been sole first if not for two surprises. First, Bernstein managed to save this desperate position against Nimzovich. In face of Black's threats of 30 . . . N-Q6! followed by 31 . . . R-K8ch, 30 . . . R-K7 followed by 31 . . . RxPch, and 30 . . . N-R6ch followed by 31 . . . Q-K6! as well as the mundane 30 . . . QxB, the betting was a kopek to a ruble that White couldn't hold the position.

"Bernstein played *30 B-R8!!*, a magical resource that protects the Bishop and restrains the Black Queen because of mate on KN7. It has been argued by some would-be analysts that 30 . . . R-K7! would win now but 31 P-N3!, N-R6ch; 32 K-R1 keeps White alive.

"Nimzovich chose *30 . . . N-Q6*, which even after *31 P-R4!* seemed decisive because of *31 . . . Q-N6*, threatening 32 . . . R-K8ch. But Bernstein came back with another fantastic saving grace in *32 R-R8, B-B1; 33 B-K4!!*, blocking the dangerous file.

"Nimzovich didn't believe it could be that simple, and his face was a torrent of consternation. He played the best plan, *33 . . . Q–B7ch; 34 K–R2, QxRPch; 35 K–N1, N–K4!; 36 BxN, QxB!*. But White came back with *37 B–R8!* and the game was drawn shortly after *37 . . . Q–K6ch; 38 K–R2, Q–B5ch; 39 K–N1, Q–N6!; 40 B–B3, Q–K6ch; 41 K–R1, Q–B5; 42 Q–Q1, Q–R3ch; 43 K–N1, Q–K6ch; 44 K–R1, Q–R3ch; 45 K–N1, Q–K6ch; 46 K–R1, QxB; 47 RxB! and 48 Q–N4ch.*

"The third tournament leader was Lasker, who did to Rubinstein what Rubinstein failed to do against Capablanca. Akiba suddenly appeared in danger of being eliminated from the finals, a horrible thought because of what it would do to our planned finale.

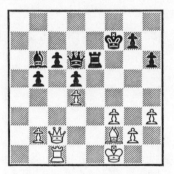

"After great maneuvering Lasker found *42 Q–B5ch, R–B3; 43 Q–K5!*. He correctly evaluated the ending as superior for him despite his slightly bad Bishop. Since Rubinstein could not allow the Queen to dominate, the game continued— *43 . . . R–K3; 44 QxQ, RxQ; 45 K–K2, K–K2; 46 K–Q3, R–N3; 47 P–KN3, R–B3; 48 P–B4, K–Q2; 49 R–K1, R–B1; 50 R–QR1, P–R4; 51 B–K3, P–N3; 52 R–KB1, K–Q3; 53 P–KN4, PxP; 54 PxP.*

"Once again Rubinstein bewildered the onlookers with an uncharacteristic endgame blunder. Was this not the Rubinstein whose play with Rook and Pawns has so astonished his rivals that they suspected he was inspired by witchcraft?

"With the routine 54 . . . K–K3 as suggested by the other masters Black should survive. Instead, Rubinstein played *54 . . . P–B4??; 55 PxPch, BxP; 56 BxBch, KxB* and began to run out of moves following *57 P–B5, PxP; 58 PxP, R–B3; 59 R–B4!, P–N5; 60 P–N3!.* Black was in zugzwang and had to concede ground with *60 . . . R–B2; 61 P–B6, K–Q3; 62 K–Q4, K–K3; 63 R–B2!!, K–Q3; 64 R–QR2, R–B2; 65 R–R6ch, K–Q2; 66 R–N6* and here the 'Pride of Poland' *Resigned.*

(Translator's note: There is something about losing an important game which psychoanalysts have never been able to explain adequately. Perhaps Petar Trifunovich, the veteran Yugoslav drawing master of the 1950s and '60s, explained it best. During a small event in his country in 1970, America's Ken Rogoff lost one of his early games but then won several in a row. "Ah, poor Rogoff," said the Dubrovnik grandmaster, "You should play like ———," mentioning the name of a Yugoslav teenager also in the tournament. Rogoff protested that the object of Trifunovich's praise had drawn several games and was thus far behind Rogoff in the standings. Trifunovich replied: "Yes, but you have lost a game and a lost game goes to your heart."

As illogical as that sounds, the pages of chess history are replete with examples of how the shock of a loss can open the floodgates to more bad play. This is exactly what happened to Rubinstein.)

"And on the following day there was more bad news for Rubinstein when he met Alekhine. Both sides misplayed the opening (1 P-Q4, N-KB3; 2 P-QB4, P-K3; 3 N-QB3, B-N5; 4 P-K3, P-QN3; 5 B-Q3, B-N2; 6 P-B3, P-B4; 7 P-QR3, BxNch; 8 PxB, P-Q4?!; 9 N-K2, O-O; 10 O-O, QN-Q2; 11 N-N3, Q-B2; 12 BPxP, KPxP; 13 P-K4?, BPxP; 14 BPxP, Q-B6; 15 B-K3, PxP; 16 PxP, B-R3?; 17 BxB, QxBch; 18 K-R1, NxP; 19 N-B5!, N-B7ch; 20 RxN, QxR; 21 Q-N4, P-N3).

"White (Rubinstein) was ready to obtain a clear superiority with 22 N-K7ch and 23 QxN. For some reason, however, he played 22 R-KB1?!, Q-N7; 23 N-R6ch?, K-N2; 24 NxP. This made sense if Black played 24 . . . RxN; 25 RxRch, KxR; 26 QxNch or 24 . . . N-B3?; 25 RxN!, KxR; 26 Q-B4ch and 27 Q-K5ch with a mating attack.

"But Alekhine coolly played 24 . . . Q-N6! and White fumbled away his chances with 25 P-Q5, N-B3!; 26 Q-Q4, RxN; 27 B-B4, Q-R5; 28 P-N4, R-QB1 29 Resigns.

"The fifth round turned out be the most exciting of the preliminaries when Marshall failed to overreact to Bernstein's pretty but disastrous tenth move.

MARSHALL–BERNSTEIN: *1 P–Q4, P–Q4; 2 P–QB4, P–QB3; 3 N–QB3, N–B3; 4 PxP, PxP; 5 N–B3, P–K3; 6 B–N5, Q–N3; 7 Q–B2, N–B3; 8 P–K3, B–Q2; 9 P–QR3, R–B1; 10 B–Q3, B–N5?; 11 O–O!, BxN; 12 PxB, N–QR4; 13 QR–N1, Q–B3; 14 KR–B1, Q–R5; 15 Q–R2, N–K5?; 16 BxN, PxB; 17 N–K5!, P–B3; 18 R–N4, RxP?!; 19 Q–Q2!!, RxRch; 20 QxR, O–O; 21 RxQ and wins.*

"But the star game was Nimzovich–Tarrasch:

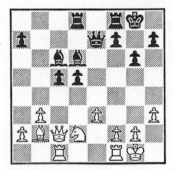

"Black's hanging pawns were, in Nimzovich's eloquent phrase, 'a curious mixture of static weakness and dynamic strength.' If White had time for 19 P–QN4 or 19 B–R3, the Pawns would be revealed as a weakness. But Black struck first with *18 . . . P–Q5!!*.

"Suddenly the Black Bishops were free and we were treated to a combination similar to the one Lasker discovered a generation ago in his 1889 game with Bauer in Amsterdam, the sacrifice of two Bishops. Our game con-

tinued *19 PxP, BxPch!; 20 KxB, Q–R5ch; 21 K–N1, BxP!* If
White accepts the second piece, he is mated by way of
22 . . . Q–N5ch and *23 . . . R–Q4.*

"Nimzo tried *22 P–B3,* and the German responded
22 . . . KR–K1!, which confined the White K to the Kingside
and made . . . R–K7(ch) available. There followed *23 N–K4,
Q–R8ch; 24 K–B2, BxR!* and since White could not permit
25 RxB, Q–R7ch, he played *25 P–Q5, P–B4!; 26 Q–B3,
Q–N7ch; 27 K–K3.* Dr. Tarrasch finished off with *27 . . .
RxNch!; 28 PxR, P–B5ch; 29 KxP, R–B1ch; 30 K–K5,
Q–R7ch; 31 K–K6, R–K1ch; 32 K–Q7, B–N4 Mate!* This
was only narrowly nosed out for the Brilliancy Prize by
Capablanca's victory over Bernstein two rounds later.
Capa's idea was original, but Tarrasch was repeating the
Lasker–Bauer game!

"Round five was also significant because it was the first
time that Dr. Lasker and Señor Capablanca had ever met
over the chessboard. The champion seemed to treat the
game lightly as he gave his worthy opponent the two-Bishop
advantage and the better Pawn structure very early. But
once again Lasker had judged just how much he could
risk without going too far. Pieces were traded off quickly
and a draw was agreed.

"So after five fairly exciting rounds we were pleased to
see Alekhine leading with 4 points; Lasker at 3½; Bernstein
and Tarrasch (with a bye) at 3; and Janowski, Marshall,
and Capablanca (with a bye) at 2½. Rubinstein had only 1
point plus the bye in five games, and Nimzovich had
only 1½.

"The only commotion in the sixth round was Capablanca's
end of our young hero's streak.

ALEKHINE–CAPABLANCA: *1 P–K4, P–K4; 2 N–KB3,
N–QB3; 3 B–N5, P–Q3; 4 P–Q4, PxP; 5 NxP, B–Q2;
6 N–QB3, N–B3; 7 O–O, B–K2; 8 N–B5?, BxN; 9 PxB,
O–O; 10 R–K1, N–Q2!; 11 N–Q5, B–B3; 12 P–QB3,
N–N3!; 13 NxBch, QxN; 14 BxN, PxB; 15 Q–B3:*

"An indifferent opening gave White only the mirage of an initiative. Capa staked a claim on concrete values with *15 . . . KR–K1!; 16 B–K3, P–B4; 17 R–K2, R–K4!; 18 QR–K1, QR–K1*. This Capablanca is young but he never misses an opportunity to seize an open file and never overlooks a trick such as 18 . . . RxP?; 19 B–Q4!

"Now White could have swapped Rooks with 19 B–B4 so that he could overcome the passivity of his pieces. However, Alekhine's penchant for speculation was satisfied only by *19 Q–N7?, QxP; 20 QxBP, Q–K3; 21 QxRP*, reminding the spectators of Capablanca's first round against Nimzo.

"As observed by Dr. Tarrasch, Black already had a forced win with *21 . . . N–Q4!; 22 K–B1, N–B5; 23 R–Q2*, and now 23 . . . Q–N5!, e.g., 24 P–B3, Q–K3; 25 BxN, RxRch; 26 K–B2, R–B8ch!; 27 K–N3, P–N4!; 28 BxNP, Q–N3; 29 K–R4, R–K4; 30 P–KB4, RxPch. But Capa played the fancier *23 . . . NxP!?* and still won after *24 KxN, Q–N5ch; 25 K–B1, Q–R6ch; 26 K–K2, RxBch; 27 PxR, QxKPch; 28 K–Q1, QxR(8)ch*, although, if truth must be told, he received some later help from his opponent.

"The seventh round saw Alekhine and Lasker fighting to a perpetual check in twenty-five moves — another bad move costing Lasker a win. So Capablanca's fifteen-move combination against Bernstein put him in a tie for first with Alekhine. Bernstein fell to sixth, and sixth place did not

count for much in the preliminaries since only five men
would survive to the finals. Rubinstein had already bitten
the dust.

"To pounce on the faltering Bernstein, Lasker served
up his favorite Berlin Defense in the eighth round and
had almost a won game after thirty-five moves.

"What happened next was passing strange. As stubborn
a believer in common sense as Dr. Lasker is, he is super-
stitious about a few things. One was having a row of cigars
placed at his right when he sat down to play. Another was
having Martha always present in the audience during
important games.

"As the third hour approached, his bride of four years
stepped out of the playing hall for a breath of fresh air after
being assured that Emanuel was crushing Bernstein easily.
Half an hour later she returned and asked if he had resigned. Yes, it was terrible, one of the onlookers said.

"Why terrible? she asked, and was told this: Black played
35 . . . Q–R7?? (instead of the solid 35 . . . Q–N6), thinking
that 36 NxN, R–R7; 37 R–K2, R–R8ch; 38 K–B2 couldn't
be played because of 38 . . . Q–N8 mate.

"But there was no mate since KN3 was vacant. Lasker
played 38 . . . PxN, and after 39 Q–N6! he had to lose a
Pawn and eventually the game. It was Lasker who had
resigned.

"Catastrophe! First Rubinstein was cut down and now Lasker appeared on the brink of elimination. Our plan of a supreme Championship finals was slipping away from our fingers as the rounds continued.

"And in the ninth round Lasker came very close to duplicating Rubinstein's feat of two crippling losses in a row ("Trifunovich's Law" — trans.) but Tarrasch allowed him to escape with a draw. Capablanca was by this time in tremendous form. His winning plan against Janowski began with the eleventh move — play P–QN5 and secure Q5 for a N. That was all he needed:

"CAPABLANCA–JANOWSKI: *1 P–K4, P–K4; 2 N–KB3, N–QB3; 3 B–N5, P–QR3; 4 BxN, QPxB: 5 N–B3, B–QB4; 6 P–Q3, B–KN5; 7 B–K3, BxB?!; 8 PxB, Q–K2; 9 O–O, O–O–O?!; 10 Q–K1, N–R3; 11 R–N1!!, P–B3; 12 P–N4, N–B2; 13 P–QR4, BxN; 14 RxB, P–QN3; 15 P–N5!, BPxP; 16 PxP, P–R4; 17 N–Q5, Q–B4; 18 P–B4, N–N4; 19 R–B2, N–K3; 20 Q–B3, R–Q2; 21 R–Q1, K–N2; 22 P–Q4!, Q–Q3; 23 R–B2, PxP; 24 PxP, N–B5; 25 P–B5!, NxN; 26 PxN, QxP(Q) 27 P–B6ch and Black Resigned in four moves.*

"In the excitement of the top boards it was easy to overlook the bizarre other games. Marshall and Blackburne, for example, set some kind of record. Marshall made eleven consecutive moves with an N while Blackburne made eleven straight moves with his Q. The N moves were better, and Marshall pulled into second place. The score stood: Capablanca 6–3; Marshall 5½; Alekhine, Tarrasch, and Bernstein 5; Lasker, 4½. Everyone but Marshall had had a bye, or rest day, already.

"Only the strongest players had any fighting spirit left for the final rounds, and this favored the World Champion. He won two easy games from his old customers, Janowski and Gunsberg. This gave him 6½, a score equaled by Tarrasch, who had to fend off Bernstein's last hurrah. The Ukrainian could have qualified for the finals if he had won, but a blunder on the seventeenth move cost him two Pawns. So with the preliminary section over, the scores were: Capablanca, 8; Lasker, Tarrasch, 6½; Alekhine, Marshall, 6; Bernstein, Rubinstein, 5; Nimzovich, 4; Blackburne, Janowski 3½; Gunsberg, 1.

"This was a creditable showing for all five finalists, a setback for Rubinstein, and what a performance by the Cuban! I must confess, we organizers had by now lost all hope of an exciting finish to our tournament. Since the points accumulated in the preliminaries were to be carried over into the finals, Capablanca began with a 1½-point lead. This surely would be insurmountable in the eight games each player had left. He could collect the prize right now, P. P. Saburow, president of the club committee, said to me.

"To say that the final stage of play at Petrograd was summed up in one game is a bit of an overstatement—but only a *bit*. The world of chessplayers now knows of the game I speak, but let me set the stage:

"*Round 12:* Capablanca had the bye, so Lasker moved to within a half-point of the lead by belittling Alekhine's Albin Counter Gambit. Marshall moved into third place with a fine tactical endgame victory over Tarrasch, who has been constantly complaining of the weather.

"*Round 13:* The weather got worse for Tarrasch, who ventured a Falkbeer Counter Gambit against Alekhine and lost in forty moves. The Capablanca–Lasker game was a bitter draw. The Cuban held a huge advantage right out of the opening, and, despite some inaccurate play, entered the endgame with two pieces against a Rook. But all Pawns were on the Kingside, with three for each player. Capablanca maneuvered his B and N for seventy moves until he conceded that he had run out of winning plans.

"*Round 14:* Tarrasch made up for Capa's lack of success in this round by turning a clearly favorable position against the Cuban into a clearly lost one in less than ten easy moves. Marshall had hit his high point in the tournament in the previous round, and here he made a horrible blunder against Alekhine. It was the kind of mistake we like to call a criminal move, and it allowed mate in two.

"*Round 15:* The tournament was already very long, but now it became a race of just two horses. Both Lasker and Capablanca won, and that left the scores with Capa at 10½ (yet undefeated), Lasker at 9, and Alekhine a point behind. Lasker still trailed by the same margin as at the beginning of the finals. And it was clear that Alekhine was no real threat to the leaders. The little inconsistencies and overly anxious flights into speculation had already begun to mar his record. This young lawyer may be champion one day, they say, but he will have to curb his imagination first.

"*Round 16:* The best of the finals' games so far was fought this day when Marshall met the Champion. 'He dared an awful lot,' Tarrasch remarked of Lasker. 'And it may well have proved fatal for him. But then, just this is his style.'

"The position was double-edged, and the betting—for Russian chess lovers are fond of wagering on games in progress—was heavy on both sides. Lasker selected 21 ... B–R5 probably counting on 22 R–Q2, R–K6!?; 23 BxR, PxB; 24 N–N5; P–KR3, or some such complication.

"Instead, the American played 22 *BxP?!* and after 22 ... *PxB; 23 B–Q8!, QxB; 24 N–N5* it was clear that Black must surrender the Queen. However, after 24 ... *QxN; 25 QxQ, BxR; 26 QxP!, B–B7!* (otherwise 27 R–B7);

27 QxB, P–Q6; 28 Q–Q1, P–R4; 29 Q–N4, R–KB1 it was equally clear that Black had more than ample compensation.

"The preponderance of Lasker's material made itself felt after *30 R–Q1, QR–K1; 31 Q–N6, R–K7!; 32 R–KB1* (32 RxP, R–K8ch; and then . . . NxR) *P–Q7!; 33 RxRch, KxR; 34 QxPch, K–N1; 35 Q–Q8ch, K–R2; 36 Q–R4ch, B–R3*–and Marshall ran out of checks and moves. Even Lasker's archrival, Tarrasch, said such games as this made the 4,000-ruble honorarium we paid the champion seem worthwhile.

"But this was only the first half-point Lasker had gained on the Cuban (who was drawing with Alekhine): Capablanca 11, Lasker 10, Alekhine 8½ at the halfway point of the finals.

"*Round 17:* Alekhine seemed to be pressing Lasker most of the way in one of those early endings that appear in the Exchange Variation of the Ruy Lopez. And then, as if by sorcery, Black forced the win of the Exchange! This put old Emanuel in a temporary tie with Capa, who had his day off. After the long and eventless Marshall–Tarrasch draw was finished, the stage was set for the showdown that we chess fans had hoped for.

"*Round 18:*

RUY LOPEZ

Emanuel Lasker	J. R. Capablanca
1 P–K4	P–K4
2 N–KB3	N–QB3
3 B–N5	P–QR3
4 BxN	. . .

"There has been much talk in the weeks since this game was played about Lasker's choice of this ancient system. The opening is better than its reputation, and its reputation is still good. Remember that Capablanca and Alekhine had earlier selected this variation when playing for a win in this tournament. And few can forget that this same Lasker played 4 BxN to begin his match with Tarrasch six years ago.

"There is an added psychological motive here. As every Russian schoolboy knows, White has the better Pawn structure after 4 . . . QPxB and should have strong winning chances if all the pieces are exchanged. This means that Capablanca, who was much disposed to share this particular point, had to seek complications. The onus was on Black already. Very clever, Dr. Lasker!

	4	. . .	QPxB
	5	P–Q4	PxP
	6	QxP	QxQ
	7	NxQ	B–Q3

"We must point out that Tarrasch played 7 . . . P–QB4 and 8 . . . B–Q2 and developed a satisfactory game with his K on the Queenside.

	8	N–QB3	N–K2
	9	O–O	O–O
	10	P–B4	R–K1?!

"And here there was considerable dispute over whether Black should stop White's daring plan with 10 . . . P–KB4; 11 P–K5, B–N5; 12 B–Q2, BxN!; 13 BxB, P–QN3 followed by 14 . . . P–B4 with a rock-solid game.

	11	N–N3	P–B3

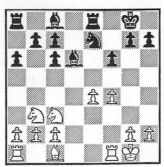

12   P–B5!?   . . .

"An exceptionally bold idea. White has chosen a most innocuous treatment of the opening. It is common, for example, for White to put his K on the Queenside. Lasker's move was considered by one and all to be a gamble. He hoped to exchange off Black's best piece, the KB, with B–B4 before Black could pile up against the very vulnerable White KP.

12   . . .   P–QN3?

"Capablanca did not take this threat as seriously as he should. The more aggressive kibitzers were waiting for 12 . . . P–KN4! so that on 13 PxP e.p., NxP; 14 RxP Black could regain his Pawn with 14 . . . B–K4 and 15 . . . BxN. This would alleviate his troubles greatly.

13   B–B4   B–N2?
14   BxB!!   PxB

"Black's second error appears to have been his failure to play 13 . . . BxB. The paradox is that Black's Pawns are much weaker now that they are undoubled. After 13 . . . BxB; 14 RxB, B–N2; 15 R–Q1, Black still has major problems because he must exchange Rooks or concede the only open file to White. And as every Russian schoolboy knows, the exchanges of heavy pieces must favor the better Pawn structure.

"The next stage of the game was easy to understand. First White placed an N on K6 and controlled the key file: *15 N–Q4, QR–Q1; 16 N–K6, R–Q2; 17 QR–Q1, N–B1; 18 R–B2, P–QN4; 19 R(2)–Q2, R(2)–K2; 20 P–QN4!, K–B2; 21 P–QR3, B–R1, 22 K–B2, R–R2.*

"The next stage of the plan was to open a Kingside-file for his more active Rooks: *23 P–N4, P–R3; 24 R–Q3, P–QR4; 25 P–KR4, PxP; 26 PxP, R(2)–K2; 27 K–B3, R–N1; 28 K–B4, P–N3, 29 R–N3, P–N4ch; 30 K–B3, N–N3; 31 PxP, RPxP.*

"Black would have done better to open the KN file on move 29 because he would have been able to fight back on that line but could not compete on the KR file. Capablanca was hoping for 32 RxP, N-B5! followed by 33 . . . N-K4ch with a fighting chance. Lasker's handling of the finish was superb.

32	R-R3!	R-Q2
33	K-N3!	K-K1
34	R(1)-KR1	B-N2
35	P-K5!!	. . .

"This was envisaged when White played K-N3 to get his K off the long diagonal of Black's Bishop. The last piece to enter the attack was White's QN, and now it could have played a decisive role on either KB6 or QB5. For example, 35 . . . BPxP; 36 N-K4, N-Q4; 37 R-R7!, B-B1; 38 R-R8!, winning a piece.

35	. . .	QPxP
36	N-K4	N-Q4
37	N(6)-B5	. . .

"Crushing. The main threat was 38 NxB and 39 N-Q6ch. The rest of the game was brief: *37 . . . B-B1; 38 NxR, BxN; 39 R-R7, R-B1; 40 R-QR1, K-Q1; 41 R-R8ch; B-B1; 42 N-B5, Resigns.*

" 'The spectators had followed the final moves breath-lessly,' Dr. Lasker recalled. 'That Black's position was in ruins was obvious to the veriest tyro. And now Capablanca turned over his King. From the several hundred spectators, there came such applause as I have never experienced in all my life as a chessplayer. It was like the wholly spontaneous applause which thunders forth in the theater, of which the individual is almost unconscious.'

"Well, that was Round 18. What some chess fans have already forgotten is that his immortal and dramatic triumph left Lasker in first place only in a technical sense. He had a bye in the nineteenth round, and Capablanca had a clear chance to resume a share of first place.

"*Round 19:* A second miracle occurred this day. With the White pieces against Tarrasch, Capablanca opened *1 P-K4, P-K4; 2 N-KB3, N-QB3; 3 N-B3, N-B3; 4 B-N5, B-N5; 5 O-O, O-O; 6 P-Q3, BxN; 7 PxB, P-Q4?!; 8 BxN?!, PxB; 9 NxP, Q-Q3; 10 B-B4, R-K1; 11 Q-B3!, PxP; 12 PxP, RxN.*

"With a choice of two Rooks to place on Q1 so to attack the Q and tactically profit from Black's piece position, Capa carelessly chose the KR. What happened then is *13 KR-Q1??, B-N5; 14 Q-N3, BxR; 15 BxR* — and suddenly the Cuban saw that *15 . . . Q-Q7!* threatened mate on the last rank and preserved the extra piece. There would have been no mate possible after 13 QR-Q1! (In Trifunovich's

SCORETABLE

	C	L	T	A	M	Be	R	N	Bl	J	G	Total
1. Capablanca	X	½	½	1	½	1	½	1	1	1	1	8–2
2. Lasker	½	X	½	½	½	0	1	½	1	1	1	6½–3½
3. Tarrasch	½	½	X	½	½	1	½	1	1	0	1	6½–3½
4. Alekhine	0	½	½	X	1	½	1	½	½	½	1	6–4
5. Marshall	½	½	½	0	X	1	½	½	1	1	½	6–4
6. Bernstein	0	1	0	½	0	X	½	½	½	1	1	5–5
7. Rubinstein	½	0	½	0	½	½	X	½	½	1	1	5–5
8. Nimzovich	0	½	0	½	½	½	½	X	0	½	1	4–6
9. Blackburne	0	0	0	½	0	½	½	1	X	0	1	3½–6½
10. Janowski	0	0	1	½	0	0	0	½	1	X	½	3½–6½
11. Gunsberg	0	0	0	0	½	0	0	0	0	½	X	1–9

FINALS	Lasker	Capablanca	Alekhine	Tarrasch	Marshall	Total
1. Lasker 6½	XX	½1	11	1½	11	13½–4½
2. Capablanca 8	½0	XX	½1	10	11	13–5
3. Alekhine 6	00	½0	XX	11	1½	10–8
4. Tarrasch 6½	0½	01	00	XX	0½	8½–9½
5. Marshall 6	00	00	0½	1½	XX	8–10

words, the eighteenth round went to his heart—trans.). This is what cost our friend from across the Atlantic his tournament.

"There were, of course, two rounds left, and Capa picked up a half-point in the twentieth when Marshall butchered an ending to him while Lasker couldn't budge Dr. Tarrasch. But in the final round both the contenders were paired with favorite 'customers'. Capablanca accepted Alekhine's Pawn offer and won in forty-five moves. Marshall didn't want to trade Queens so early in his game with Lasker and later complained somewhat sadly that 5 Q–K2 took all the fun out of his favorite opening:

"LASKER–MARSHALL Rd. 21: 1 P–K4, P–K4; 2 N–KB3, N–KB3; 3 NxP, P–Q3; 4 N–KB3, NxP; 5 Q–K2, Q–K2; 6 P–Q3, N–KB3; 7 B–N5, B–K3; 8 N–B3, QN–Q2; 9 O–O–O, P–KR3; 10 B–R4, P–KN4; 11 B–N3, N–R4; 12 P–Q4!, NxB; 13 RPxN, P–N5?; 14 N–KR4, P–Q4?; 15 Q–N5!, O–O–O; 16 Q–R5, P–R3; 17 BxP, PxB; 18 QxRPch, K–N1; 19 N–N5, N–N3; 20 R–Q3, Q–N4ch; 21 K–N1, B–Q3; 22 R–N3, KR–K1; 23 P–R4, B–KB4; 24 N–R7!, B–Q2; 25 P–R5, Q–Q7; 26 PxN, R–K8ch; 27 K–R2!, P–QB3; 28 N–N5!, PxN; 29 Q–R7ch, Resigns.

"Thus ended one of the greatest meetings of chess talent the world had ever witnessed. The final banquet was an exceptional treat. There were mounds of Beluga caviar and gallons of vodka and French wines. Two incidents stood out during the lengthy meal.

"First, Martha Lasker appealed to her husband to make peace with Capablanca. Instantly he got up from his chair, carried a glass of champagne to the Cuban master, and drank to his health. After they shook hands, the entire table of guests applauded the reconciliation.

"The second instance came when Czar Nicholas, who had taken an avid interest in the progress of the tournament to which he had contributed 1,000 rubles, arose to speak. Our beloved leader said that the five finalists had reached a point of expertise which placed them in a class of their own. These men, I believe he said, have given so much to the game that they deserve a professional title — Grandmaster. There may be others to warrant the title, he said, but Lasker, Capablanca, Alekhine, Tarrasch, and Marshall will always be remembered as the first.

"And on that festive note we close our chronicle of the Petrograd Masters' tournament."

J. J. Sossnitsky
July 11, 1914

IV

The Old Man,
The New Idea

Q: Dr. Lasker?

A: Yes?

Q: Dr. Lasker, I'm Jeffrey Lee of the *New York Globe.* I'd like to interview you about the chess match.

A: Ah, Mr. Lee — you're not a relative of F. J. Lee of England, are you? I played him twenty-five years ago at the London tournament. Won both games.

Q: No, Dr. Lasker. About the match . . .

A: Tournament, my boy, not match. And as you can see, it is still going on. Réti is trying to squeeze the last ounce of blood out of Janowski.

Q: Sir, could you tell our readers about the tournament and how you came to win it?

A: Well, I must write Martha but . . . to begin with I was as surprised as anyone here that the top prize was granted to me. It was a surprise to me, a shock to some of my colleagues . . . and a thunderbolt, I'm sure, to Señor Capablanca.

106

Q: Why didn't you think you would win?

A: Well, there are many reasons. First, let me recall a little ancient history. You must understand what has happened since the last great tournament, the one at St. Petersburg just before the War. Even the Czar was present. A very keen man, the Czar, but not a first-rate mind. No, I'm afraid he would never have made a chessplayer. . . .

I went straight home after the tournament banquet. But Alekhine, Marshall, and Tarrasch headed for Mannheim, where a modest tournament was set to start in late July. A fairly good event—it had Spielmann, Milan Vidmar, and young Tartakover also. It got under way on July 20th, I recall, but at the end of one week other events overtook chessplay.

The Austrian ultimatum following the assassination of Archduke Ferdinand was presented to the Serbs on the 28th while Alekhine was leading. Spielmann and Vidmar were tied with him when the Czar called for general mobilization of the troops. On August 1st Alekhine was in clear first place. But by then Germany had declared war and the tournament ended with the eleventh round.

All of the foreigners were escorted either to the nearest westbound train or to the nearest jail. Janowski, Alekhine, Bogolyubov of the Ukraine, plus a few other Russians— Flamberg, Selesniev, and so on—were jailed at Rastatt and then at Triberg . . .

Q: I'm afraid I don't see what all this . . .

A: Wait just a minute, young man. Always so impatient, this new generation. . . . Now the chessplayers were all confined together and left to amuse themselves—which meant, of course, to amuse themselves with chess.

They played constantly and were even allowed to conduct tournaments. Some of the Austrian citizens—Vidmar, Breyer, Réti, and Duras—were staying nearby, and they were allowed to compete. Together, they debated the great issues of strategy that had been taken for granted since the days of Steinitz. Naturally they came up with new answers. For example, they analyzed the Fianchetto Defense to

1 P–Q4 and also the reply 1 . . . N–KB3 to 1 P–K4. They questioned so deeply that when the Armistice was signed each of them had improved immensely in depth and they were ready to test their new theories on an unsuspecting chess world. It was the "New Idea" of chess, they called it.

Q: What about you?

A: I played little chess. It contented me to work on my verse-drama and my philosophical works. Martha and I got along.

It wasn't so easy for some of the others. Schlechter, the poor man, literally starved to death in 1918 shortly after a tournament in Berlin that I won. Tarrasch lost two sons in the early days of the fighting, and I'm afraid he has changed greatly. Rubinstein's emotional problems have only been exacerbated by the war.

Q: But even after you lost the World Championship title in 1921 you were still considered Capablanca's coequal?

A: Yes, other people wanted me to fight to get my title back, but I said no. Too much trouble over something that wasn't worth all that it's reputed to be. This tournament here in New York was originally planned to be a match between Capablanca and Alekhine. But there were not enough backers who wanted to see Alekhine. Many wanted me. So the organizers arranged for this amusing event as a substitute.

Q: And yet you didn't think you could win?

A: As I told my good friend Edward Lasker, this "New Idea" may not be as good as everyone claims, but it is challenging. Even if you find over-the-board the best method of combatting such a strategy with its attacks from the wings and apparent disregard of the center, you have probably spent the better part of two hours doing so. Then, when you need time to think of improving your game, you have none.

Q: How good is this "New Idea"?

A: See for yourself. No one had ever heard of this fellow Selesniev, but he finished fourth at a very strong outing at Mahrich Ostrau in Czechoslovakia last year. I won the tournament ahead of Réti and Gruenfeld, but this Russian came in before Euwe, the young Dutchman, Tartakover, Tarrasch, Spielmann, and Rubinstein. Bogolyubov has scored two reasonable firsts—at Pistyan in '22 and at Carlsbad last year. And, of course, this young dynamo Réti won at Gothenburg 1920 and Teplitz-Schonau 1922. And Alekhine won the first Soviet Championship four years ago and took first at Hastings. . . .

Q: I'm afraid these names and dates don't mean very much to me.

A: Yes, but this was not the success of individuals. It was supposed to be the success of a style. Tartakover called it the Neo-Romanticism. Others call it Hypermodernism. I prefer the "New Idea."

Q: I understand this is the first strong American tournament in a generation.

A: Quite so. The last was at Cambridge Springs in Pennsylvania, where Mr. Marshall surprised everyone. I must say I prefer New York. This fine hotel, the Alamac, has just been finished, and it is an excellent venue. I understand the general manager of the hotel even contributed $2,500 or about one-fourth of the projected cost of the event. . . . Señor Capablanca's popularity, I think, had something to do with it.

Q: Capablanca was therefore the favorite?

A: Certainly. He is Mr. Chess as far as the American public and even much of Europe is concerned. People who know nothing of Rooks and Bishops know who Capablanca is. He is handsome, healthy, even witty—the kind of man we need as ambassador to the nonplayers of the world. Or so they say.

The most impressive thing about the Cuban—and you should know that I am not apt to spread many good words about him—is that when play started on March 16, Capablanca had not lost a game in eight years. In fact, he's lost only four games of 126 from St. Petersburg to New York. Not bad . . . for a youngster.

Q: You mentioned his youth and his health. Is this important?

A: If it were not so, why has Capablanca already begun

to propagandize in favor of five-hour playing sessions instead of four. Even with a slight case of the grippe before the tournament began, Capablanca meant to outlast us all.

Q: There were eleven players altogether, I understand?

A: Yes, Capablanca, me, Marshall and Edward Lasker from America, Alekhine and Bogolyubov from Russia, Réti of Czechoslovakia, old Maroczy of Hungary, Tartakover of Vienna, Janowski of France, and Frederick Yates of England. With eleven players competing there was always someone sitting out each day. That's why my early score was deceptive. I had the bye in the first round.

Q: Were there any surprises at the start?

A: The trend was clear from the first day. There were two examples of the Triberg Opening — that is to say, the King's Indian Defense. . . . Réti against Marshall and Maroczy against Edward Lasker. Both were drawn. Aside from Alekhine's easy destruction of the English attacker, Yates, the only decision was Tartakover vs. Bogolyubov. White chose a truly original idea, truly "neo-romantic": 1 P-K4, P-K4; 2 P-KB4, PxP; 3 B-K2!? Of course, Black had nothing really to fear, but he blundered criminally in a Rook and Pawn ending. These youngsters will never go anywhere until they learn the ending.

Q: What were your thoughts when you met Capablanca in the second round?

A: I thought, "He thinks I want revenge for the World Championship match so badly I will attack prematurely. But I can wait." As it turned out, neither of us could do very much with my Ruy Lopez, and we drew in thirty moves.

The feature of the round, however, was the first victory of the "New Idea," and it put Alekhine in sole possession of first place. Let me show you on this board here.

MAROCZY–ALEKHINE: *1 P–K4, N–KB3; 2 P–Q3?!, P–K4; 3 P–KB4, N–B3; 4 N–KB3, P–Q4!; 5 KPxP, NxP; 6 PxP, B–KN5; 7 B–K2, BxN; 8 BxB, Q–R5ch; 9 K–B1?, O–O–O; 10 N–B3, B–B4; 11 N–K4, N–K6ch; 12 BxN, BxB; 13*

Q–K1, Q–R3; *14* N–N3, N–Q5; *15* Q–N4, P–QB3; *16* Q–R4, K–N1; *17* R–Q1, KR–K1; *18* P–R4, Q–B5; *19* R–R3, P–QN4!; *20* N–R5, PxQ; *21* NxQ, BxN; *22* P–B3, NxB; *23* RxN, BxP; *24* RxP, R–KB1 *25* Resigns.

Q: Very impressive. Did you consider him a dangerous rival?

A: Dangerous, yes. A rival, not entirely. You see, Alekhine is 32 now and not at all the young man I met at St. Petersburg. But he has one weakness he hasn't been able to correct. He can't play dull chess. That is, he can't play the kind of humdrum positions that occur most often between top players. He must attack. Even when he must defend, he decides to attack.

In the third round I had the Black pieces against him, and he began with a speculative eighth move followed by adventurous tenth and fifteenth moves:

1 P–Q4, P–Q4; *2* P–QB4, P–K3; *3* N–KB3, N–KB3; *4* N–B3, QN–Q2; *5* PxP, PxP; *6* B–B4, P–B3; *7* P–K3, N–R4; *8* B–Q3?, NxB; *9* PxN, B–Q3; *10* P–KN3, O–O; *11* O–O, R–K1; *12* Q–B2, N–B1; *13* N–Q1, P–B3!; *14* N–K3, B–K3; *15* N–R4, B–QB2; *16* P–QN4, B–N3; *17* N–B3, B–KB2!

White's opening plan of sinking a Knight on K5 has failed. Now he should have been worrying about his weak QP

and Kingside. But he chooses to open a new line with
18 P–N5? Now I provoked another weakness with *18 . . .
B–KR4!; 19 P–N4, B–KB2; 20 PxP, R–B1; 21 Q–N2, PxP;
22 P–B5, Q–Q3!*

Q: Why did he play P–B5? It only weakened his Kingside
more.

A: He had to stop . . . N–K3–KB5. There is an old expression, "For want of a nail a shoe was lost. . . ." Now I
had control of the diagonal leading to his KR2 and was
threatening both . . . Q–B5 and . . . B–B2.

Q: So?

A: So he tried *23 N–N2, B–B2; 24 KR–K1* and after
*24 . . . P–KR4!; 25 P–KR3, N–R2!; 26 RxRch, RxR; 27
R–K1, R–N1* he had no way of preventing *28 . . . N–N4.*
Alekhine became desperate: *28 Q–B1, N–N4; 29 N–K5*
and I replied *29 . . . PxN; 30 QxN, P–K5; 31 P–B6, P–N3!;
32 P–B4, RPxP!; 33 B–K2, PxP; 34 B–R5, R–N7!; 35 N–R4,
QxP(5)*, and after a trade of Queens he conceded.

Q: What was happening to Capablanca while all this was
going on?

A: Nothing but draws. When he drew with Edward
Lasker on the third day, I asked my German-American
friend why he could accept a draw in such a difficult position which offered him winning chances. He said that it
was very complicated and, besides, his opponent was
Capablanca. It doesn't matter, I recall telling Edward, the
player with the better position "has a moral obligation to
play for a win."

The real surprise in the early rounds was Tartakover, who
had 3–1, followed by Alekhine, Bogolyubov, and myself.
Tartakover is a wit and a charmer. He was born in Rostov-
on-Don, but like so many former subjects of the Czar, he
now makes his home beyond the Soviet borders. At 37 he
has already written extensively on the game and with an
acute sense of irony. He was the one who noted that Réti
studies mathematics but is not a dry mathematician, that
he represents Vienna without being Viennese, was born in
old Hungary but cannot speak Hungarian, speaks rapidly

only to appear more mature and deliberate, and will become the best player in the world without becoming World Champion.

Ewfim Bogolyubov is two years younger and is a totally different man. Where Tartakover is cynical, 'Bogo' is ebullient. Where Tartakover is a pessimist, the Ukrainian brims with optimism. Some say that his chess is too speculative in the manner of Alekhine. But I think he prefers simplicity. For example, in the fourth round he had White against Réti:

1 P–K4, P–K3; 2 P–Q4, P–Q4; 3 N–QB3, N–KB3; 4 B–N5, B–N5; 5 N–K2!?, PxP; 6 P–QR3, B–K2; 7 BxN, BxB; 8 NxP, B–Q2?; 9 Q–Q3, B–B3; 10 O–O–O, BxN; 11 QxB, Q–Q4; 12 Q–K3, O–O; 13 N–B3, Q–QR4; 14 N–K4, N–Q2; 15 P–KR4, B–K2; 16 P–KN4, P–QN4.

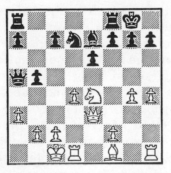

Q: Black's King looks safer than White's. I know a little about the game.

A: Perhaps, but White has no intention of attack when he can play *17 P–N4!, Q–N3; 18 N–B5, NxN; 19 QPxN, Q–N2;* and now *20 B–Q3, P–QR4; 21 Q–K4!!.* A very deep move that enables White to use his advantage in space during the endgame despite the Bishops of opposite color.

After a few moves it was clear that Black's QNP was hopelessly weak and that White's control of the open files was decisive. The game continued *21 . . . QxQ; 22 BxQ, QR–Q1; 23 P–QB3, PxP; 24 RPxP,* and now Black tried to blockade the position with *24 . . . P–B4!?; 25 PxP, P–K4,* but lost anyway after *26 P–R5, B–N4ch; 27 K–B2, K–B2; 28 B–B6.* Bogo eventually invaded along the QR-file.

Meanwhile, my namesake, Edward, was blundering horribly to Janowski. "I would probably have taken cyanide that night," he told me later, "had I been a few years younger." The bravado of youth.

Q: It's no secret that the big story of the fifth round was Capablanca's loss to Réti. How did you feel about it?

A: It didn't surprise me as much as it did the others. I thought, "Now you are no longer the undefeatable superman. Now you can start playing to win every game again." That loss was probably the best thing that happened to him. Just look at what happened after that, he won ten and drew five.

Q: But to lose to Réti? . . .

A: Don't minimize our friend from Czechoslovakia. For the last year he has been the terror of Europe. He is the artistic leader of the "New Idea" people. You know what they said about the Italian Independence movement — Garibaldi was the sword, Mazzini the heart, and so on. Well, Alekhine's iron successes have acquired for him the reputation of the sword of the new style of play. Nimzovich, with his theoretical conclusions, is the mind. But Réti, who said "We, the young players, are not interested in the rules but in the exceptions," he is the heart.

His big surprise in this tournament was the Double Fianchetto of the Bishops. This gave him no advantage with White against Capablanca:

1 N–KB3, N–KB3; 2 P–B4, P–KN3; 3 P–QN4!?, B–N2; 4 B–N2, O–O; 5 P–N3, P–N3!; 6 B–N2, B–N2; 7 O–O, P–Q3; 8 P–Q3?!, QN–Q2; 9 QN–Q2, P–K4; 10 Q–B2, R–K1; 11 KR–Q1, P–QR4; 12 P–QR3, P–R3; 13 N–B1, P–B4; 14 P–N5, N–B1!

Q: It doesn't look like White is better.

A: No, he should have played 8 P–Q4. But it offends Réti's senses to move a center pawn to the fourth rank this early. Black's thirteenth move was a clever offer: 14 PxRP, RxP; 15 NxP, BxB; 16 NxN would favor Black after 16 . . . B–B3; 17 NxNch, BxN; 18 BxB, QxB because of his strength on both sides of the board.

Q: Would Capablanca have accepted a draw at this point?

A: Probably, if White continued routinely with 15 P–K4, N–K3; 16 N–K3, N–Q5 and N–Q2–B4 after . . . NxN and White recaptures with the BP. But White played *15 P–K3?, Q–B2; 16 P–Q4,* and Capablanca had reason to play for more with *16 . . . B–K5!* After *17 Q–B3, KPxP; 18 PxP* Black could have seized a superior game due to his strong piece play in the center with 18 . . . N–K3; 19 PxP, QPxP.

But, as happens when you believe you are invincible, he tried to capitalize on the long diagonal with *18 . . . KN–Q2?* thinking that *19 Q–Q2!* was unplayable because it lost a Pawn. Instead of the necessary defensive action, the World Champion jumped in with both feet: *19 . . . PxP?; 20 BxP, QxP; 21 BxB, KxB; 22 Q–N2ch!* (protecting the QNP), *K–N1; 23 RxP, Q–B4; 24 QR–Q1, R–R2; 25 N–K3, Q–R4* (else 26 N–N4); *26 N–Q4!*

Q: So this is just the kind of position the Hypermodernists have been talking about?

A: Yes. White controls the strongest file and strongest diagonal. The Black defenses crumble. Capa had counted on 26 . . . BxB; 27 KxB, RxN; 28 PxR, QxR, but just then he noticed 29 N–B5! So he shortened the game with *26 . . . BxB; 27 KxB, Q–K4?; 28 N–B4, Q–QB4; 29 N–B6, R–B2; 30 N–K3, N–K4; 31 R(1)–Q5* and *Resigned* in face of 31 . . . N–B5; 32 RxQ, NxQ; 33 R–B2, N–R5; 34 N–Q5!

The fifth round ended with Bogolyubov and Tartakover in first, myself in third . . . and Capablanca tied for eighth place.

Q: Is it true that your spectacular sixth-round game with Edward Lasker was your first serious game with him?

A: More or less. We've known each other since the old days in Berlin, but we've rarely spoken of chess. He introduced me to Go, the Japanese game, and we played for many hours. And, as is my custom, I spent the morning hours before each game taking long walks. My companion during these jaunts through Central Park was Edward. But we never talked of chess.

Q: Should he have won?

A: No one "should" have won any game! No, it is a fight from start to finish, and if you make a mistake, you score no points for moral victory. If you mean that with correct play my position was hopeless, that may be true.

He had the Black pieces and sacrificed a Pawn on the fifteenth move, and after fifteen very complicated moves he nearly had a winning position. But he blundered at the end of the first time-pressure session. Then it was my turn to blunder at move 37 when I had a clearer line than the one I played. It secured two pieces for a Rook, but . . .

Then I discovered that his Rook was too powerful, and I sacrificed one of my Knights for his Kingside Pawns and the attack. But this petered out by the sixtieth move, and I foolishly rejected several drawing continuations. In the third session of play I could not avoid the exchange of Queens, and just before the third time control Edward had this position:

Black's winning chances involve the sacrifice of his QRP and the advance of his last pawn. But to do that he must force the White Knight back. The correct method was 72 . . . R–Q2!; 73 N–B6, R–Q1; 74 K–K5, P–R4!; 75 PxP, P–N5; 76 N–K4, R–Q4ch!; 77 K–B6, R–Q6! and Black queens.

I should mention at this point that this lengthy game was of great interest to our colleagues. You see, there were two groups, or factions, of contestants. Alekhine and Bogolyubov were longtime rivals in their country, and so they were on opposite sides here. Capablanca joined Alekhine, I think, because I got along with Bogo so well. The World Champion and I don't get along. And Réti was the third member of the rival group. So Capablanca, Réti, and Alekhine were watching my game with great interest — or rather, great anticipation.

When Edward played *72 . . . R–R1* instead of *72 . . . R–Q2*, these three onlookers went into a fury of intense calculation, hoping it would force an immediate resignation. However, after *73 N–K3, R–K1ch; 74 K–Q4, R–Q1ch; 75 K–K4, P–R4* he found that I, too, had a passed Pawn: *76 PxP, P–N5; 77 P–R6!, K–B4; 78 P–R7!, P–N6; 79 N–Q1!*. Even though I lost my remaining Pawns, I could set up an impregnable blockade of his Pawn. A draw was agreed on the 103rd move in the fourteenth hour of play.

That meant that Tartakover's loss to Capablanca left Savielly in a three-way tie for first place with Alekhine and myself. The Cuban finally showed signs of life with a most impressive ending, surely one of the greatest Rook-and-Pawn finishes of all time:

White was obviously going to lose his QBP. But Capa saw that the combination of a White rook on the seventh rank, a passed Pawn, and an active King were worth at least two pawns.

White played *34 BxN, PxB; 35 K–N3!!* and Black was lost! Tartakover played *35 . . . RxPch; 36 K–R4, R–B6* after seeing that *36 . . . R–B8; 37 K–R5, K–N1; 38 R–Q7* was hopeless. Now Capa followed with *37 P–N6, RxPch; 38 K–N5, R–K5* (*38 . . . RxP; 39 K–B6, K–N1; 40 R–Q7* is a mate); *39 K–B6, K–N1; 40 R–N7ch, K–R1; 41 RxP*, and Black could not avoid one of three dangers: (*a*) a last-rank mate; (*b*) the advance of the KNP; or (*c*) the loss of all Queenside Pawns. He resigned on the fifty-second move.

While all this was going on, the "New Idea" claimed another victim. You should have seen the expression on some of the masters' faces after White's twelfth and thirteenth moves!

RÉTI-YATES: *1 N-KB3, P-Q4; 2 P-B4, P-K3; 3 P-KN3, N-KB3; 4 B-N2, B-Q3?!; 5 P-N3, O-O; 6 O-O, R-K1; 7 B-N2, QN-Q2; 8 P-Q3, P-B3; 9 QN-Q2, P-K4; 10 PxP, PxP; 11 R-B1, N-B1; 12 R-B2, B-Q2; 13 Q-R1!, N-N3; 14 KR-B1, B-QB3?; 15 N-B1, Q-Q2; 16 N-K3, P-KR3?!; 17 P-Q4!, P-K5; 18 N-K5, BxN, 19 PxB, N-R2; 20 P-B4!, PxP e.p.; 21 PxP, N-N4; 22 P-B4, N-R6ch; 23 K-R1, P-Q5; 24 BxP, QR-Q1; 25 RxB!, PxR; 26 BxBP, N-B7 ch; 27 K-N2, QxB; 28 QxQ, RxQ; 29 BxR, N-K5; 30 P-K6!, R-Q7ch; 31 K-B3 Resigns.*

Q: It was at this point that you began to assert your lead, wasn't it?

A: Yes, in the seventh and eighth rounds the only points of interest were Marshall's first victory (after an uncommonly poor start of 2-4) and Bogolyubov's third loss in a row, this time to me. By this time I had 5½ points followed by Alekhine at 5, Capablanca 4½, and Réti and Tartakover at 4.

I was beginning to wonder if we were going to repeat the St. Petersburg tournament here in New York but with the roles of Capablanca and myself reversed. Suddenly, the World Champion returned to fine form with the brilliant annihilation of White's Queenside pawns in his ninth-round encounter with Bogolyubov.

BOGOLYUBOV-CAPABLANCA: *1 P-Q4, N-KB3; 2 N-KB3, P-Q4; 3 P-K3, P-K3; 4 B-Q3, P-B4; 5 P-QN3, N-B3; 6 O-O, B-Q3; 7 B-N2, O-O; 8 QN-Q2?, Q-K2; 9 N-K5, PxP; 10 PxP, B-R6!; 11 BxB, QxB; 12 QN-B3, B-Q2; 13 NxN, BxN; 14 Q-Q2, QR-B1; 15 P-QB3?, P-QR3; 16 N-K5, B-N4; 17 P-B3, BxB; 18 NxB, R-B2; 19 QR-B1, KR-B1; 20 R-QB2, N-K1; 21 KR-B1, N-Q3; 22 N-K5, Q-R4; 23 P-QR4, Q-N3!; 24 N-Q3, QxNP; 25 N-B5, Q-N3; 26 R-N2, Q-R2; 27 Q-K1, P-QN3; 28 N-Q3, R-B5; 29 P-R5, PxP; 30 N-B5, N-N4!; 31 R-K2, NxQP!; 32 PxN, R(1)xN 33 Resigns.*

Position after 23 . . . Q–N3.

Notice that 24 R–N2 would not have stayed the execution because of 24 . . . N–B4! 25 R(2)–N1 (otherwise 25 . . . NxP), P–B3; 26 N–N4, P–K4!. So Capa gained a half-point on me as I drew with Marshall.

Q: Some of the other players have spoken about your luck. . . .

A: Rubbish. What they mean by "luck" is one player's ability to take full use of his chances and another player's failure. Whenever you have hard-fought chess, you have errors. The better players know how to take advantage of these slips.

As you can see, this was an exceptionally hard-fought event. More than seventy of the 110 games ended in a victory.

Q: Perhaps this is due to the younger generation, who . . .

A: Not at all. The average age here is 42. I am 56, as is Janowski. Maroczy, "the last of the Steinitzians," is 54. Why, the youngest player in New York is Alekhine, and he is already 32. Compare that with Hastings, where the average age was 38 and the percentage of draws was about the same. It was higher at St. Petersburg, where the average age was 40.

I will admit that against Marshall in the ninth round I had good fortune when the American failed to make the most of his chances in the first session. And then in the second session . . .

. . . he could have won simply with 52 QxP, the most obvious move on the board. After 52 . . . BxN; 53 KxB, Black has only a few checks. His K is badly placed for a Q-and-P ending.

But Marshall played *52 NxP?* and allowed me a miraculous saving grace in *52 . . . Q–B7ch; 53 K–B3, B–Q7!!.* Now 54 Q–B2, Q–Q6ch; 55 K–N2ch, K–K1 doesn't ensure progress. So he tried *54 Q–B1, QxPch; 55 K–K2ch, K–K1; 56 Q–B5,* winning a piece. But it was not good enough after *56 . . . Q–B5ch; 57 KxB, QxPch; 58 K–K2, Q–B5ch; 59 K–B2, Q–B4ch; 60 K–N2, Q–Q3; 61 K–B3, K–Q1!; 62 K–K4, Q–K3ch! Draw.*

That was simply Marshall's failure, not luck. Capablanca had some good fortune a few rounds later when Alekhine with the White pieces could not make any progress after 1 P–Q4, P–Q4; 2 P–QB4, P–QB3; 3 N–QB3, N–B3; 4 P–K3, B–B4?; 5 PxP, PxP; 6 Q–N3, B–B1!

But this did not make up for my own comeback in the same round, the twelfth. This illustrated one of my favorite observations: The player who obtains a slight disadvantage is stimulated to hard work, but the player with a superior game becomes lazy. The result is that often the defender turns the tables.

Against Janowski I surrendered the two Bishops by the thirteenth move and fought for air through two time controls. On the thirty-eighth move he had exerted so much pressure that I conceded the QP. For some inexplicable

reason Janowski didn't take it. He moved one of his at-
tacking Rooks away and moved it back the following move.
Again, I could do nothing but allow him to capture the
QP. Again he refused!

Thirteen moves later, Black (Janowski) had played the
useless 53 . . . R–N6?, and I went on the attack with
*54 N–Q1!, R–Q2; 55 R–N3, R(2)–N2; 56 N–B3!, B–K6;
57 N–Q5, R–N7.*

This was tricky because now on 58 NxB, RxR; 59 R–N6ch,
K–B2 he could meet 60 NxB with 60 . . . R(2)–N7, and 60
RxPch, K–B3!; 61 RxR with 61 . . . PxN! So I chose *58 RxB!,
PxR; 59 R–N6ch, K–Q2; 60 NxP,* a superior line that left
him with one resource.

He had to play 60 . . . R–K7!, so that on 61 NxB, R(2)–N7
or 61 RxPch, K–B3; 62 RxR, RxN he would be safe. However, Janowski again played inexplicably: *60 . . . K–B2??,*
after which *61 NxB* won shortly.

Q: What was happening in the scoretable while this was
happening?

A: Oh, let's see. After thirteen rounds I had increased my
lead to 1½ points, just the margin that Capablanca had ten
years ago. It was Lasker 9½, Réti 8, Capablanca 7½, and
Alekhine 7.

Q: You really wanted to win this tournament, I assume?

A: Of course, what is the point of playing if you don't
try to win? Naturally, there was the money consideration
as well. You may have heard that after the war I was ill-

advised to put my money in German marks. A mark was worth twenty American cents before the fighting, but last fall each mark was down to about one quadrillionth of a penny.

I must tell you how eager I was to play here. Just before the tournament I was touring Scandinavia. I had calculated things so closely that my boat from Finland back to Hamburg would leave me just enough time to board the *U. S. S. Cleveland*, which was taking the players to America. But my boat in Finland could not sail because of frozen waters.

There was nothing to do but march across the ice to a train station several miles away and make the journey by rail. Not bad for a man of 56.

Q: Back to the tournament—in the fourteenth round the spectators got a treat.

A: Yes, because Capablanca had his way with the tournament committee and put in another rule. As with the Hastings event of '95, we had the drawings for each round made by lot. Therefore, no one knew who they were playing on a given day and no one could prepare an opening for the Cuban, who rarely prepares his own openings.

So the fans were pleased when we were paired in the fourteenth round and I had Black. After a difficult opening in which both of us sought to overcome the drawishness of the Pawn structure, a complex middlegame was reached. White's only winning idea was Kingside attack via P–KN4. But if we reach an ending, Black is better because of his Bishops.

Now with 23 ... Q–Q2, 23 ... B–B2 or some other preparatory move I could have anticipated 24 P–KN4, N–K5ch!; 25 BxN, BPxB. Then the White Q cannot easily penetrate to the Kingside. But I played the indifferent *23 ... N–K5ch* immediately, and after *24 BxN, BPxB; 25 Q–N4!* I was in trouble because of threats of 26 P–B5, 26 N–N6ch, or 26 QxP.

Play continued: *25 ... P–B4; 26 NxBP!, PxN; 27 QxP, P–KR4; 28 P–KN4, R–B3*—and here he erred with 29 *P–N5?*, a nasty error that should have been punished by 29 ... R–Q3!; 30 P–KN4; K–N1; 31 PxP, Q–Q2!; e.g. 32 Q–K5, Q–N5!

However, I chose the equally erroneous *29 ... K–N1?*, and after *30 NxQP, B–B2; 31 NxBch, QxN; 32 P–KN4* again missed a safe draw with 32 ... R–B7ch; 33 K–N3, R–K7; 34 P–N6, P–R5ch!; I tried the riskier *32 ... PxP; 33 Q–R7ch, K–B1; 34 R–R6!, B–N1!?; 35 Q–B5ch, K–N2; 36 RxR, PxR; 37 K–N3.*

This was another opportunity for me to sit and wait. The key point is that 38 QxNP, P–B4! gives me perpetual check opportunities. And the Black Q is also activated after 38 ... B–Q4; 39 QxNP, Q–N2!; 40 P–N4, Q–R3. Alekhine suggested 37 ... B–B2!! as the strongest because 38 KxP?? is, of course, unplayable, and 38 ... Q–K3; 39 KxP?, B–R4ch was threatened.

But I erred once more with 37 ... Q–K3?; 38 KxP!, QxQch; 39 KxQ, B–Q4; 40 P–N4, P–R3; 41 K–N4! (41 K–K5??, K–N3), B–B5; 42 P–B5, B–N6; 43 K–B4, B–B7; 44 K–K5, K–B2; 45 P–R4!!. The Black B can't dance at two weddings, not to mention three. I resigned after 45 ... K–N2 (45 ... BxP; 46 KxP is easier); 46 P–Q5!, BxP; 47 P–Q6, P–B4; 48 PxP, B–B3; 49 K–K6, P–R4; 50 P–B6ch. Capablanca was within a game of first place, and the memory of St. Petersburg flashed before everyone's eyes. This was especially true because I had the bye in the following round and Capa's crush of Janowski put him in a tie for first place temporarily.

Q: So your game with Réti in round 16 was very dramatic.

A: Drama is an overworked word. I would say that it was a critical time for me. I had the Black pieces and was unsure what to do against the feared "New Idea" opening. The game began with *1 N–KB3, P–Q4; 2 P–B4, P–QB3; 3 P–KN3, B–B4; 4 P–N3, N–B3; 5 B–KN2, P–K3; 6 B–N2, QN–Q2; 7 O–O, B–Q3; 8 P–Q3, O–O.*

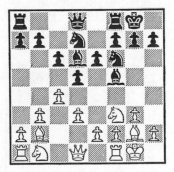

In the twelfth round Bogolyubov had tried a similar formation, but there were a few differences. Black played ... R–K1 instead of developing his QB, which was still on QB1. And since White's K4 was not under fire from a Black B, Réti played P–Q4 instead of P–Q3. That game, which I'm sure will win the Brilliancy Prize, went 9

QN-Q2, N-K5?; 10 NxN, PxN; 11 N-K5, P-KB4; 12
P-B3!, PxP; 13 BxP, Q-B2; 14 NxN, BxN; 15 P-K4, P-K4;
16 P-B5!, B-KB1; 17 Q-B2, PxQP; 18 PxP, QR-Q1;
19 B-R5!, R-K4; 30 BxP, RxKBP; 21 RxR, BxR; 22 QxB,
RxB; 23 R-KB1, R-Q1; 24 B-B7ch!, K-R1; 25 B-K8!!,
Resigns.

This was the third impressive game Réti had won with
this opening, but even he is not an expert in its intricacies.
For example, in our position he should have played 9 N-B3
so to meet 9 . . . P-K4 with 10 P-K4! This inaccuracy allowed me to equalize in the center: *9 QN-Q2?, P-K4!;
10 PxP, PxP; 11 R-B1* (more consistent was 11 P-K4, PxP;
12 PxP, BxP!; 13 N-B4!), *Q-K2; 12 R-B2, P-QR4!; 13
P-QR4, P-R3.*

This was the kind of formation I had envisioned. Black's
last move cuts off another square for the White KN and
threatens . . . P-K5 at some stage. It also provides a retreat
square for the QB. Black must time . . . P-K5 very carefully
or Réti will have full control of the center, as he did against
Capablanca and Yates.

Play proceeded *14 Q-R1, KR-K1; 15 KR-B1, B-R2!,*
and now White prepared to sacrifice the Exchange with
16 N-B1, P-K5; 17 PxP, PxP; 18 N-Q4, P-K6; 19 NxP,
BxR; 20 RxB. But after *16 N-B1* I answered *16 . . . N-B4.*

Réti was in difficult shape, and he correctly fought back
with *17 RxN!, BxR; 18 NxP, QR-B1; 19 N-K3, Q-K3; 20*

P–R3. There now followed a curious pair of errors. I chose
20 . . . B–Q3? instead of the much clearer *20 . . . P–QN3.*
But then Réti replied *21 RxR, RxR; 22 N–B3?* instead of
the powerful *22 N(5)–N4!,* which would have won a second
pawn, either the KNP or QP.

Both sides having made their first silly error, we got into
the kind of fighting game that I enjoy: *22 . . . B–K2; 23
N–Q4, Q–Q2; 24 K–R2?, P–R4!; 25 Q–R1, P–R5; 26 NxP,
PxPch; 27 PxP, NxN; 28 BxN, B–B3! 29 BxP, R–B4.*

Suddenly White has more than ample material compensation, but he can't get out of the entanglement of pieces.
Réti was very resourceful in finding *30 B–R6, B–N3; 31
Q–N7, Q–Q1; 32 P–QN4!, R–B2! 33 Q–N6,* but after *33 . . .
R–Q2!; 34 QxQch, RxQ;* he was lost since *35 N–B6, R–Q3;
36 BxB, RxN* would cost a piece. Réti chose *35 P–K3, PxP;
36 K–N2, BxN; 37 PxB, B–B4; 38 B–N7, B–K3* and resigned
on the fourth-fifth move.

Q: So that decided the tournament?

A: Not exactly. It did give me a half-point lead over Capa,
who only drew with Marshall in a winning position. And
in the following round Capa had the bye, so I went ahead
by 1½ points by walking over Yates. Alekhine was two points
back in third place, and Réti was just behind in fourth.

It narrowed a bit in the eighteenth round as I drew with
Alekhine and the Cuban defeated Edward Lasker. This
Hypermodernism is contagious. Capa answered 1 P–K4
with 1 . . . P–KN3. Even Alekhine called it the "joke
opening."

Q: How was Capablanca playing at this point?

A: His usual irritatingly good technique. On April 12,
the nineteenth round, he didn't have to do much but use
technique against Tartakover.

TARTAKOVER–CAPABLANCA: *1 P–K4, P–K4; 2 P–KB4,
PxP; 3 B–K2, P–Q4; 4 PxP, N–KB3; 5 P–B4, P–B3; 6
P–Q4, B–N5ch!; 7 K–B1, PxP; 8 BxP, PxP; 9 BxN, N–Q4!;
10 K–B2, RxB; 11 BxP, O–O; 12 N–KB3, N–B3; 13 N–B3,
P–QN4; 14 B–Q3, N–N5ch; 15 K–N1, B–N2; 16 B–B5,*

*BxN; 17 PxB, N-K6; 18 BxPch, K-R1; 19 Q-Q3, BxN;
20 PxB, N-Q4; 21 B-K4, N-B5; 22 Q-Q2, Q-R5; 23
K-B1, P-B4; 24 B-B6, R-B3; 25 P-Q5, R-Q1!; 26 R-Q1,
RxB; 27 PxR, RxQ; 28 RxR, N-K3; 29 R-Q6, Q-B5ch;
30 K-N2, Q-K7ch Resigns.*

You see the humor here? Tartakover thought he was
winning a piece after 9 . . . RxB; 10 Q-R4ch.

Q: Now, it was Lasker at 13, Capablanca at 12, and
Alekhine 11, with three rounds to go. Is that right?

A: Yes. Actually the twentieth round was sufficient to
decide the event. It all boiled down to this game.

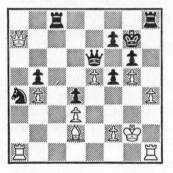

Maroczy played this strange system with Black, 1 P-K4,
P-K3; 2 P-Q4, P-Q4; 3 N-QB3, B-N5, and obtained the
better of the middlegame. But then he began to allow
exchanges that favored my chances in the endgame. On
the thirty-fifth move I played a very careless move, grabbing
his QRP and allowing him this strong attack.

36 . . .   QxP?

The attack would have been *too* strong if he had played
36 . . . R-B7!; 37 QR-Q1, Q-Q4ch; 38 P-B3 (or 38 K-N3,
RxB; 39 P-K6, P-B5ch), QxP; 39 K-B1, (39 KR-K1, RxBch)
N-B6. The same goes for 37 B-B4, Q-Q4ch; 38 K-N3,
N-B6; 39 KR-K1, RxRP!; 40 KxR, Q-B6!; 41 R-KN1,
Q-R4ch; 42 K-N3, Q-N5ch; 43 K-R2, Q-R5ch and mates.

37	QR–K1	Q–Q4ch
38	K–N3!	KR–K1
39	P–R5!	PxP
40	RxR	RxR
41	RxP	N–B6?

Maroczy missed a second golden chance in 41 . . . P–B5ch!!, a move virtually everyone but Alekhine over-looked. Then if 42 BxP, R–K8 or 42 KxP, R–K7, Black wins. Best, our Russian friend says, is 42 K–R4! followed by 42 . . . Q–R8ch; 43 K–N4, Q–N7ch; 44 K–B5, Q–Q4ch; 45 K–N4, R–K7; 46 Q–N8! with a draw.

| 42 | Q–N6 | N–K7ch |
| 43 | K–R2 | Q–K3?? |

And this third error lost all hope, whereas by 43 . . . R–K3; 44 Q–N8, Q–Q3ch, a drawn ending was available.

White continued *44 QxNP, Q–Q3ch; 45 K–N2, N–B5ch; 46 BxN, QxB 47 QxR, Q–N5ch; 48 K–B1, QxR; 49 Q–K5ch,* and after *50 QxBP* Maroczy saw it was hopeless and re-signed. Combined with Capablanca's failure to defeat Yates in a greatly favorable position, my lead grew to 1½ points.

Q: You couldn't be stopped then.

A: Not really. The clinching game was the following day against Tartakover.

Some people claimed I spent most of the game toying with him. He had a promising game on the Queenside with White if he continued 14 P–QN4. But he misjudged the nature of an advantage in space. That led to the opening of the KB-file after *14 P–B4?, PxP; 15 BxP, NxB; 16 RxN.*

There are those who believed I was in great danger because of the threats of QR–KB1 followed by Q–Q3–KN3 or P–KN4–5. But almost any position is defensible, and this one is especially rich in resources. I responded with *16 . . . B–K2!; 17 QR–KB1, R–B1!* so that on 18 P–KN4, P–KR3; 19 P–KR4, N–R2 the attack would be caught dead in its tracks.

Tartakover chose the slower *18 Q–Q3, B–K1; 19 Q–N3, Q–Q1; 20 N–Q1,* and following *20 . . . N–Q2!* Black stood very well indeed. I had protected all of my weak spots and was ready to counterattack. Tartakover misjudged this and played *21 N–K3?,* after which *21 . . . B–KN4!; 22 R–N4, P–KB3; 23 Q–B2, P–KR4!; 24 R–N3, P–R5; 25 R–N4, B–R4* won the Exchange and inevitably the game.

After he resigned, my victory was flashed to chess enthusiasts all over the world, including a group in South America that was receiving every move of the tournament by special cable. Despite the cheers, I retired to my room and wrote a letter to Martha in Berlin.

Q: Therefore, Capablanca's last two victories must have been an anticlimax?

A: Yes, he was still 1½ points away when they took down the tournament site ropes. Alekhine fought well to finish third because Marshall put on a very determined finish.

Q: And Réti was fifth.

A: Yes. As Hermann Helms wrote in *The New York Times,* "This New Idea may be a world beater but it does not play itself." The new players have made some good suggestions, and it is for the rest of us to digest their ideas and adjust to them. Those of us who adjust best will be the most successful. If you'll notice, my score with Réti was 2–0 and with Alekhine 1½–½. Capablanca could only score 1–1 with

SCORETABLE

	Em. L	C	A	Mars	R	Maro	B	T	Y	Ed. L	J	Total
1. Lasker, Em.	XX	½0	1½	½1	11	11	11	½1	½1	½1	11	16–4
2. Capablanca	½1	XX	½½	½½	01	½1	11	11	1½	½1	½1	14½–5½
3. Alekhine	0½	½½	XX	½½	10	1½	½½	½½	11	½½	11	12–8
4. Marshall	½0	½½	½½	XX	½1	0½	01	½0	½1	1½	11	11–9
5. Réti	00	10	01	0½	XX	½½	01	11	10	10	10	10½–9½
6. Maroczy	00	½0	0½	1½	½½	XX	01	½½	11	½1	10	10–10
7. Bogolyubov	00	00	½½	10	10	10	XX	01	11	½1	01	9½–10½
8. Tartakover	½0	00	½½	½1	00	½½	10	XX	10	½0	½1	8–12
9. Yates	½0	0½	00	½0	01	00	00	01	XX	11	½1	7–13
10. Lasker, Ed.	½0	½0	½½	0½	01	½0	½0	½1	00	XX	0½	6½–13½
11. Janowski	00	½0	00	00	00	01	10	½0	½0	1½	XX	5–15

them, and that explains my margin of victory as well as anything else.

Q: Dr. Lasker, your final result was 80 percent. I'm no expert on these matters, but I understand no one has scored that well in such a strong competition in decades.

A: It was enough to win. That is all that matters.

V

The End of Chess?

"Pit two players against each other who both have
perfect technique, who both avoid weaknesses, and
what is left? — a sorry caricature of chess."

— EMANUEL LASKER, 1925

From the vantage point of half a century later, the 1920s
appear to have been the golden age of tournament chess.
For much of the world it was an era of economic boom and
artistic ferment. These two factors almost always help promote the game.

It was also an era of superstars. Lasker, Capablanca, and
Alekhine were all World Champion during the decade, and
all were in, or close to, their prime. It was also a period of
grand and exotic tournaments: the first modern Hastings in
1920, two great Carlsbad events organized by Czechoslovak
enthusiasts in '23 and '29, and tournament sites with names
like Baden-Baden (1925), Bad Kissingen (1928), Mahrisch-
Ostrau (1923), and Pistyan (1922).

But none of these highest-class competitions were so
dominated by one person — and none so potentially dangerous for chess — as the quadruple-round grandmasters'
event in New York during the spring of 1927.

There was no suspense in the closing rounds of New

133

York 1927. Not since Lasker's runaway victories at London 1899 and Paris 1900 had someone scampered off so effortlessly with first prize in a field of the world's best. But Capablanca did it.

It was potentially dangerous because the game was not meant to be dominated. When Babe Ruth virtually discovered the home run in baseball and Bobby Jones seemed in these years to be the only human who could win a golf tournament, those sports prospered. But with Lasker in semiretirement again and Capablanca apparently too good for anyone else, chess naturally suffered.

What was worse was the way Capa won. At its higher levels the game became just an application of technique to old problems. The openings were increasingly the same — Queen's Gambit Declined, more often than not. A master got the slightest advantage and the rest was technique. Capablanca set the standard and everyone followed.

The great burst of creativity of the Hypermoderns actually encouraged this deadening of the game. In his *Manual of Chess* Lasker characterized the dangers of the "scientific" approach to play by quoting Réti's notes on a 1925 game. After 1 P-K4, P-QB4; 2 N-KB3, N-KB3; 3 P-K5, N-Q4; 4 N-B3, NxN; 5 QPxN, Réti condemned White's recapture as inferior to 5 NPxN and added, "The game will show how by modern chess technique a minute but clear positional advantage incurred in the opening can be easily converted into a win."

"Easily converted into a win"? So much for the fighting element in chess.

It was in this atmosphere — in which one of the strongest players in the world could claim that a minor error on the fifth move could decide a game — that subversive thoughts grew. Capablanca himself suggested in 1925 that there wasn't much left to the old rules anyway and that maybe we should add a few more squares to the board and a few more pieces to jazz the game up again. On the lower levels, even among masters, there was still a lot of play to be found. But at the pinnacle — where Capablanca played — the game was becoming boring. And it was only a matter of time, some said, before Capablanca's deadly, efficient technique filtered down into everyone's games. Maybe the rules *should* be changed. Maybe . . .

The original purpose of the 1927 event was the familiar one of choosing a World Championship challenger. Since Capablanca had not defended his title in six years, the organizers hoped to bring half a dozen of his most capable successors together for a match tournament to select the best of the lot.

When Lasker first proposed this idea two years before, no one jumped at it. Events appeared to be handling themselves. The Champion announced in 1926 that Aron Nimzovich, the winner of the powerful Dresden event of that year, had the best claim as challenger. Capa gave Nimzovich, then a Danish resident, until January 1, 1927, to deposit a $500 forfeit fee to maintain his title claim.

Failing that, the Argentine Chess Club was offering $10,000 in prize money to host a Capablanca–Alekhine match. So, when Nimzovich unaccountably let the New Years' deadline slide by, Alekhine pressed the Buenos Aires offer. Capa gave his informal OK.

The New York organizers didn't have a challengers tournament, but they had something better—a preview of the World Championship itself. Capablanca and Alekhine, both well liked in New York, had already accepted invitations by late 1926. The other places in the scoretable were easily filled with Nimzovich, the Yugoslav master Vidmar, Spielmann of Austria, and New York's own Marshall.

A strong tournament, certainly, but it was robbed of the highest status by events.

First there was the business with Bogolyubov. After winning the great Moscow 1925 tournament ahead of both Lasker and Capablanca, Bogo defected to Germany and settled down in Triberg with a German wife. Having been invited to what could have been one of the strongest events in chess history, he cabled back to New York: "Instead of

mediocre tournament, propose match myself and Capablanca." So much for Bogolyubov. Actually, he told friends,
he was holding out for more money.

But there was a far more serious flap over Lasker. Two
versions of the story of Lasker's noninvitation are told. In
one, the winner of the 1924 tournament was solicited at the
very last minute but refused to play. In the other version
Lasker was never officially invited.

When the fans began to question Lasker's absence, the
former Champion complained to an Amsterdam newspaper
that (1) he had been cheated out of fifteen minutes in his
second game with Capablanca three years before because of
a defective clock; (2) he had not been given his customary
appearance fee then; and (3) he was cheated out of a surplus
of the 1924 gate receipts. The tournament officials of 1927
were the same as those of three years before, and they were
"only tools in the hands of Mr. Capablanca," Lasker charged.

The New Yorkers, led by the tournament secretary,
Norbert L. Lederer, fired back with a denunciation of
Lasker as a master of gamesmanship. There had been no
surplus, they said, but a deficit. There was no $500 hono-
rarium for Lasker because he was no longer World Champion in 1924. And the reason Lasker lost fifteen minutes in
that controversial game was that the old man simply had
failed to notice that his clock was running.

Not content with these words, Lederer, a noted chemist,
author, and American representative for Alekhine, turned
the dispute into what the local press called "The Great
Cigar Smoke Scandal." Lasker loves to smoke cigars,
Lederer said. But he consumes only the foulest stogies at
the board and saves his prize Havanas for his private hours.
Why? Simply to indulge in "virtual gas attacks on his opponents," he charged.

There was more. Remember that crucial win over Maroczy
in the twentieth round in 1924? Lasker had upset the Hungarian by jumping up repeatedly to ask the spectators to
keep quiet, Lederer alleged. And against Janowski, another

old-timer vulnerable to psychological tactics, Lasker had tried the "two-repetition" gambit.*

Lasker replied that if he was guilty of these things, why didn't someone — either the players he offended or the organizers — make a complaint at the time they occurred? With this counter, and a little more huffing and puffing, the controversy died out. The six invited masters sat down at the Alamac Hotel in early February to play chess.

The first round saw Capablanca vs. Spielmann and Alekhine vs. Vidmar both follow a new idea in the Queen's Gambit (1 P–Q4, P–Q4; 2 P–QB4, P–K3; 3 N–QB3, N–KB3; 4 N–B3, QN–Q2; 5 B–N5, B–N5, followed by . . . P–B4). It wasn't surprising because the foreign masters had analyzed the variation on their Atlantic voyage. Today it is called either the "Manhattan Variation," after the tournament site, or the "Westphalia Variation," after the name of their ocean liner.

Both games were drawn. But Nimzovich drew first blood against the old swindler, Marshall. This was one of the 50-year-old American's last strong tournaments, and it was clear that time and chess theory had overtaken him. With White Marshall could not find the right handle for the attack

---

* That is, he allegedly claimed a draw when the same position had occurred twice, not three times as the rules require. The most ingenious exploitation of this rule was used by Alekhine in his famous victory over Réti at Baden-Baden 1925. On the sixteenth move Alekhine played . . . B–KR6, seeking either to trade off White's Fianchettoed KB or to force the B–KR1 retreat that would allow an attack with . . . P–KR4.

But Réti played 17 B–KB3. The game continued 17 . . . B–N5; 18 B–N2, B–R6; 19 B–B3; and Alekhine claimed a draw. No, the position has only occurred twice, said Réti. Three times, said Alekhine, now walking away from the board. Twice, shouted the excitable Czech. No, three times, Alekhine replied as he put on his coat.

It took the tournament committee half-an-hour to get both players together, reconstruct the game, and verify that Réti was right. So, after the delay, Alekhine sat down to play 19 . . . B–N5!!. Réti, who had argued in favor of continuing the game, felt honorbound to play 20 B–R1. Alekhine responded 20 . . . P–KR4 and won one of the most beautiful games ever played.

after *1 P-K4, P-K3; 2 P-Q4, P-Q4; 3 N-QB3, B-N5; 4 PxP, PxP; 5 N-B3, N-K2; 6 B-Q3, QN-B3; 7 P-KR3, B-K3; 8 O-O, Q-Q2; 9 B-KB4?!, BxN! 10 PxB, P-B3; 11 R-N1, P-KN4?!; 12 B-N3, O-O-O.*

White's treatment of Winawer's 3 . . . B–N5 was considered correct until the 1920s, when Maroczy, Alekhine, and Nimzovich showed that 4 PxP was harmless. White should try the more positional 5 B–Q3 in coordination with KN–K2, or later redeploy his forces with 9 N–K2 and P–QB3. But Marshall had to attack.

After Black's provocative 11 . . . P–KN4, instead of the secure 11 . . . N–Q1 and 12 . . . P–B3, White had opportunities. The right plan was 13 N–Q2!, threatening to hop to QN3 and B5. For example, 13 N–Q2, B–B4; (or 13 . . . N–B4; 14 N–N3, P–N3; 15 N–B5!) 14 N–N3, P–N3; 15 N–B5, Q–K1; 16 BxBch; and 17 Q–Q3.

But White played *13 Q–K2?* with the idea of 14 B–R6!. However, Nimzovich's *13 . . . QR–K1!* foiled that since 14 B–R6, PxB; 15 QxPch, K–Q1; 16 R–N7, N–B4!; 17 RxBP, QxR would leave him with a material edge.

Marshall continued with *14 KR–K1, N–B4; 15 BxN?*, another dubious idea, and after *15 . . . BxB; 16 Q–N5, N–Q1* he missed the last chance of 17 Q–R5 (so that on 17 . . . K–N1 he has 18 P–B4!). Marshall chose *17 Q–B5?, P–N3; 18 Q–R3, K–N2; 19 Q–N3* and Black's game was winning after *19 . . . N–B3; 20 N–Q2, N–R4!* because there was no longer an attack to be afraid of. Nimzovich eventually scored the point in sixty moves, but the result appeared clear after *21 Q–N2, RxRch; 22 RxR, R–K1; 23 RxR, QxR; 24 Q–N1, K–B1; 25 Q–Q1, Q–K3; 26 N–N3, N–B5!; 27 N–Q2, N–R6; 28 N–B1, NxP; 29 Q–R5, B–Q6; 30 Q–Q1, Q–K5; 31 N–Q2, Q–K7!*

Nimzovich was the kind of player who often scored better with the Black pieces. This became apparent in the second round during one of the classic demonstrations of the power of open files and ranks:

NIMZOVICH–CAPABLANCA: *1 P–QB4, N–KB3; 2 N–KB3, P–K3; 3 P–Q4, P–Q4; 4 P–K3, B–K2; 5 QN–Q2, O–O; 6 B–Q3, P–B4; 7 QPxP?, N–R3!; 8 O–O?!, NxP; 9 B–K2, P–QN3; 10 PxP?, NxP; 11 N–N3, B–N2; 12 NxN, BxN; 13 Q–R4, Q–B3; 14 B–R6, BxB; 15 QxB, N–N5; 16 Q–K2, KR–Q1; 17 P–QR3, N–Q6; 18 N–K1, NxN; 19 RxN, QR–B1; 20 R–N1, Q–K4; 21 P–KN3.*

White's silly seventh move led him into a policy of Exchanges. To slow down Black's initiative, Nimzovich traded wood in the hope of securing a draw by exhaustion of material. But Black has reached the maximum point of development and must use his advantage in space. First he tried *21 . . . Q–Q4!*, which threatened *22 . . . Q–R7; 23 B–Q2, BxRP.*

Nimzovich was forced into weakening his Queenside with 22 *P–QN4, B–B1; 23 B–N2, Q–R7!* In the face of . . . *P–QR4!* he responded with a series of bad moves: *24 R–R1, Q–N6; 25 B–Q4, R–B7; 26 Q–R6?*

Capablanca understood the principles of open lines better than anyone between the era of Tarrasch and the arrival of Fischer. He quickly tore apart White's defenses with a series of hammer blows: *26 . . . P–K4!; 27 BxKP, R(1)–Q7; 28 Q–N7* (not *28 R–KB1, QxKP!!*), *RxP; 29 P–N4, Q–K3; 30 B–N3, RxP!*. If the R is taken, Black can mate with *31 . . . QxNPch; 32 K–R1, Q–R6.*

The Danish master had nothing better than *31 Q–B3, R(R)–N7ch; 32 QxR, RxQch; 33 KxR, QxNP; 34 QR–Q1*, after which the advance of Black's two RP's left White without a defense on either side of board. Resignation came on the forty-second move.

The third indication of the way of things was an exceptionally hard-fought ending between Alekhine and Spielmann in the second round. After Black had established a simple R-and-P victory by the thirty-seventh move, Spielmann got a second wind and with great ingenuity could have squeezed out a draw at move 47. But he erred and had to find another series of saving moves. These would have permitted him to draw at move 56. But another blunder left this position on the board at move 61:

Thanks to that pessimistic epigram ("All Rook and Pawn endgames are drawn") White can still hold the game. But salvation is available only if White can keep the Black K from reaching KN7. If the Black K penetrates, the last White Pawn is threatened and a path is cleared for Black's own Pawn.

61 R–K4ch?   . . .

So much easier is 61 K–K2! so that on 61 . . . R–R8; 62 R–K4ch, K–R6; 63 R–K3ch, K–R7; 64 R–K7, P–B4; 65 R–KN7, R–KN8; 66 R–R7ch, K–N7; 67 R–R6! winning the pawn. On 62 . . . K–B4 in this line White cuts off the Black K with 63 R–QR4. And on 62 . . . K–R6; 63 R–K3ch, K–N7 White drives the K off with 64 R–N3ch, K–R7; 65 R–N5.

61 . . .   **K–R6**
62 R–KB4??   . . .

Even here 62 K–K2! draws, e.g. 62 . . . R–R5; 63 R–K3ch and 64 R–KN3. White now immobilizes his R.

62 . . .   **P–B4**
63 R–B3ch   . . .

On 63 K–K2 or 63 R–QR4, Black is already able to play 63 . . . K–N7 safely, e.g. 63 K–K2, K–N7; 64 R–B3, R–R6!; 65 R–B4, R–R6; 66 K–K1, R–R7 winning the pawn.

63 . . .   **K–R7!**
64 R–B4   **R–R6ch**
Resigns

It was no good to play 64 R–N3 because of 64 . . . R–R6. In the final position White must lose because 65 K–K2,

K–N7; 66 R–QR4, R–QN6; 67 R–R2, R–N1, followed by a check on the K-file or the seventh rank, will win the White P depending on what White's R does.

Rudolf Spielmann at 44 was the last of the great Viennese masters. During the final years of the Dual Monarchy of Austria-Hungary all of the great players of Eastern Europe could be found at the Café Central or the Wiener Schachklub. On a given day you might find Réti and Duras from Prague, Tartakover from Russia, Schlechter, Georg Marco or Adolf Albin, whom we met at Hastings, the great Hungarian Geza Maroczy, or the lesser masters like Heinrich Wolf or Dr. J. Perlis.

Spielmann was the last of the generation that had made Vienna the center of the chess world in the first two decades of the century. He was also the last Romantic player. Spielmann's greatest success came typically during the Gambit tournaments of Abbazia 1912 and Baden 1914, when Marco, speaking for the organizers, decreed that every player must open with a gambit variation when he had White.

In the previous year Spielmann had won a strong event at Semmering and might have won the even greater Carlsbad 1929 gathering ahead of every leading master of Europe had he not oversimplified in a winning position against the rank outsider, Hermann Mattison.

The last incident was typical of the kindly, well-remembered Spielmann. He could beat anyone on a given day. In the 1923 Carlsbad tournament he crushed Alekhine in the next-to-last round and drove the Russian out of first place. This was the tournament at which Spielmann won the prize for the fewest draws by the simple expedient of losing twelve of his games en route to last place.

But while he was always a dangerous player, Spielmann could never put together a really commanding string of victories. It was a lack of passion in dull positions, like that R-and-P ending. Alekhine put Spielmann's weakness down as "a slightly exaggerated good-naturedness which at times could not be distinguished from indifference."

Spielmann should have lost in the third round also, but an oversight by Vidmar led to a drawn Bishop-of-opposite-color ending. Marshall gave Capablanca the only full point in that round when on the twenty-fourth move he blundered away a Pawn in a mildly inferior position. That put Capablanca at 2½–½, just ahead of Alekhine's 2–1, and the even scores of Nimzovich and Vidmar.

Capablanca could have increased his lead the next day, but Vidmar encountered good luck. In just the kind of dominating position the Cuban loved — an ending in which his rooks were active and Vidmar's were passive — he didn't try hard enough, and it dwindled to a draw. Nimzovich moved up in what should be called today the Nimzo-Larsen opening.

NIMZOVICH–SPIELMANN: *1 N-KB3, P-Q4; 2 P-QN3, P-QB4; 3 B-N2?, N-QB3?; (3 . . . P-B3!) 4 P-K3, N-B3; 5 B-N5, B-Q2; 6 O-O, P-K3; 7 P-Q3, B-K2; 8 QN-Q2, O-O; 9 KBxN, BxB; 10 N-K5, R-B1; 11 P-KB4, N-Q2; 12 Q-N4, NxN; 13 BxN, B-B3; 14 R-B3, BxB; 15 PxB, Q-B2; 16 Q-R5.*

·Here Black can defuse the attack with 16 . . . B-K1!, e.g. 17 R-R3, P-KR3; 18 N-B3, P-B4 or 17 R-B6!?, Q-R4!;

18 N-B3, P-KR3; 19 RxRP?, PxR 20 QxRP, P-B3; 21 PxP, R-QB2.

But Spielmann picked a bizarre defense: *16 . . . P-KR3?!; 17 QR-KB1, P-KN3?*, which overlooked White's nineteenth move. Even 17 . . . B-K1 was better, although after 18 R-N3, P-B4; 19 QxRP, QxKP; 20 Q-B4! and 21 N-B3, it was not good.

Nimzovich responded with *18 QxRP, QxP; 19 R-B6!*, and Spielmann realized to his regret that there was no way of averting the mate threat of R-KB3-KR3 except by trading Queens: *19 . . . Q-R4; 20 QxQ, PxQ; 21 N-B3, R-B2; 22 R-R6, P-B3; 23 N-R4, B-K1; 24 R(6)xBP*, and White won with his P.

After four rounds it was Capablanca 3-1, followed by Alekhine and Nimzovich a half-point back. But the fifth round brought the first showdown between the two men who would play for the world title in the fall. Consider Capa's own opinion of Alekhine, given just before the tournament began:

He has what is probably the most marvelous chess memory that ever existed. . . . He certainly knows by heart all of the games ever played by any of the first-class masters. . . . The writer believes that he has not the proper temperament for match play . . . not the proper combative spirit. Furthermore he is extremely nervous. . . ."

Capa recalled that he first met the Russian at the 1914 St. Petersburg event, when Alexander and his brother Alexei were Capa's constant companions. "Then he was not very good in the play for position in the middlegame," Capa said, and "very weak in the endings." But now in 1927, "he has what is perhaps the best rounded game of the masters."

With White Alekhine began: *1 P-Q4, N-KB3; 2 P-QB4, P-K3; 3 N-KB3, P-QN3; 4 P-KN3, B-N2; 5 B-N2, P-B4?!; 6 P-Q5, PxP; 7 N-R4, P-N3; 8 N-QB3, B-N2; 9 O-O, O-O; 10 B-B4?, P-Q3; 11 PxP, N-R4; 12 B-Q2, N-Q2.*

Alekhine's tenth move was an attempted improvement over a 1926 game between two lesser masters, Vajda and Monticelli, which gave White a secure superiority. In the Benoni-type position White should play for P–K4, P–KB4 and P–K5. For example, 13 P–K4 now would be good because it carries the tactical trick of 14 N–B5. Play continued:

| 13 | P–B4? | P–QR3 |
| 14 | B–B3? | . . . |

Alekhine loses the thread of the game here. He should still develop with 14 P–K4 or 14 P–R4 although 14 P–R4, P–B5!; 15 P–K4, P–QN4; 16 PxP, PxP; 17 RxR, BxR is not particularly pleasant after 18 N–B5 (18 QNxP?, Q–N3ch) PxN; 19 QxN, P–N5; 20 N–Q1, PxP and 21 . . . N–B3. Best play is 14 P–R4, P–B5!; 15 B–K3! and 16 N–B3 as Alekhine later said.

| 14 | . . . | KN–B3 |
| 15 | P–QR4 | P–B5! |

To be followed by either . . . N–B4–N6 or 16 . . . P–QN4; 17 PxP, PxP with a powerful Queenside initiative.

| 16 | B–K3 | Q–B2 |
| 17 | P–KN4? | . . . |

As usual, Alekhine's greatest flaw is the inability to restrain himself from dubious or desperate attacks. Now Black took complete control of the board with just a few moves: *17 . . . N–B4; 18 P–N5, KN–Q2; 19 P–B5, KR–K1; 20 B–B4, B–K4; 21 B–N4, N–N6!; 22 PxP, RPxP; 23 R–N1, BxN!; 24 PxB, Q–B4ch; 25 P–K3, N–K4!*. Black must win the QP, and he has excellent chances of grabbing the KP or QRP as well. And 26 BxN? would concede the KNP also.

Alekhine tried *26 B–B3, N–Q6!; 27 K–R1, BxP; 28 RxN, NxB; 29 R–QN1, RxP; 30 N–N2, RxB!; 31 RxR, NxN; 32 KxN, R–K1; 33 K–B1, BxR; 34 QxB, QxP* and *Resigned* in a few moves. Not a very good sign for Alekhine's fans.

The other incident of this round involves one of the great chess stories. It's been told in many forms, but the version Milan Vidmar chose went like this:

Nimzovich had the Black pieces against Vidmar and asked his old friend not to smoke because of the usual effect on the hypernervous Nimzo. Vidmar agreed, but during the game's complications, he absent-mindedly pulled out his pack of cigarettes. Nimzovich at once headed for the tournament director to complain. The TD was Geza Maroczy, and he reminded Nimzovich with typical legal-mindedness that Vidmar had not broken his word because he had not yet smoked the cigarette. Yes, said Nimzovich, I know that, but I also know he is thinking about doing it. "And as an old chess player you must know that the threat is stronger than the execution."

The game itself was fascinating because it appeared that White never made an error and yet was swept off the board in thirty moves. After the first seventeen moves White has iron control of the only open file and the advantage of the two bishops:

VIDMAR–NIMZOVICH: *1 P–Q4, N–KB3; 2 N–KB3; P–K3; 3 P–B4, B–N5ch; 4 B–Q2, Q–K2; 5 N–B3, O–O; 6 P–K3, P–Q3; 7 B–K2, P–QN3; 8 O–O, B–N2; 9 Q–B2, QN–Q2; 10 QR–Q1, BxN; 11 BxB, N–K5; 12 B–K1, P–KB4; 13 Q–N3, P–B4; 14 N–Q2, NxN; 15 RxN, P–K4!; 16 PxKP, PxP; 17 P–B3.*

Alekhine observed in the tournament book that 6 Q–B2! would have allowed White to continue with B–Q3 and therefore not worry about . . . P–K4–5. The Russian emigré also pointed out that 10 N–KN5! followed by 11 B–B3 would neutralize the long diagonal and secure equality.

17 . . .	**P–KN4!!**

With this enormously powerful move, Black forces open a kingside file. By attacking White's KB3, Nimzovich will either open up his QB's diagonal or secure K5 for his N. The remarkable feature of this plan is that Black can ignore the two bishops and the Q-file.

18	B–B2	N–B3
19	KR–Q1	QR–K1
20	Q–R4	B–R1!

This anticipates 21 R–Q7, which would now be met by 21 . . . NxR; 22 RxN, Q–B3; 23 QxP, P–R3.

21	R–Q6	Q–KN2
22	B–B1?	. . .

This is the only clear mistake in the entire game. With 22 B–K1 White could meet 22 . . . P–K5 with 23 B–B3 and 22 . . . P–N5; 23 PxP, NxP; with either Alekhine's suggestion, 24 BxN, QxB; 25 Q–B2, or Nimzovich's, 24 R–Q7, Q–N4; 25 BxN.

After Black's 22 ... *P–K5!* Vidmar's position was untenable since 23 PxP, NxP; 24 R(6)–Q3, QxP or 23 P–B4, PxP and 24 ... P–K6. So he gambled on a counterattack with 23 *B–K1, PxP; 24 B–B3,* but after *24 ... Q–K2!* (threatening 25 ... QxPch and mate in four) *25 R(6)–Q3, PxP; 26 BxP, BxB; 27 BxN, Q–K5!; 28 R(1)–Q2, B–R6; 29 B–B3, Q–N5ch* and Black mated in two moves.

Nimzovich was 41 then, afflicted by a lung ailment that accentuated his hypertension. Capablanca said his problem was the inability "to carry into effect, in a practical way, his, at times, very profound conceptions." Nimzo was a very original thinker, Capa said. However, the champion added, "His strength is his weakness; he plays such bizarre openings and such complicated games that very often he is just as much puzzled as his opponent, if not more so, as to the best course to follow."

Yet he was still the most opinionated of masters, already a legend. One example of his attitude, told by Harry Golombek, should suffice:

Nimzovich grew up in the same cultural milieu as another talented East European, David Przepiorka of Warsaw. They were both young, Jewish, and exceptionally good at the game. They must have seen each other at dozens of tournaments. But they never spoke, never shook hands, never recognized one another.

It wasn't Przepiorka's fault. He was everyone's friend — everyone, that is, but Nimzovich. Finally, after a quarter-century of this, both men were playing at Liege 1930 when Nimzo came over to congratulate the Pole for a fine game and a fine illustration of Nimzovich's principles. The ice broken, Przepiorka asked why Nimzovich had been so cold over all these years.

Oh, very simple, Nimzovich replied. "I always thought you were a member of the Tarrasch school."

Only the first cycle of five rounds had been played, but the pattern was already set. Capa led with 4–1 followed by Nimzovich at 3½, Alekhine at 2½, Vidmar 2, and the attacking masters, Spielmann and Marshall at 1.

Capablanca then settled back and relaxed for the next five rounds. He easily beat Marshall in the sixth round when the American dropped a Knight with the White pieces after eleven moves (1 P–Q4, N–KB3; 2 N–KB3, P–K3; 3 B–N5, P–B4; 4 P–B3, Q–N3; 5 Q–B2, PxP; 6 NxP?, N–B3; 7 P–K3, P–Q4; 8 N–Q2, B–Q2; 9 QN–B3?!, N–K5; 10 B–KB4, P–B3; 11 B–Q3??, P–K4; 12 BxN, PxB(K); 13 QxP, O–O–O).

After that the World Champion played four uneventful draws in a row. Alekhine drew four after losing to Nimzovich. Marshall finally won a game (over Vidmar), and it turned out to be his only victory in the tournament. The only excitement of the second cycle was that of Nimzovich, who put up a stiff challenge to Capablanca's lead. He received a gift point in Round 9 after an atrocious opening.

SPIELMANN–NIMZOVICH: *1 P–K4, N–QB3; 2 N–KB3, P–K3; 3 P–Q4, P–Q4; 4 P–K5, P–QN3; 5 P–B3, QN–K2?!; 6 B–Q3, P–QR4?!; 7 Q–K2, N–B4; 8 P–KR4!, P–R4; 9 N–N5. P–N3?; 10 N–Q2, KN–K2; 11 N–B1, P–B4; 12 P–B3, P–B5; 13 B–B2, P–N4; 14 P–KN4!, N–N2; 15 N–N3, N–B3; 16 Q–N2, B–K2?; 17 PxP, PxP; 18 R–KN1, R–QR2.*

Alekhine makes an interesting proposal in the tournament book of 19 K–K2!, a high-class waiting move. On 19 . . . B–B1, for example, White can play 20 N–R7. The main point of the K–move is to avoid . . . BxKRPch after the White N moves.

19 NxBP!?   KxN

White's sacrifice is undoubtedly sound, but the question is, Which followup? With 20 B-N6ch, K-N1 (20 . . . KxB; 21 NxPch mates); 21 NxP Black complicates matters with 21 . . . BxPch. Another try is 20 N-K4, BxPch; 21 K-K2, but again 21 . . . K-N1 is unclear.

20 NxP??   . . .

Alekhine's suggestion of 20 N-K2! looks convincing, e.g., 20 . . . BxPch 21 K-Q1, K-N1; 22 N-B4!, R-KB2; 23 N-N6, B-K2; 24 NxR, KxN; 25 Q-N6.

But the line played by the Austrian loses: *20 . . . BxPch; 21 K-K2, NxN; 22 B-N6ch, K-Q2!; 23 BxN, K-Q2!* and the Black K walked away. Nimzovich survived to enjoy his extra piece after *24 Q-N7ch, B-K2; 25 B-B7, R-R7 ch; 26 K-Q1, K-B2; 27 B-B4, RxP; 28 Q-R7, K-N3!; 29 R-N8, Q-B2; 30 Q-R8, N-Q1.*

This put Nimzovich in first place, tied with Capablanca at 6½–2½, for one brief round. The next day . . .

NIMZOVICH–VIDMAR: *1 P-K3, P-Q4; 2 N-KB3, N-KB3; 3 P-QN3, B-N5!; 4 B-N2, QN-Q2; 5 P-KR3, B-R4; 6 B-K2, P-K3; 7 N-K5, BxB; 8 QxB, B-Q3; 9 NxN, QxN; 10 P-QB4, P-B3; 11 O-O?, O-O-O!; 12 N-B3.*

As with his first game with Capablanca, Nimzo has done nothing with the White pieces except trade them off. Now Black played the fine *12 . . . B–B2!* so that he could answer 13 P–Q3 with *13 . . . Q–Q3; 14 P–B4, P–Q5.*

Instead, White chose *13 P–Q4, P–KR4; 14 P–B5?* in the mistaken belief that his Queenside play with P–QN4–5 was faster than Black's Kingside attack. The game continued—*14 . . . P–KN4; 15 P–QN4, P–R5; 16 P–N5, QR–N1!; 17 PxP, PxP*—and Nimzovich saw that Black's King could run to Q1 if necessary.

So there was nothing to do but defend the Kingside, a policy that led to *18 P–B3, N–R4; 19 P–K4, P–B4!; 20 PxQP, KPxP; 21 QR–K1, P–N5!; 22 RPxP, PxP; 23 PxP, RxP.* He desperately tried *24 NxP,* but Vidmar finished him off with *24 . . . P–R6!; 25 N–K7ch, K–N2; 26 R–B3, RxPch; 27 QxR, PxQ; 28 P–Q5, Q–N5!,* and White resigned shortly afterward when he realized how far he was behind.

After ten rounds and two cycles, the scores read: Capablanca, 7; Nimzovich, 6½; Alekhine, 5; Vidmar, 4½; Marshall, 4; Spielmann, 3½. The third cycle was Capa's meat. After nearly three weeks·of play his rivals were exhausted, but he was fresh. It was at this point that the combination of Capa's tremendous energy and his effortless technique began to pay off. There was good technique (as opposed to dull "bad" technique), the critics said, meaning exciting games like Capablanca's thirteenth round versus Spielmann: *1 P–Q4, P–Q4; 2 N–KB3, P–K3; 3 P–B4, N–Q2; 4 N–B3, KN–B3; 5 B–N5, B–N5; 6 PxP, PxP; 7 Q–R4!?*

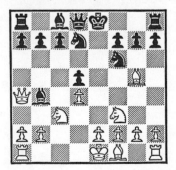

In the first round Capablanca played 7 Q–N3, P–B4; 8 P–QR3, BxNch; 9 QxB, and had no advantage after 9 . . . P–B5.

7 . . .	BxNch?

The point of 7 Q–R4 is to answer 7 . . . P–B4 with 8 PxP, BxNch; 9 PxB, O–O with 10 Q–Q4 holding the Pawn. However, 7 . . . Q–K2; 8 P–QR3, BxNch; 9 PxB, O–O; 10 P–K3, P–B4; 11 B–Q3, Q–K3! should equalize.

8	PxB	O–O
9	P–K3	P–B4
10	B–Q3	P–B5
11	B–B2	Q–K2?!

There was a slightly better alternative in 11 . . . P–QR3; 12 N–K5, P–N4, although 13 Q–R3! is strong. Best is Alekhine's suggestion of 11 . . . R–K1; 12 O–O, R–K3 intending 13 . . . R–R3.

12	O–O	P–QR3
13	KR–K1	Q–K3

Spielmann's plan is to occupy K5 with an N and control the march of his Queenside majority. It fails nicely.

14	N–Q2	P–N4
15	Q–R5!	N–K5?

Last chance for defense with 15 . . . B–N2; 16 Q–B7, Q–B3.

16	NxN	PxN
17	P–QR4	Q–Q4

The failure of Black's plan is that White has too much Queenside pressure, e.g. 17 . . . R–N1; 18 KR–N1, Q–Q4; 19 B–B4, R–N3; 20 PxP, RxP; 21 RxR, PxR; 22 B–R4.

| 18 | PxP!! | QxB |
| 19 | BxP | R–N1 |

Capablanca won another Brilliancy Prize (New York 1916) for beautiful variations that never occurred. Here he is rewarded for similar lines such as 19 . . . R–R2; 20 P–N6!, QxQ; 21 PxR, QxR; 22 RxQ, N–N3; 23 P–R8(Q).

The Cuban now used his last pawn to win back the piece with interest. This was a marvelous example of technique: *20 PxP!, R–N4; 21 Q–B7, N–N3; 22 P–R7, B–R6; 23 KR–N1!, RxRch; 24 RxR, P–B4; 25 B–B3, P–B5; 26 PxP, Resigns.*

Oddly enough, Capablanca didn't think highly of his chances in the tournament. He wrote that he was actually a better player eight years before when defeating Boris Kostich, an early Yugoslav grandmaster, in a short Havana match. He said that at St. Petersburg 1914 he was filled with ambition but lacked confidence. "Today we have plenty of confidence . . . but most of the ambition is gone. . . . Then we were very nervous and easily upset. Today we are cool and collected and nothing short of an earthquake will ruffle us. We have now more experience, but less power."

What was most disturbing about his lack of ambition was

that the Cuban could still beat the best players with his dry consolidation of forces and endgame technique. He finished the third cycle of play with a masterpiece of heavy-piece technique against Nimzovich who, clearly in an exhausted state, had scored only one point in five rounds.

Nimzovich (White) again did nothing with the first move advantage:

1 P–K4, P–QB3; 2 P–Q4, P–Q4; 3 P–K5, B–B4; 4 B–Q3, BxB; 5 QxB, P–K3; 6 N–QB3, Q–N3; 7 KN–K2, P–QB4; 8 PxP, BxP; 9 O–O, N–K2; 10 N–R4, Q–B3; 11 NxB, QxN; 12 B–K3, Q–B2; 13 P–KB4, N–B4; 14 P–B3?, N–B3; 15 QR–Q1, P–KN3?!

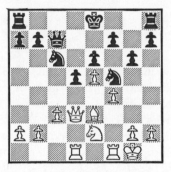

Black is perfectly safe as long as White doesn't try for the P–QB4 break. Nimzovich played an incredibly naive positional move: *16 P–KN4??.* After *16 . . . NxB; 17 QxN, P–KR4!* he had to choose between allowing the KR-file open or to close the position. He picked *18 P–N5* and after *18 . . . O–O!* Black had an excellent endgame.

The next stage of play involved a good deal of maneuvering. Basically, Black strove to double R's on the half open file and play his knight to KB4. It went: *19 N–Q4, Q–N3; 20 R–B2, KR–B1; 21 P–QR3, R–B2; 22 R–Q3, N–R4; 23 R–K2, R–K1; 24 K–N2, N–B3; 25 R(2)–Q2, R(1)–QB1; 26 R–K2, N–K2; 27 R(2)–Q2, R–B5; 28 Q–R3?, K–N2; 29 R–KB2, P–QR4; 30R–K2, N–B4.*

By putting his Q on KR3 instead of KB2, Nimzovich has made possible the destruction of his Q4 outpost. He cannot allow the QB-file to be opened, e.g. 30 R(2)–Q2, NxN; 31 RxN, RxR; 32 PxR, R–B5; 33 Q–K3, P–R5 followed by the approach of the Black K and a timely . . . Q–N6!.

So the game continued:

31 NxNch   NPxN

With the idea of 32 QxRP, R–KR1; 33 Q–B3, R–R5 and crushing pressure for Black on the Kingside. White's overextended Pawns are grabable once an additional file or rank is opened.

32 Q–B3   K–N3
33 R(2)–Q2   R–K5!

The next stage is doubling Rooks on the fifth rank.

34 R–Q4   R–B5
35 Q–B2   Q–N4!

And now the target is K7, which can be reached via 36 . . . R(B)xR; 37 RxR, R–K7. On 36 RxR(B), QxR; 37 R–Q4, Q–N6 White can only temporize with Q–Q2–KB2–Q2 or make K-moves. That, however, is his best.

The game continued: *36 K–N3, R(B)xR; 37 PxR, Q–B5;*

38 K–N2, P–N4; 39 K–N1, P–N5; 40 PxP, PxP; 41 K–N2, Q–B8! and White ran into zugzwang after *42 K–N3, Q–KR8!; 43 R–Q3, R–K8; 44 R–KB3, R–Q8; 45 P–N3, R–QB8!.*

On a K-move White falls into 46 ... R–B7!; 48 QxR, QxR and mates. White actually played *46 R–K3* and *Resigned* following *46 ... R–B8* because 47 Q–N2 loses the Q to 47 ... R–KN8 and any other Q-move hangs an R after 47 ... Q–N8ch.

This classic of grind-it-out play completed the fifteenth round with the standings: Capablanca, 11; Alekhine, 8; Nimzovich and Vidmar, 7½; Spielmann, 6; and Marshall, 5. In the next round Capa stretched his lead to 3½ points by walking over Marshall.

What followed was, in Lasker's words, a sorry caricature of chess. The Cuban had virtually clinched first place and only needed a few draws. Therefore, he told the tournament referee to inform his last four opponents that he was offering them each a draw in advance!

At the preliminary players' meeting Capa had insisted that all draw offers be communicated through the tournament officials, and thus they were agents to the champion's joke on the chess world. First, he met Spielmann.

After allowing his opponent several chances for advantage, Capablanca (Black) urged a draw with 27 ... N–B4; 28 R–N4, N–Q3; 29 R–N3, N–B4. Of course, Black is better if he plays 27 ... QR–R1.

Then came Round 18 versus Vidmar. Capablanca had great respect for the first Yugoslav master to gain an international reputation. He had predicted that Vidmar would finish at least third in the event.

Again, Black stands better and can open up the game with . . . P–N5. Black's good Bishop leaves him plenty of room for maneuver. On 22 R–QR1 intending P–QR4, Black can play 22 . . . R–QN1, for example. Nevertheless, Capa offered a draw and his opponent eagerly accepted.

The next round produced another incident. This time the opponent was Nimzovich.

With 21 N–Q5 Black (Nimzovich) can defend simply with 21 . . . K–N2. However, 21 R–Q6!, K–N2; 22 N–Q5,

NxN; 23 KPxN is very favorable. Alekhine considers 23 . . . R–K1; 24 R–Q7, P–K5; 25 K–B2! as very strong in the tournament book.

The champion naturally saw 21 R–Q6. But instead of playing it, he wrote a note to his opponent: "Please make better moves. I don't know how to avoid a win." The tournament referee took it two feet to his opponent while Capablanca played *21 K–B2?*. It was sufficiently weak as to allow Black to draw.

The last round was a real game for Capablanca since Alekhine was playing for a win. However, in twenty-six moves, the two men had traded almost everything off the board, and a draw was agreed.

SCORETABLE

	Capa.	Alek.	Nimz.	Vidm.	Spiel.	Marsh.	Total
1. Capablanca	XXXX	1½½½	1½1½	½½1½	½½1½	11½1	14–6
2. Alekhine	0½½½	XXXX	½01½	½½½½	1½½1	½1½1	11½–8½
3. Nimzovich	0½0½	½10½	XXXX	100½	11½½	1½½1	10½–9½
4. Vidmar	½½0½	½½½½	011½	XXXX	½½½½	½01½	10–10
5. Spielmann	½½0½	0½½0	00½½	½½½½	XXXX	½½11½	8–12
6. Marshall	00½0	½0½0	0½½0	½10½	½½0½	XXXX	6–14

When Capablanca returned to Havana in time for the fall match with Alekhine, he was mobbed by enormous crowds and recognized as his country's most famous personality. His New York success confirmed the widely held feeling that the difference between Capablanca and the rest of the chess world was very great.

And on September 16 the "Chess Machine," the unbeatable World Champion, the master of the latest advances in chess technique, sat down against a player whom he had beaten eight times, drawn with seven times, and never lost to. And somehow, and probably for the good of chess, Capablanca lost.

VI

Last Round

Noon, August 28, 1936/Nottingham, England: The final round is nearly three hours old. Five men are still in range of first place, and two more are capable of squeezing as close as third. Among the competitors are three former World Champions, the incumbent titleholder, and a future Champion.

And yet blunder follows blunder in an amazing array of errors by the best players in the world. Max Euwe, the current champion, should have lost a piece on the twenty-second move, but his rabbit opponent overlooked the simple win. Salo Flohr's mistake is even worse, and only a return blunder by Tartakover saves the Czech from his third major disaster in the tournament. Botvinnik of Russia is completely outplayed by the tail-ender, Willie Winter, who then offers a draw. That puts the pressure on José Raoul Capablanca.

He has White against Bogolyubov and is clearly winning. Victory means clear first in the strongest tournament in twelve years. It would establish Capa as the next World Champion challenger after the return match between Alekhine and Euwe. It would, in effect, mean another shot at the world title that he once held so firmly. On the other hand, defeat would mean tying with others for a place as low as sixth.

With 25 Q–N5! White could win a pawn after 25 . . . R–QN1; 26 NxP or 25 . . . R–R2; 26 Q–N6. If Black plays 25 . . . BxNch; 26 KxB, P–B6ch; 27 K–K1 Capablanca would win easily on the Queenside. Capa continued:

25	NxP!?	B–K4
26	N–K6	QR–R1!

Black loses even faster on 27 . . . R–K1; 28 BxP!, KxB; 29 Q–B1ch. Bogolyubov places his faith in two Bishops and the KB-file.

27	NxRch	RxN
28	Q–N5?	. . .

Now, with first place in his grasp, Capablanca completely overlooks Black's threat. With 28 B–K3, B–R7; 29 R–KN2!, BxRch; 30 KxB, B–K4; 31 K–B1 it would be a job for White's perfect technique.

28 . . .   BxP!

Threatening mate, of course, and nearly turning the tables 180 degrees. White is in dire trouble, so he plays . . . well, let's wait until we get to that.

Nottingham 1936 was a landmark. It was Lasker's last tournament, the last good showing for Capablanca, the last accomplishment by the generation that emerged before the first World War. Even at 44 Alekhine was in decline, and by the time he faced a field of such grandmasters again — at AVRO 1938 — he could only manage an even score. The ebullient Bogolyubov never played in a major event after this, and Vidmar turned to tournament direction.

On the other hand, there was a new generation, born in this century, composed of people no one had ever heard of until a few years before — Botvinnik, Flohr, the young Americans Fine and Reshevsky. When another war interrupted tournament chess — midway through the international team event at Buenos Aires in 1939 — the players went into hibernation for six years. When it was over, Capablanca and Lasker were dead and Alekhine was on the verge. Thus, Nottingham was one of those rare face-to-face meetings of chess generations.

Bogolyubov later explained why he got off to a bad start. For three consecutive nights, he said, he dreamed he was Alderman J. N. Derbyshire, a British industrialist. The Alderman was a chessplayer and had won one of the minor tournaments held in connection with the Nottingham Congress of 1886 (the major event was won by Amos Burn). Derbyshire was footing the bill for a large portion of the fiftieth anniversary tournament. The thought of spending so much money on anything inevitably led to Bogolyubov's breaking out in a cold sweat, he explained. Bogo had defected from the USSR eleven years before, and his materialism was not quite dialectical.

Because of Alderman Derbyshire's generosity it was the finest English tournament since Hastings '95. Play was held in the Great Assembly Hall of Nottingham University. There were separate rooms for displays of problems, of historic chess sets, for the players' own analysis, and even a room for table tennis at which the 25-year-old Reshevsky excelled.

The English themselves were well represented by a remarkable variety of competitors. There was the athletic patrician, 55-year-old Sir George Thomas, whose mother had won the first international women's tournament at the first Hastings. Almost a direct opposite of Thomas was William Winter, a 38-year-old carelessly, almost slovenly dressed, nervous, chain-smoking, and exceptionally perceptive chess writer. Winter became a chessplayer after his doctor told him to give up politics. He had been an active Communist Party organizer and served six months in jail for sedition on one occasion.

Also playing were Conel Hugh O'Donel (C.H.O'D) Alexander and Sir Theodore Henry Tylor. Alexander, an Irish mathematics professor and attacking genius, was, at 27, the youngest in the tournament. He later served in several prominent posts in British Intelligence, before dying in late 1973. Tylor, a correspondence champion and university legal scholar, was the only blind player to represent his country in the international team championships. But these were the rabbits and, in many ways, the least interesting personalities of 1936.

The first round began on August 10 on a somber note. Word had come that Tartakover, the last to arrive for the event, had sunk with a Dutch liner in the Thames the night before. All lives were thought lost in a severe storm.

Capablanca was paired with the doctor, then a Parisian resident, in the first round and watched as tournament director A. F. Mackenzie made the formality of starting Tartakover's clock at the usual time. After twenty minutes, however, the "late" Tartakover strode into the room and pushed his QP two squares.

More than ruffled by the appearance of a ghost, Capablanca offered a draw after nineteen moves. The tournament was played under a new rule that forbade draws in less than thirty moves. When Mackenzie asked Capablanca what he should do, the Cuban replied, "If two masters of the caliber of Dr. Tartakover and myself were to appraise the position as even, I would accept their opinion with the slightest hesitation." Draw agreed.

It turned out that Tartakover had taken a different route from the Continent — a boat from Rotterdam to Hull rather than to London. This, he thought, was a shortcut, but was only a lifesaver.

An odd mistake by Alekhine opened the first round. After *1 P-K4, P-K3; 2 P-Q4, P-Q4; 3 N-QB3, B-N5* he picked up the wrong piece and played *4 B-Q2* instead of the intended *4 P-K5*. Then after *4 . . . PxP* he chose *5 NxP?, QxP 6 B-Q3* instead of the complex and superior *5 Q-N4*. Flohr made up for it with *6 . . . BxBch; 7 QxB, Q-Q1?* when *7 . . . QxP!* would have left White minus two Pawns and with compensation for only one. The former Champion won in fifty-seven moves.

The clearest sign of the times was Lasker's loss to Reuben Fine, the recent victor at Zandvoort ahead of Euwe and Keres. Black's tenth and fourteenth moves ruined his Pawn structure — 10 . . . QN-Q2 and 14 . . . K-R2 were recommended.

FINE–LASKER: *1 P-Q4, P-Q4; 2 P-QB4, P-K3; 3 N-KB3, N-KB3; 4 N-B3, B-K2; 5 P-K3, O-O; 6 B-Q3, PxP; 7 BxP, P-B4; 8 O-O, P-QR3; 9 Q-K2, P-QN4; 10 B-Q3, B-N2?; 11 PxP!, BxP; 12 P-K4, QN-Q2; 13 B-N5, P-R3; 14 B-R4, P-N5?; 15 N-R4, B-K2; 16 KR-Q1, N-R4; 17 BxB, QxB; 18 QR-B1!, QN-B3; 19 P-KN3, P-R4; 20 N-B5, KR-B1; 21 NxB, QxN; 22 N-K5, RxR; 23 RxR, R-QB1; 24 RxRch, QxR; 25 Q-B2!, Q-N2; 26 Q-B6, Q-R2; 27 Q-B8ch, K-R2; 28 N-B6, Q-B4; 29 P-K5ch, P-N3; 30 PxN, NxBP; 31 Q-N7; K-N1; 32 B-K2, N-Q4; 33 N-K5 Resigns.*

"Young man, you play well," said the 68-year-old Lasker to an opponent who was born half a year after St. Petersburg 1914.

The second round provided a matchup no one had witnessed for nine years—Alekhine vs. Capablanca. After their 1927 match Alekhine strenuously avoided a confrontation. If Capablanca was invited to a tournament, Alekhine informed the organizers he would not play. Soon organizers knew better than to invite the two enemies, who had become embittered by negotiations for a rematch.

The absence of Capa allowed Alekhine, then a Paris-based married man, to score his greatest victories–thirteen wins and two draws at San Remo 1930 and 5½ points ahead of the field at Bled 1931. But Euwe had upset Alekhine in their 1935 match, and Alekhine was no longer powerful enough to deny the Cuban a place at Nottingham.

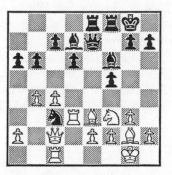

A few minor inaccuracies by Capa gave Black (Alekhine) the better side of a Dutch Defense. As he pointed out later, Alekhine could have kicked White around with 24 . . . B–QR5; 25 Q–Q2, N–K5; 26 Q–K1, P–KN4!

But Black miscalculated this variation: 24 . . . P–B5?; 25 PxP, B–B4; 26 Q–Q2, BxR; 27 PxB, P–B4?; 28 RxN, BxR; 29 QxB, thinking he was the double Exchange ahead. In fact, Capa had three minor pieces for the two Rooks and an overwhelming game. When the game was due to be adjourned, a depressed Alekhine committed a second blunder. He made his thirty-eighth move on the board when, according to the rules, it should have been sealed.

The two players and referees argued about it until an official ruling a week later. Then Alekhine resigned almost unnoticed. But Capablanca had had his revenge.

The standings showed Euwe in the lead with 2–0, followed by Botvinnik, Capablanca, and Fine at 1½. The third round included another flap, this time between Flohr and Capa. The Cuban survived a bad opening and by his thirty-seventh move was holding easily.

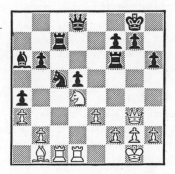

The former Champion gave this explanation to *64,* the Russian weekly. "Both players were very short of time. When four moves remained to be made our table was surrounded by a crowd of journalists, participants and others. . . . Max Euwe, who stood close to the table, spoke several times to Flohr, telling him the number of moves remaining to be made, as both players had stopped writing down the moves. As I requested him to keep quiet, he started to argue with me and tried to persuade me that he was entitled to speak . . . as a result of this interference I made a grave error, losing the Exchange."

Black played *37 . . . Q–B1?* overlooking the strength of *38 N–B5!.* Capa immediately responded *38 . . . R–N3,* and after *39 N–Q6, RxQ; 40 NxQ* had to lose material since *40 . . . R–N4* allows *41 NxP.* Black gave up the Exchange with *40 . . . RxPch; 41 KxR, RxN; 42 B–R2, R–B3; 43 BxP* and surrendered in the third session of play.

The only problem with Capablanca's version of the incident is that the time limit was thirty-six moves in two hours, not forty. This would mean that Black's blunder came after the time control.

Tartakover and Lasker played a tepid draw in that round after which the old man said, "With the onset of age, I must always keep in mind the factor of increasing entropy."

He was still the center of attention although until the Zurich tournament of 1934 he hadn't played in nearly a decade. One fan at Nottingham recalled bringing a Lasker enthusiast to the university for a day's play (*Chess 1936*):

He sat down in front of the demonstration board bearing Lasker's game—and there I left him. Several times I returned always to find him gazing with steadfast eyes at the game of the idol of his youth.

At 4 P.M. I asked him should we return home. No reply. At 4:30 I repeated the question. "Wait a minute," he barked. At 5 it became serious. . . . "If you must go, then go," replied my friend. "I am staying here until Lasker makes his next move."

How could I explain that Lasker had resigned over an hour ago?

Like Steinitz at Hastings, Lasker was playing for the money. He had tried making a living by teaching—not chess, but contract bridge. The Laskers had decided to live in Russia for the time being after the 1936 Moscow tournament. In fact, the old master would have lived out his days as a Soviet citizen if his wife hadn't asked him to return to America as her 70th birthday present.

Meanwhile, Botvinnik had taken the lead at 2½-½ due to his victories over Alexander and Bogolyubov. The New Soviet chess man forged forward the next day, August 13.

OLD INDIAN DEFENSE

M. M. Botvinnik	S. Tartakover
1 N–KB3	N–KB3
2 P–B4	P–Q3
3 P–Q4	QN–Q2

4	P-KN3	P-K4
5	B-N2	B-K2

Tartakover was especially fond of this opening, which is not bad, just out of fashion since the advent of the King's Indian.

6	O-O	O-O
7	N-B3	P-B3
8	P-K4	Q-B2

Another plan, probably better, is 8 . . . P-QR3 intending 9 . . . P-QN4. Naturally on 9 P-QR4, P-QR4! Black secures an excellent outpost for an N at QN5, or QB4 after a subsequent . . . KPxP.

9	P-KR3	R-K1
10	B-K3	N-B1?!

Black follows an older idea that doesn't generate enough central energy. He hopes to play the opening like a Philidor's Defense with . . . B-Q2, . . . QR-Q1 and . . . B-B1 before upsetting the tension in the center. His next move is not necessary for that plan.

11	R-B1	P-KR3
12	P-Q5	. . .

Beginning a middlegame strategy that may involve 13 PxP and 14 P-QN4-5 to secure control of Q5.

12	. . .	B-Q2
13	N-Q2	P-KN4?

Another piece of a bad puzzle. Black wants to restrain P-KB4, but 13 . . . N-N3 does that just as well.

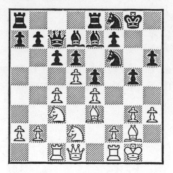

| 14 | P–B4! | NPxP |
| 15 | NPxP | K–N2 |

How else does Black protect the KRP against the BPxP threat?

| 16 | BPxP | QPxP |
| 17 | P–B5! | . . . |

The threat of 18 P–Q6 can draw off another Kingside piece and bring White's QN into play. Black cannot allow the steamroller of Pawns on Q5 and QB5. Alekhine urges 17 . . . Q–B1; 18 P–Q6, B–Q1 in his notes.

| 17 | . . . | PxP |
| 18 | NxP | Q–B3 |

A concession that Black is in a bad way. Botvinnik could win the KRP now with 19 NxN, BxN; 20 Q–R5 but after 20 . . . N–N3 resistance is possible. White has reason to expect more.

| 19 | N–QB4! | N–N3 |
| 20 | N–Q6! | . . . |

Another strong tactical idea. Not only 21 NxRch but the more dangerous 21 NxN, followed by 22 RxB and 23 Q–B3ch is threatened.

| 20 | ... | B–K3 |
| 21 | NxB! | NxN |

Black loses a piece on 21 ... RxN; 22 N–B5ch, BxN; 23 PxB, opening an attack on the Black Q.

| 22 | RxN! | ... |

Obvious, yes, but very impressive, considering White's winning method. He could have won a Pawn four moves ago or the Exchange two moves ago, but instead he prefers to sacrifice material.

| 22 | ... | KxR |
| 23 | Q–R5 | N–N3 |

The threat was 24 QxRPch, N–N3; 25 B–N5 mate. Tartakover's move prepares the K's escape via K2.

| 24 | N–B5! | R–KN1 |

Again 24 ... BxN; 25 PxB wins a piece. White's main threat is 25 QxRP. Against 24 ... R–R1 there was a simple win with 25 R–B1, Q–R5; 26 BxP, and a complex one with 25 P–KR4, BxP; 26 R–Q1, QR–Q1; 27 B–N5ch and mates.

25   QxP   BxP

There was no other way to prevent mate at KN5 except to create a flight square. The game was finished with *26 R–Q1, QR–Q1; 27 Q–N5ch, K–K3; 28 RxR, P–B3; 29 RxR, N–B5; 30 Q–N7, Resigns,* and won a deserved Brilliancy Prize.

Mikhail Moiseivich Botvinnik was 25 and trying for his first foreign success. He already had plenty of credits in Soviet events. He had been Soviet Champion at 20 and second-place winner behind Capablanca at the Moscow International just two months before Nottingham. But in his only previous European venture Botvinnik placed a dismal fifth at Hastings 1934–1935.

His reputation among the foreign players was considerable, nevertheless. Bogolyubov, playing cards one day with Vidmar and Tartakover, remarked to them, "You are all patzers. I lose to you just out of bad luck." Then he noticed Botvinnik in the room and added, "Ah, but him, he beat me fair and square."

Another story, probably apocryphal, involves the same participants at AVRO two years later. The tournament was organized by a Dutch radio station for the purpose of choosing a challenger to Alekhine after his restoration to the Championship throne. A reporter asked each of the players who they thought were the best and second best players in the world. Alekhine: "I am the best, of course." And second best? "Botvinnik." And Capablanca said, Well, yes, Capablanca was the best player, but he figured that the young Russian, Botvinnik, was his closest rival. And so said Flohr and Euwe and everyone else down the line. Botvinnik was everyone's choice of second best to this revealing question.

Botvinnik had already developed many of his usual habits — sipping fruit juices during the round, cleaning his glasses, and taking long impassive "thinks" at the board.

Alekhine, on the other hand, would shift his body nervously from side to side, curl his hair, and frequently cough. The two men met in a tactical delight on the following day.

ALEKHINE–BOTVINNIK: *1 P–K4, P–QB4; 2 N–KB3, P–Q3; 3 P–Q4, PxP; 4 NxP, N–KB3; 5 N–QB3, P–KN3; 6 B–K2, B–N2; 7 B–K3, N–B3; 8 N–N3, B–K3; 9 P–B4, O–O; 10 P–KN4!?*

Alekhine said he picked up this idea from Jan Foltys, the Czech master who played at the Podebrady tournament that year. The plan is 11 P–N5, or 11 P–B5 followed by 12 P–N5 to confuse Black's Kingside defenders. In the Foltys-Eliskases game Black continued 10 . . . N–QR4!?; 11 P–N5, N–K1?; 12 B–Q4, R–B1; 13 P–KR4!, N–B5; 14 BxN, RxB; 15 Q–Q3, R–B1; 16 O–O–O with an effortless attack. Alekhine thought he had prepared a surprise.

But Botvinnik responded *10 . . . P–Q4*, following a game he had played in the Moscow tournament against Grigory Levenfish. That game continued 11 P–K5, P–Q5!; 12 NxP (12 PxN, BxP), NxN; 13 BxN, NxP, with a better game for Black because the center is more valuable than the Kingside.

The whole line was revived by Fischer twenty-five years later, and for the reasons Bobby enumerated, 10 . . . N–QR4! is recommended as superior today, e.g. 11 P–N5, N–Q2!;

12 B–Q4, P–B3; 13 P–KR4, PxP!; 14 BxB, KxB; 15 N–Q4, B–N1 with a sound position.

The game continued—*11 P–B5, B–B1; 12 KPxP, N–N5* and here White played *13 P–Q6,* "doubtless the best move," according to Alekhine. But Fischer, following a suggestion of Czechoslovakia's Ludek Pachman, obtained a winning position against Reshevsky in a 1961 match game with 13 B–B3!, PxP; 14 P–QR3, PxP; 15 B–N2 (even better is 15 PxN!), N–R3; 16 Q–Q3, P–K3; 17 O–O–O.

The point of 13 P–Q6 is to meet 13 . . . QxP with 14 B–B5 and 13 . . . PxP with 14 P–N5 and 15 P–B6. Botvinnik fearlessly played *13 . . . QxP!; 14 B–B5, Q–B5!* rather than 14 . . . QxQ; 15 RxQ!, NxPch; 16 K–Q2. Now it appeared that Black was ready to take over with 15 . . . N–K5 and exploit the exposed White position.

But White still had punch: *15 R–KB1!, QxRP; 16 BxN,* and Black saw that 16 . . . BxP; 17 PxB, Q–R5ch; 18 R–B2, QxB; 19 B–Q3 or 16 . . . Q–N6ch; 17 R–B2, NxP; 18 N–K4! was a loss for him. He played *16 . . . NxP!* and after *17 BxN, Q–N6ch; 18 R–B2, Q–N8ch; 19 R–B1, Q–N6ch; 20 R–B2, Q–N8ch* they drew since White cannot risk 20 K–K2??, QxBch, or 20 K–Q2??, B–R3ch.

One-third of the way into the tournament saw Botvinnik and Euwe tied at 4–1; Fine and Reshevsky at 3; Alekhine, Capablanca, Vidmar, and Tylor (!) at 2½; followed by the also-rans—like Lasker. But since Euwe, Capablanca, and Vidmar had already had a bye round, they had a potential lead on the others. Euwe had, in fact, won his first four games against Reshevsky, Winter, Vidmar, and Alexander.

Euwe paralleled Botvinnik in his methodical and modest view of the world and the role of chess in it. His reputation before defeating Alekhine rested on several matches he lost. That is probably why Alekhine had chosen him as his 1935 challenger—Euwe had been a good loser when he faced Bogolyubov, Réti, Alekhine, and Capablanca.

Few things rattled Euwe. A year later, at the return match with Alekhine, his opponent tried to upset him with little annoyances—slamming doors when he walked away from the board or bringing in a brace of his pet Siamese cats. But it only encouraged Euwe, who thought, "Here you have the powerful Alekhine, unbeatable in the chess world, and still he makes use of such little tricks. He must have more esteem for my play than I thought he would have."

In the sixth round a humorous episode occurred. Fine drew a fairly simple game with the current champion in nineteen moves, but at different points during the session both Capablanca and Alekhine whispered suggestions into the American's ear. Both wanted to see Euwe do badly so that their own prestige would be enhanced. After six rounds it was Botvinnik and Euwe in first place, followed by Fine and Reshesvky.

Fine and Reshevsky, Reshevsky and Fine. The United States had waited thirty years to produce another grandmaster equal in stature to Marshall—and then it produced two. Reshevsky, a schoolboy prodigy who emigrated to America from Poland when he was 9, was 25 at Nottingham. Fine, a New York City-born product of the Marshall Chess Club, was 22. For the previous five years, despite competition from strong masters like Arthur Dake, Herman Steiner, A. I. Horowitz, and the internationally experienced Isaac Kashdan, the Fine–Reshevsky rivalry was the talk of American chess. Reshevsky renewed his adolescent interest in the game in 1931, when he won the American Chess Foundation Championship. The next two years Fine won, with Reshevsky second. In 1934 they tied. Reshevsky went to Europe and won at Margate and Great Yarmouth in England in 1935. Fine also went and took first at Hastings 1935–1936. One did well, and the other tried to surpass him.

And then just four months before Nottingham the slight but wiry Reshevsky won the U.S. Championship in a star-studded tournament arranged after Marshall retired in early '36. Fine was third.

Good will was wearing thin even among countrymen in the exceptionally tense event at Nottingham. Round Six was played on a Saturday, August 5. On the following day, a

free day, Fine and Reshevsky were to play off an adjournment from the fifth round. The tournament officials noted
that Euwe had to act as a friendly party to bring the two
Americans together after the first session because of some
bitterness. And during the second session of play the
tournament controller stood by, "lest Fine's sarcasms at
his opponent's carrying on attempts to win an undoubted
draw game should lead to a breach of the peace." They drew
before a third session was necessary.

Alekhine maintained his miserable form into the seventh
round, when he was paired with Reshevsky. "He was thin,
jerky in his movements, and his eyes flickered from side to
side," Botvinnik recalled. "He was still drinking wine and
lost to Reshevsky only because he drank a whole bottle of
wine before dinner. But he was a Chess Player with capital
letters."

After twenty-eight moves Reshevsky forced a series of
trades into a minor-piece ending that favored his two N's.
Alekhine began to tire in the fourth hour of play and missed
several good moves that would have restrained the Black
cavalry. Now, with 39 B–Q4, Black still had to prove he
had a win, but Alekhine makes "another terrible move."

49 B–R3?   P–K4!

Black polishes off the game quickly after this because of Knight forks and the activity of his K. For example, 50 PxP, N(2)xPch; 51 NxN, NxNch; 52 K–K4, K–K3 should be an easy win, e.g. 53 B–B5, N–N5; 54 P–R4, N–B3ch; 55 K–Q4 (else 55 . . . K–Q4), K–B4 scooping up the Kingside P's.

50	K–K3	K–K3
51	B–N2	K–Q4
52	N–R4	N–N3!
53	B–B1	N–B5ch
54	K–B2	N–N5!

Threatening another N-fork. The key point of Black's maneuver is that 55 . . . N–R7 will grease the path of the QNP. White will not even get a chance to sacrifice a piece for it if the Pawn gets to the sixth rank. The game proceeded with 55 *K–K2, N–R7; 56 B–Q2, P–N5; 57 PxP, P–N6; 58 K–Q1, NxP!*.

There was a last Alekhine trap in 58 . . . P–N7??; 59 K–B2, NxB; 60 KxP, N–N5; 61 K–B3 forking the pieces. But Black's move threatened . . . K–B5–Q6 or . . . N–Q6–B7ch followed by . . . P–N7. Alekhine tried *59 N–N2, K–K5; 60 P–R4, N–Q6; 61 B–R5, N–N7ch;* and *resigned* because 62 K–K2, N–B5! would either Queen the P or win the White B.

A quarter-century later Reshevsky said this and his 1955 victory over Botvinnik in the U.S.–U.S.S.R. match were his two favorite games.

After seven rounds Alekhine had a negative score (3–4), and another former champion, Capablanca, was 3½–2½ with a bye. The leaders continued to be the remarkable Botvinnik and Euwe with 5 points, followed a half-point back by the two Americans. Since only Euwe among the four leaders had had a bye, he was effectively in the top spot.

The eighth round was marked by Fine's positional piece sacrifice against Winter, another Euwe victory, and by the return of Capablanca. With the Black pieces against Thomas, the Cuban risked nothing and won with typical technique:

1 P–K4, P–K4; 2 N–KB3, N–QB3; 3 B–N5, P–QR3; 4 B–R4, P–Q3; 5 BxNch, PxB; 6 P–Q4, P–B3; 7 B–K3, N–K2; 8 N–B3, N–N3; 9 Q–Q2, B–K3; 10 P–QN3?.

White's position demands Queenside castling followed by P–KR4. Otherwise, Black's Bishops and more solid center will grow to be overwhelming in no time.

| 10 | ... | P–Q4! |

Alekhine says the best Thomas could do now would be 11 KPxP, BPxP; 12 N–QR4, P–K5; 13 N–N1, but that was hardly palatable.

| 11 | O–O | QPxP! |
| 12 | QNxP | B–Q4 |

This wrecks the Kingside since 13 Q–Q3, P–KB4! would cost a piece.

| 13 | N–N3 | BxN |
| 14 | PxB | N–R5! |

Black must win a P after this because 15 Q–K2, Q–Q4; 16 N–K4, Q–K3! followed by 17 . . . Q–R6 is crushing. The rest was a devastating example of Capablanca's best style: *15 Q–Q3, NxPch; 16 K–R1, NxQP; 17 Q–K4, Q–Q4!; 18*

QxQ, PxQ; B19 BxN, PxB; 20 QR–Q1, B–B4! (not 20 . . .
P–QB4?, which would endanger the win after 21 *P–QB3!);
*21 N–B5, K–B2; 22 NxQP, KR–K1; 23 P–QB3, R–K4; 24
R–Q3, QR–K1; 25 P–QR4?, BxN!; 26 RxB, P–QB4; 27
R–Q2, R–QN1; 28 R–QN1, P–QR4; 29 K–N2, K–K3; 30
R–B2, K–Q3; 31 P–B3, P–N4; 32 K–N3, P–R4; 33 P–R4,
PxPch; 34 KxP, R–K6; 35 K–N3,* and now 35 . . . *P–B5; 36
P–N4, PxP; 37 PxP, R–N6!* forced immediate resignation.

"Nottingham was just the tournament for Capablanca,"
Botvinnik later wrote. The time limit and relatively few free
days for analysis of openings and adjourned games were
very beneficial. "He never was a chess professional, his
talent was so great that he was always confident that he
would find the right answer at the board."

In the next two rounds Capa disposed of Reshevsky and
Vidmar and was challenging Botvinnik for the tournament
lead. That came about because on the 20th, after a rest day
with a trip to Alderman Derbyshire's manor, a garden
party, and some afternoon Shakespeare, Alekhine took the
steam out of Euwe's drive. A long but fascinating endgame
with Queens gave the former Champion a victory in eighty-
one moves. This revenge gave Alekhine another burst of
energy for his final charge up from ninth place. He followed
it with a sparkling victory over Winter in Round 10. The
Englishman played one of the most drawish of opening
variations with the White pieces: *1 P–K4, P–K3; 2 P–Q4,
P–Q4; 3 PxP?!, PxP; 4 B–Q3, N–QB3; 5 N–K2, B–Q3; 6
P–QB3, Q–R5!; 7 N–Q2, B–KN5; 8 Q–B2, O–O–O; 9 N–B1.*

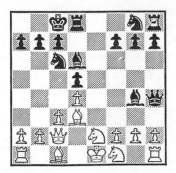

Black always has chances for upsetting the symmetry in this system despite its reputation. Alekhine's first step was the elimination of his slightly inferior QB: 9 . . . P-KN3!; 10 B-K3, KN-K2; 11 O-O-O, B-KB4!; 12 N(1)-N3, BxB; 13 QxB, P-KR3.

Here Winter played a positional horror, 14 P-KB4??, which worsened his Bishop and created golden chances for Black on the K-file. The next stage for Alekhine was to seal the Kingside and shift power to the Queenside: 14 . . . Q-N5!; 15 P-KR3, Q-Q2; 16 KR-B1, P-KR4; 17 N-N1, P-R5; 18 N(3)-K2, N-B4; 19 N-B3, P-B3.

The third stage was to mine the K-file with all the energy Black held: 20 N-R2, QR-K1; 21 B-Q2, R-K3; 22 N-N4, KR-K1; 23 QR-K1, R(1)-K2!; 24 K-Q1, Q-K1. White was hardly able to move anything. So he prepared for 26 N-B1 by playing 25 Q-B3.

Alekhine began the final assault with 25 . . . N-R4!; 26 P-QN3, (26 QxP, RxN; 27 RxR, RxR; 28 QxQN, N-N6!!), N-B5!!. Winter could not accept the offer because of 27 . . . Q-R5ch; 28 K-B1, B-R6ch; and 29 . . . Q-B7. And since 27 N-B1 would lose an R to 27 . . . NxB, White played 27 B-B1.

The rest was essentially mopup: 27 . . . QN-K6ch; 28 BxN, NxBch; 29 NxN, RxN; 30 Q-B2, Q-N4; 31 N-B1, RxBP; 32 RxR, BxR; 33 Q-K1, K-Q2; 34 P-B5, R-K6!; 35 Q-B2, P-N4; 36 R-K1, R-K5; 37 RxR, PxR; 38 K-Q2, B-Q3; 39 K-B2, B-B5, and Winter resigned.

One of the hardest things to do in a strong tournament, even against a rabbit, is to beat a worthy master who is playing for a draw with the White pieces. And Alekhine made it look easy.

The only other occasions of interest in the tenth and eleventh rounds were the postponement of the Capablanca—Vidmar game at the Yugoslav's request because of an upset stomach and Lasker's draw with Botvinnik. The game was set for the next rest day, but problems developed. In the meanwhile Alekhine's fine attack against Alexander (which won a prize) and Reshevsky's exploitation of

Lasker's mishandling of a tricky attack left the scores Botvinnik, 7½; Euwe, Fine, and Reshevsky, 7; Flohr and Alekhine, 6½; Capablanca, 6; with one game delayed. Only Reshevsky and Alekhine had not yet had a bye.

Seven of the players signed a protest petition to the tournament director insisting that the Capablanca–Vidmar game be played off quickly. Instead of the next free day just before the penultimate (fourteenth) round, they wanted it finished before the 11th. Capablanca refused, saying, "I did a favor for a colleague when he was ill. Surely Vidmar can understand that it is out of the question for me to cancel a date with a lady?" The lady in question was Olga Chegodaeva, the widow of a White Guard officer. Capa had sent her a letter saying he was lonely and needed companionship. She came at once and they later married.

The Lasker-Botvinnik affair was potentially more disruptive. After a relatively quiet middlegame, Lasker sealed his move in a slightly inferior position. Then Botvinnik made one of his rare lapses in chess etiquette. During the two-hour break he became convinced that the minor-piece ending was hopelessly drawn if Lasker sealed the right move.

So the Russian offered a draw just before resumption based on the condition that it could be accepted only if the obvious, drawing move was sealed. What could Lasker do? He wanted to draw. Therefore it was obvious that his refusal to accept the offer meant that he had sealed a different reply. An embarrassed Botvinnik offered to let Lasker hold his (Botvinnik's) pocket set so that the Russian could not reanalyze the position and consider other sealed moves. Fortunately for everyone involved, Lasker held the position easily and even stood better at the end when a draw was agreed.

With four rounds to go, the jitteriness of the tournament began to materialize in blunders. Nottingham was in fact one of the most blunder-filled events ever held with such talented players. In the third round against the lowly Tylor, Alekhine had refused a sacrifice of a piece which, if accepted, would have won for the ex-Champion easily. Instead, the refusal drew by force. Tylor was rewarded the very next round when Flohr, once considered to be Alekhine's next title challenger, committed a worse error in trying to squeeze blood out of a hopelessly drawn ending. Tylor won, and Alekhine remarked that a player who tries to win by exhausting a physically weaker opponent deserves to lose.

But no one was prepared for the next few rounds. In the twelfth round Flohr again was the victim.

On 50 . . . R–B4 Black (Flohr) could meet 51 N–B7 with 51 . . . R–KR4. White's best would be 51 P–K7, BxP; 52 RxB, P–R7; 53 R–K1, but would surely lose the Exchange down.

Inexplicably, Flohr missed Alexander's threat and played *50 . . . P–R7??* after which *51 N–B7, B–Q3ch (forced); 52 RxB, RxN; 53 PxRch, KxP; 54 R–Q1* was a hopeless ending for Black.

Even worse was Winter's catastrophe against Capablanca. Capa pressed an unsound attack a bit too far, and as time control loomed ahead he had only a glimmer of hope.

White can defend the threat of 37 ... Q–K5ch with the obvious 37 Q–B4. The win would then be academic. But Winter was unaware that the time control had been reached because he wasn't keeping score. Just to make sure, he played an extra move. It was *37 Q–R7ch??*.

What he apparently overlooked was that *37 ... K–N5; 38 P–R3ch, KxP; 39 R–N1ch* could be met by *39 ... QxRch!*. Even *39 ... K–B7* may have won for Black. Winter resigned on the next move because he couldn't stop mate.

A fighting draw between Botvinnik and Reshevsky left the scoretable with Botvinnik and Euwe, 8; Fine and Reshevsky, 7½; Capablanca (with the Vidmar game hanging in the air) and Alekhine, 7; and Flohr 6½. The thirteenth round featured Botvinnik's merciless crush of Vidmar, who was losing his enthusiasm for the tournament.

BOTVINNIK-VIDMAR: *1 P–QB4, P–K3; 2 N–KB3, P–Q4; 3 P–Q4, N–KB3; 4 B–N5, B–K2; 5 N–B3, O–O; 6 P–K3, QN–Q2; 7 B–Q3, P–B4; 8 O–O, BPxP; 9 KPxP, PxP; 10 BxP, N–N3?!; 11 B–N3, B–Q2; 12 Q–Q3, N(N)–Q4; 13 N–K5, B–B3; 14 QR–Q1, N–QN5?; 15 Q–R3!, B–Q4; 16 NxB, QNxN?; 17 P–B4!, R–B1; 18 P–B5, PxP; 19 RxP, Q–Q3; 20 NxP!!, RxN; 21 QBxN, BxB; 22 RxN, Q–B3; 23 R–Q6, Q–K1; 24 R–Q7 Resigns.*

On 20 ... KxN White has 21 BxNch and on 21 ... NxB there was 22 RxN, BxR; 23 QxRch. Though this won the prize for best game of the round, the chief topic of concern was Lasker–Euwe. White had a slightly inferior position because of the weak QP, but his offer of a draw was reasonable.

Euwe played 23 ... B–R4??, overlooking 24 P–QN4!, BxP; 25 N–B2, winning a piece and the game. This cost Euwe the tournament, as it turned out.

With the Capablanca-Vidmar game finally finished, the effect of this loss was to put Euwe in a three-way tie for fourth place with Fine and Alekhine, behind Botvinnik and Capablanca, who led with 9, and Reshevsky, who was third with 8½.

Even the next round had its share of errors. According to Botvinnik, his game with Euwe was adjourned with equal chances although Alekhine thought Euwe was always better. Before the game was resumed, Botvinnik offered a draw. Euwe wanted to look at the position more, but Botvinnik, thinking the offer accepted, showed him the Russian's analysis and Euwe disappeared with a pocket set. Fifteen minutes later Euwe decided to play on, not realizing the misunderstanding. At the board after two hours:

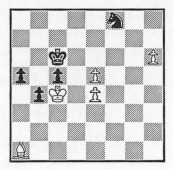

Euwe could try to grab the point with 56 K–N3! since Black has no useful move. His N can't move and his only useful K move, 56 . . . K–N4, allows 57 P–K6, P–R5ch; 58 K–R2, N–N3; 59 P–R7, K–B3; 60 P–K7, K–Q2; 61 B–B6, P–B5; and now 62 K–N1!! wins through zugzwang—62 . . . K–K1; 63 P–K5, K–B2; 64 P–K6ch, K–K1; 65 B–N5!, N–R1; 66 B–R4!, N–N3; 67 B–B6!

Actually Euwe played *56 P–K6* and, after *56 . . . K–Q3*, agreed to a draw. Alekhine won a forceful game with Tartakover to finish out with 9–5. On the eve of the final round it was Botvinnik and Capablanca at 9½; Alekhine at 9; Euwe, Fine, and Reshevsky at 8½; and Flohr with 8.

As we noted earlier, the last round was an anticlimax of thud-and-blunder. The most shocking error was Thomas–Euwe:

Black had a slightly better game because he could exploit the weakened White Kingside — *once the Q-file was neutralized*. Euwe failed to notice that White's last move, 22 Q–Q3, contained a threat. Black played 22 . . . N–K3??

Thomas may have seen 23 RxB but dismissed it because of 23 . . . RxR; 24 QxR, R–Q1. However, White had the reply 25 N–Q7!, keeping his extra piece and winning easily. White played 23 P–N3??

Less than ten moves later, in a position in which Alekhine stressed that Black was not threatening anything, Thomas butchered his position with a random advance of his K. Meanwhile, Fine was winning only due to several ghastly endgame moves by Tylor, and Lasker was beating Alexander because of a careless loss of the Exchange by the Britisher. Here we return to Capablanca–Bogolyubov.

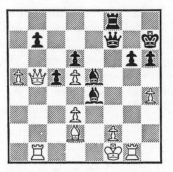

Capa played 29 QxNP, BxPch; 30 K–N2, B–K5ch and chose the inspired 31 P–B3!. Clearly 31 K–B1, BxR was taboo. The real danger was 31 K–R3, B–B4ch, followed by 32 . . . B–Q2!, avoiding an exchange of Q's.

Bogo took the offer with 31 . . . BxPch; 32 K–R3, BxP, and after 33 QxQch, RxQ; 34 KR–KB1 White had just enough play to draw. A memorable last round.

So, with a little luck, Capablanca revived his claim to the world title. And with two kinds of luck, Euwe finished in a tie for third.

SCORETABLE

	Bot	C	E	Fi	R	Alek	Fl	L	V	Bog	Ta	Ty	Alex	Th	W	Total
1–2. Botvinnik	X	½	½	½	½	½	½	½	1	1	1	1	1	1	½	10–4
1–2. Capablanca	½	X	½	½	1	1	0	½	1	½	½	1	1	1	1	10–4
3–5. Euwe	½	½	X	½	1	0	½	0	1	½	1	1	1	1	1	9½–4½
3–5. Fine	½	½	½	X	½	½	½	1	½	1	½	1	1	½	1	9½–4½
3–5. Reshevsky	½	0	0	½	X	1	½	1	1	1	½	1	1	1	½	9½–4½
6. Alekhine	½	0	1	½	0	X	1	½	½	1	1	½	1	½	1	9–5
7–8. Flohr	½	1	½	½	½	0	X	1	1	1	½	0	0	1	1	8½–5½
7–8. Lasker	½	½	1	0	0	½	0	X	½	1	½	1	1	1	1	8½–5½
9. Vidmar	0	0	0	½	0	½	0	½	X	1	½	½	1	½	1	6–8
10–11. Bogolyubov	0	½	½	0	0	0	0	0	0	X	½	1	1	1	1	5½–8½
10–11. Tartakover	0	½	0	½	½	0	½	½	½	½	X	0	0	1	1	5½–8½
12. Tylor	0	0	0	0	0	½	1	0	½	0	1	X	½	½	½	4½–9½
13. Alexander	0	0	0	0	0	0	1	0	0	0	1	½	X	½	½	3½–10½
14. Thomas	0	0	0	½	0	½	0	0	½	0	0	½	½	X	½	3–11
15. Winter	½	0	0	0	½	0	0	0	0	0	0	½	½	½	X	2½–11½

Even Lasker performed well — 1½ points off the pace after fifteen rounds was an astonishing performance for a man of 68. But the real winner was Mikhail Botvinnik.

The August 29 issue of Pravda noted, "In the remotest corners of our land, in isolated villages, collective farms, in the hill settlements of Daghestan, in the hamlets of the Central Asian republics, there exist chess clubs. . . . Seated at the chess table in Nottingham, Botvinnik could feel the entire country supporting him and wishing him success." He was awarded the Mark of Honor and became the first Soviet citizen to star in the chess world. It was the beginning of an era that lasted for nearly four decades.

VII

Schachmat!

Scene: Room 713, Moscow University, Department of Physical Culture and Sport, Class #501—"The Development and Significance of Soviet Domination in Chess." Prof. I. I. Groznitsky presiding.

GROZNITSKY: Now, class, we come to the most interesting period we will consider, the flowering of Soviet chess. You may recall that at the time of Nottingham 1936 the decadence of Western European chess was already apparent. The new masters from America, Fine and Reshevsky, tried to prop up the tottering mass of bourgeois chess theory. They were destined to fail like the other neo-colonialists.

To give some historical perspective, in August 1936, when the Nottingham event was held, Mikhail Botvinnik was a 25-year-old engineering student about to obtain the degree of Candidate of Technical Science from Leningrad Polytechnic Institute. His victory in England was the first

success of the Soviet School and its scientific approach. . . .
Yes, Ivan Stepanovich?

I. S.: But Comrade Professor, was not the victory of E. D.
Bogolyubov at the Moscow tournament of 1925 the first
Soviet success? . . .

GROZNITSKY: You are deceived, Ivan Stepanovich. No
such person as E. D. Bogolyubov existed. He is a myth
created by our capitalist enemies. As I was saying . . .

At the time of Nottingham, Vassily Vasilyevich Smyslov
was a 15-year-old First Category player in the Moscow
House of Young Pioneers. David Jonovich Bronstein was a
12-year-old member of the Kiev Pioneers. And 7-year-old
Tigran Vartanovich Petrosian had not yet learned the moves
in his native Tiflis. Neither Mikhail Nekhemyevich Tal nor
Boris Vasilyevich Spassky had been born.

Yet these were the men who virtually dominated chess
from the end of the Great Patriotic War onward. Consider
this, my students:

Because of the provocations by the American fascists,
virtually the only tournaments after the war with the best
Western and Soviet players competing were those directly
related to the World Championship. In the interzonal
tournaments, usually with twenty to twenty-two players,
the Soviet representatives took six of the top seven places
at Stockholm 1948, all five top places at Saltsjobaden 1952,
and four of the five top prizes at Goteborg 1955. In the
triennial cycle to select World Championship challengers,
several Candidates tournaments were held with eight to
ten players. Our Soviet masters took the top four positions
at Budapest 1950, five of the first six at Zurich 1953, the top
six at Amsterdam 1954, and again at Bled-Zagred-Belgrade
1959.

Perhaps you have to go back to the English hegemony of
the Staunton era to recall a time when the players of one
nation were head and shoulders above those of the rest of
the world. And this inevitable success—inevitable, of
course, because of the historical dialectic of Marxist-

Leninism, became clear for the first time at the World Championship Tournament of 1948.

Not since Philidor's time had the world been without a recognized Best Player. The death of Alekhine in Lisbon during March 1946 created a vacuum that all players wanted to fill. Our national chess authorities argued correctly that since Alekhine had agreed to play a match with Botvinnik in 1947, Mikhail Moiseivich had the best claim. The Dutch offered a proposal at the FIDE meeting of 1946 to name Euwe as interim champion since he was the only living former titleholder. Even Reuben Fine has since claimed to be 'unofficial cochampion' on the curious grounds that by tying for the highest prize at AVRO 1938, he and Paul Keres were designated as Alekhine's next opponents and therefore his heirs.

FIDE, the international federation, had been founded in Paris in 1924 but was politely ignored by the stronger grandmasters of the West. Year after year the international body would request Alekhine or Capablanca to play a title match with such-and-such a challenger and would not receive a reply. But the death of Alekhine left power in the streets and like V. I. Lenin, FIDE picked it up! Henceforward, FIDE argued, the World Championship would be organized by representatives of all its members in a majority vote, not by one champion.

In the summer of 1946 the organization made tentative plans for a six-man Championship Tournament to be held in Holland with Dr. Euwe, two Americans, and three Soviet players competing. But if any new names popped up by the spring of 1948, FIDE suggested they might be added as late starters. This didn't turn out to be necessary because the strongest postwar event, Groningen 1946, was convincingly won by Botvinnik with Euwe second and Smyslov third. Botvinnik, Smyslov, and Paul Keres, who had wisely taken Soviet citizenship, were already designated as our representatives.

The Americans were supposed to be Samuel Reshevsky

and Fine. But Fine, who said he never received a formal invitation anyway, was too busy with his doctoral thesis to get away. There was some idle chatter among organizers in the West to invite Miguel Mendel Najdorf of Argentina on the basis of his fourth-place tie at Groningen and easy victory at Prague 1946. But Najdorf, who was Polish until the War broke out during the 1939 Buenos Aires team tournament, and his supporters could not force the tournament organizers to rewrite the rules with just a few weeks to go. It remained a five-man battle.

The prizes were exceptionally high—$5,000 for first place and an honorarium of $250 per player for traveling expenses. This was a major jump from the $550 first prize at AVRO, when the players were motivated by love of art. The 1948 event was divided between The Hague and Moscow at the leisurely pace of three games per week plus one bye every fifth game because of Fine's withdrawal. No, the organizers would not repeat the insult of AVRO, where the eight contestants were led a merry chase throughout the Netherlands, playing one day in Rotterdam, the next in Amsterdam, and a few days later at The Hague. Incredibly, there were no rest days in 1938. As Mikhail Moiseivich declared, it was the worst tournament he had ever competed in.

There could be no better illustration of the difference between the honored position this game holds in the Soviet state and its neglect in the West than the arrival and preparations for the great 1948 event. Our group arrived early and came in force. Since the second Alekhine–Euwe match the organizers had recognized the need for "seconds" to assist players. At The Hague, Vyacheslav Ragozin analyzed for Botvinnik, Vladimir Alatortsev for Smyslov, and Alexander Tolush for Keres. These worthy masters were also accompanied by Botvinnik's longtime confidant, Salo Flohr, Igor Bondarevsky, and Hungarian emigré Andre Lillienthal, who served as grandmaster-correspondent for the press. Mikhail Moiseivich also brought his wife, a Bolshoi ballerina, his daughter, and his Moscow doctor. Altogether there were some twenty or so members of our delegation.

By comparison, Reshevsky arrived alone. The embarrassed Dutch attached local master Lodwijk Prins to be his second. Euwe, the hometown hero, was aided by his friend T. D. Van Scheltinga, who had tied with him in the previous year's Dutch championship. And for a touch of nostalgia, Milan Vidmar was the chief referee.

On March 1 the pomp and ceremony of the rules meeting was held in the Town Hall. Botvinnik drew number one in the pairings and earned another day of rest because it meant he had a bye in the first round. Euwe made the first initial move, and the 54-year-old schoolteacher lost no time in securing a big advantage against Keres:

1 P-K4, P-K4; 2 N-KB3, N-QB3; 3 B-N5, P-QR3; 4 B-R4, P-Q3; 5 P-B3, B-Q2; 6 P-Q4, KN-K2; 7 B-N3, P-R3; 8 QN-Q2, N-N3; 9 N-B4, B-K2; 10 O-O, O-O; 11 N-K3, B-B3; 12 N-Q5, PxP; 13 NxP!, R-K1; 14 NxBch, QxN; 15 P-B3, N-B5; 16 NxN, BxN; 17 B-K3, QR-Q1; 18 Q-Q2, N-N3; 19 B-Q4, Q-K2; 20 QR-K1, Q-Q2; 21 P-QB4, B-R5; 22 BxB, QxB; 23 Q-B3, P-KB3.

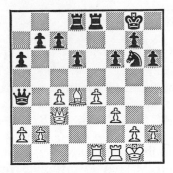

Euwe had an excellent position, but he lacked a plan. What was he to do? Petya Evgenyevich?

P. E.: White could try to play on the Kingside with P–KN3, K–R1, P–KR4, and R–KN1 in preparation for P–KN4–5. . . . Or he could double Rooks on the Queen file and prepare for, perhaps, P–QB5.

GROZNITSKY: Excellent, Petya Evgenyevich. However, Euwe continued:

	24 P–B4!?	K–R2

Black responded to the threat of 25 BxP!, PxB; 26 QxP followed by 27 R–KB3. He had no time for 24 . . . P–QB4.

	25 P–QN3	Q–Q2

Now 26 . . . P–QB4 is a threat, as well as 26 . . . P–QN4 with the idea of opening up a Queenside line, White should have maintained his strength with 26 Q–N3 followed by P–KR4–5 and P–K5!

	26 Q–B3?	P–N4!
	27 Q–Q3?	PxP
	28 QxP?	. . .

Three bad moves in a row have given Black the better game. He could play the simple 28 . . . P–Q4; 29 PxP, RxR. But there is more.

	28 . . .	RxP!
	29 RxR	P–Q4

Here White maintained material equality with *30 QxRP*, but his game collapsed quickly after *30 . . . PxR; 31 B–K3, Q–N5; 32 Q–B4, R–Q6!; 33 B–B1, N–R5!; 34 QxPch, P–B4*, followed by . . . *R–QB6–7*. White overstepped the time limit on the fifty-sixth move.

Two days later Mikhail Moiseivich made his first appearance in the tournament hall. It was the Direntuin, formerly the Grote Zaal (Great Hall) of the Zoological

Gardens before the War. The distinguished building was some distance from the Kurhaus hotel in Scheveningen, where the players lived and where adjourned games were occasionally played off. Botvinnik arrived with Ragozin, reminding himself, "It is always pleasant to win in the first round. . . . Your combatitive spirit develops, the sureness of your strength and confidence is bolstered."

It was an historic occasion. Botvinnik had never defeated Euwe, although he should have drawn the two previous games he had lost to the Dutchman and should have won three of the four games they drew.

On the seventeenth move our hero offered a Pawn, which Euwe should have ignored. White Bishops suddenly scissored across the board when the Queens departed. Despite Botvinnik's time pressure—fourteen moves for nineteen minutes—he could confidently relax and sip his fruit juice.

BOTVINNIK-EUWE: *1 P-Q4, P-Q4; 2 P-QB4, P-K3; 3 N-KB3, N-KB3; 4 N-B3, P-B3; 5 P-K3, QN-Q2; 6 B-Q3, B-N5; 7 P-QR3, B-R4; 8 Q-B2, Q-K2; 9 B-Q2, PxP; 10 BxBP, P-K4; 11 O-O, O-O; 12 QR-K1!, B-B2; 13 N-K4, NxN; 14 QxN, P-QR4; 15 B-R2!, N-B3; 16 Q-R4, P-K5; 17 N-K5!, BxN?; 18 PxB, QxKP; 19 B-B3, Q-K2; 20 P-B3!, N-Q4; 21 QxQ, NxQ; 22 PxP, P-QN3?; 23 R-Q1, N-N3; 24 R-Q6, B-R3; 25 R-B2, B-N4; 26 P-K5!, N-K2; 27 P-K4, P-QB4; 28 P-K6, P-B3; 29 RxNP, B-B3?; 30 RxB, NxR; 31 P-K7ch, R-B2; 32 B-Q5 Resigns.*

An impressive victory, but it was overshadowed by Keres' lightning attack versus the relatively unknown Smyslov. Paul Keres had been the youngest invitee at AVRO, a cherubic 22-year-old who looked 16. His surprise victory at Semmering-Baden 1937 ahead of Fine, Capablanca, Reshevsky, and Flohr led him to AVRO and from there to worldwide fame. Two years later he played in the first of many Soviet championships, and despite being trapped in Central Europe by the Naxis for most of the War, has been one of our most honored masters since then.

Vassily Smyslov also scored a success in 1938 — winning the All-Union schoolboy championship and tying for first in the Moscow city championship. In an atmosphere that encouraged chess — Vassily's father, Vasily Osipovich, defeated Alekhine in a tournament game in 1912 — he progressed quickly. It was a sensation when the unknown schoolboy defeated Reshevsky in both games of the U.S.S.R.–U.S.A. radio match of 1945.

However, he had a lot to learn in 1948, especially in his opening against Keres, in which he combined the "oil" of 6 . . . NxP with the "water" of 8 . . . P–N3:

1 P–QB4, N–KB3; 2 N–KB3, P–B3; 3 N–B3, P–Q4; 4 P–K3, P–KN3; 5 P–Q4, B–N2; 6 PxP, NxP; 7 B–B4, O–O; 8 O–O, P–N3?!; 9 Q–N3, NxN; 10 PxN, B–QR3; 11 B–R3, BxB; 12 QxB, R–K1; 13 P–K4, P–QN4; 14 Q–N3, N–Q2; 15 P–B4.

White's last move is not quite good enough. Why? Igor Stepanovich?

I. S.: Because Black can liquidate in the center with 15 . . . P–QB4 or 15 . . . PxP; 16 QxP, Q–R4! Better was 15 QR–Q1 with the idea of advancing one of the two central pawns.

GROZNITSKY: I see you have studied your homework well, Igor Stepanovich. Smyslov lost the thread of the game here and played:

15	...	R–N1?
16	QR–Q1	Q–R4

Now there is no pin after . . . P–QB4. And 16 . . . PxP; 17 QxP, Q–R4 could be met by 18 R–Q3, Q–QN4; 19 Q–B2. Black should now try 17 . . . Q–R5!?

17	P–B5	P–N5
18	B–N4	P–K4!?

Though this move greets a tactical blitz, Black has to worry about 19 P–K5 or 19 N–N5. Attack in the center is his only counter.

19	N–N5!	R–K2
20	P–B4!	...

Just as White's center crumbles, he develops strong threats of 21 NxBP! and 21 P–B5. On 20 . . . PxBP, for example, he can play 21 P–K5 followed by P–K6 or N–K4.

20	...	PxQP
21	P–B5!	NxP?

Our brilliant analyst David Jonovich Bronstein has shown that 21 . . . QxBP!! was a better try since 22 NxBP, P–Q6ch; 23 K–R1, Q–QB7!; 24 N–R6ch, K R1; 25 QxQ, PxQ; 26 RxN can be handled, not by 26 . . . RxR; 27 P–B6!!, BxN; 28 P–B7ch, but by 26 . . . P–B8(Q)!.

The right answer to 21 . . . QxBP is 22 P–K5!, e.g. 22 . . . P–Q6ch; 23 K–R1, Q–QB7; 24 P–B6, or 22 . . . NxP; 23 P–B6, BxP; 24 RxB, P–Q6ch; 25 K–R1, N–N5; 26 RxKBP, or 22 . . . QxP!; 23 BxP, Q–N4; 24 BxB, KxB; 25 PxP, QxN!; 26 RxPch, KxP! with chances for both sides. As usual the analyst-doctor is too late to save the patient-player.

22	Q–KR3	P–R4

And here Black's position was ravaged by *23 P–B6, B–R3; 24 PxR, BxN; 25 Q–KB3, P–B3; 26 BxP, N–Q2; 27 P–KR4!*. Black resigned in face of *27 . . . BxP; 28 Q–KR3* or *28 Q–B4*.

But Keres' star faded in the third round on March 8, when he challenged Reshevsky to a time-trouble battle. Both men had three minutes for eight moves. However, the American not only had a superior game but was a more experienced blitz player. The move just before time control saw Keres permit his first rank to be penetrated by Q and R. He resigned in face of mate.

Yet he who lives by the sword shall die by the sword, to borrow from the West. Reshevsky's second time battle in the following round was a reversal. This was the round that also saw Euwe brilliantly sacrifice two N's against Smyslov only to throw away a forced win with one move and a draw with the next. This was the doctor's third straight loss, and it later became four.

In the Botvinnik–Reshevsky game we see Black develop excellent Queenside counterplay early on:

1 P–Q4, N–KB3; 2 P–QB4, P–K3; 3 N–QB3, B–N5; 4 P–K3, P–Q4; 5 P–QR3, B–K2; 6 N–B3, O–O; 7 P–QN4, QN–Q2; 8 B–N2, P–B3; 9 B–Q3, PxP; 10 BxP, B–Q3; 11 N–K2, P–QR4!; 12 P–N5, N–N3; 13 B–Q3, PxP; 14 BxP, B–Q2; 15 Q–N3, P–R5; 16 Q–Q3, R–R4; 17 N–B3, Q–K1!; 18 BxB, QxB; 19 O–O, R–B1; 20 P–K4, N–B5; 21 B–B1, P–K4; 22 R–Q1, PxP; 23 QxP, Q–K3; 24 R–R2, P–KR3; 25 P–KR3, R–R3; 26 N–Q5.

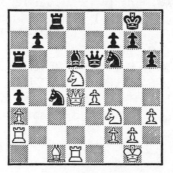

After the American's last move he had ten minutes left to play fifteen moves. Mikhail Moiseivich had sixteen minutes. Reshevsky quickly grabbed the KP here but overlooked the powerful 26 . . . N–K4!, which pinned the White QN and threatened 27 . . . R–B5. On 27 NxNch (or 27 N–Q2?, B–B4; 28 Q–R1, N–Q6!) Black recaptures with his KNP. Then 28 NxN, BxN; 29 Q–Q2 (29 Q–Q5, R–Q3), R–Q3; 30 Q–K2, RxRch; 31 QxR, RxB! should win. Better was 28 Q–Q5, but Black must be favored after 28 . . . NxNch. However . . .

26	. . .	NxP?
27	R–K2	P–B4
28	P–N4	B–B4?

Black spent three to four minutes over this doubly costly move. It is the typically naïve trick of a speed player—29 QxQN, BxPch. Why didn't he play 28 . . . N–N4?, I'm sure some of you will ask. Even Salo Flohr wrote that, since 29 Q–Q3, NxNch; 30 QxN, PxP leaves Black a P ahead, White's best was 29 RxQ, NxNch; 30 K–N2, NxQ; 31 RxN, PxP; 32 RxNP.

However, 29 NxN!, QxR; 30 N–B6ch!! draws, and this may be what Reshevsky wondered about. White obtains a perpetual check after 30 . . . PxN; 31 Q–Q5ch, K–R1; 32 N–B7ch, K–R2; 33 QxPch! (not Flohr's 33 N–N5ch), K–N2; 34 BxPch!, KxN; 35 Q–Q7ch, B–K2; 36 Q–Q5ch, and 36 Q–R5ch. Black can play 35 . . . Q–K2 in this line, but 36 QxR is not at all clear. By rejecting drawing lines, Reshevsky prepared for a losing blunder.

| 29 | PxP | QxP? |

This loses. There was a likely drawn ending in 29 . . . BxQ; 30 PxQ, BxPch; 31 RxB, NxR; 32 KxN, RxP. But after *29 . . . QxP?; 30 QxN(K), QxP; 31 N–R2, R(1)–B3; 32 N–B4,* Black forefeited in a hopeless position: 32 . . . Q–N6; 33 R–Q8ch, B–B1, 34 RxBch mates anyway.

The fifth round and the end of the first cycle came on

March 11, when more than 1,200 spectators turned out to see the current U.S.S.R. champion, Keres, meet tournament leader Botvinnik. Since AVRO, where they drew twice, Botvinnik had always maintained the upper hand in their encounters. Three months before The Hague Botvinnik defeated Keres in a tough R-and-N ending at a Moscow tournament. He had a big plus score already, and it increased when Keres tried too hard in the first game at The Hague. The opening Keres chose was strange for him (*1 P–QB4, P–K3; 2 P–KN3, P–Q4; 3 B–N2, P–Q5; 4 P–QN4, P–QB4; 5 P–N5?!, P–K4; 6 P–Q3, B–Q3; 7 P–K4?!, Q–B2; 8 N–K2, P–KR4; 9 P–KR4*). After Botvinnik castled Queenside, Keres became confused and allowed Black to win a P. The Estonian hung on into a K-and-P ending, but it was hopeless.

Once the first cycle was over and everyone had had their bye, the enormity of Botvinnik's charge became apparent. He led with $3\frac{1}{2}$–$\frac{1}{2}$, a full point ahead of Reshevsky and $1\frac{1}{2}$ in front of Keres and Smyslov. Poor Euwe, obviously outclassed, was 0–4 before a hometown audience.

Mikhail Moiseivich was already an established hero in the land of the Soviets. He lost games occasionally but never his national stature. Botvinnik's approach to chess was notable. He spent half his time—usually six straight months of a year—on chess and the rest on his engineering work. "I can only play good chess when I have had a rest from it and my chess hunger has been reawakened," he explained. His science and his game were really all he needed: "I am a very solitary person and have very few relations with the outside world."

The second cycle was more relaxed than the first. There were fewer blunders, less time pressure, and, typically, fewer wins. In the sixth round Euwe won a pawn from Keres but couldn't do anything with it. Nor could Reshevsky, who accepted a piece sacrifice from Smyslov that round. On the 18th of March Keres and Reshevsky drew a peaceful game in which Black's twenty-four moves included twelve with his KN. Another typical draw was

Botvinnik–Smyslov, which began the same day and lasted seventy-seven moves before Botvinnik agreed that his Exchange was not sufficiently better than Smyslov's two extra pawns. Mikhail Moiseivich escaped from a difficult position on the 25th against Reshevsky, who was surprised to have more time than his opponent in a time scramble and misplayed.

The youngest and oldest players met on the 23rd for an exceptionally fine endgame won by Smyslov over Euwe in eight hours. The last round at The Hague, played on the 25th, proved to be the most interesting session so far. Reshevsky defended brilliantly against Euwe after adjournment. The American's King was in danger, and he was a piece behind, but he managed to draw in fifty-seven moves. The star game, however, was:

NIMZO–INDIAN DEFENSE

M. M. Botvinnik	P. Keres
1 P–Q4	N–KB3
2 P–QB4	P–K3
3 N–QB3	B–N5
4 P–K3	O–O
5 P–QR3	BxNch
6 PxB	R–K1

An interesting idea. Black will play . . . P–K4 and delay . . . P–QB4 in favor of . . . P–K5 and . . . P–Q4. This is directed against the aggressive placement of a White B on Q3.

7 N–K2	P–K4
8 N–N3	P–Q3?!

This begins a bad opening plan that doesn't fit in with 6 . . . R–K1. Black could obtain good play with 8 . . . P–K5 followed by the Fianchetto of his QB . . .

9 B–K2	QN–Q2

Or he could try 9 . . . P–B4 and 10 . . . N–B3 to work on
the QP. Keres incorrectly thinks that he can obtain sufficient
counterplay against the QBP with . . . N–N3, . . . P–B4xP
and . . . B–K3.

10	O–O	P–B4

Last chance for 10 . . . P–K5, e.g. 11 P–B3, P–QN3!;
12 PxP, B–N2 as suggested by Boleslavsky.

11	P–B3!	BPxP?

This is another dubious move which opens up vistas for
White's Bishops. It is hard to see now that White will have
enormous strength on the QR1–KR8 diagonal in five moves,
but it occurs because of 11 . . . BPxP. Better was a waiting
move such as 11 . . . N–B1.

12	BPxP	N–N3
13	B–N2	PxP

14	P–K4!!	. . .

If Black is not positionally lost after this strategic refutation of Keres's opening, he is very close to it. Black only
considered 14 BxP or 14 PxP, either of which would give
him adequate play after 14 . . . P–Q4.

14 ...	B-K3

Hoping for 15 QxP, N-R5!; 16 B-B1, Q-N3.

15 R-B1!	R-K2?

This was just not Keres's day. This clumsy move was in preparation for . . . N-K1 and . . . P-B3 to protect himself on the long diagonal. Though this is the kind of defense that worked in the first round against Euwe, this position is too open. Better here was 15 . . . R-QB1; 16 QxP, N-R5; 17 B-R1, N-B4.

16	QxP	Q-B2
17	P-B5!	PxP
18	RxP	Q-B5
19	B-B1!	Q-N1
20	R-KN5!	...

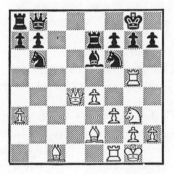

The immediate threat is 21 QxKN. The best Black can do is hold his losses to a P with 20 . . . N-K1; 21 N-R5, P-B3; 22 NxPch, NxN; 23 QxN, Q-KB1.

20	...	QN-Q2
21	RxPch!	KxR
22	N-R5ch	K-N3

There was no way of avoiding the loss of heavy material now: 22 . . . K–R1; 23 NxN, Q–K4; 24 B–N2! or 22 . . . K–B1; 23 NxN, NxN (23 . . . Q–K4; 24 B–R6 mate); 24 QxN, K–K1; 25 B–N5ch.

23 Q–K3!   Resigns

As they left The Hague, the players stood thus: Botvinnik, 6; Reshevsky, 4½; Keres and Smyslov, 4; and Euwe 1½. Notice that if Keres had won this last game, he would have been tied for first place. Whenever Botvinnik seemed to be in danger in this tournament, he reestablished himself by defeating Keres. On to Moscow.

It was not easy for anyone, even the most determined chessplayers, to ignore what was going on in the outside world. On February 25, less than one week before play began, President Benes of Czechoslovakia agreed to the legitimate demands of his nation's Communists. Throughout the West, there were threats and warnings of war. It was in this atmosphere that the tournament was held.

The entire group of some three dozen people from The Hague moved across the tightened borders to the East in early April. At the Polish border the Dutch representatives were detained because they did not have visas. No one passed through Poland without permission, a local general told them, leading Harry Golombek, the chess journalist, to note that the general showed "an easy forgetfulness of recent history." But Botvinnik defused a potential international incident by telephoning Moscow to expedite matters. The Dutch proceeded without visas.

The second tournament hall was worthy of the event. The Hall of Columns of the House of Unions could hold 2,000 enthusiasts. Outside this architectural marvel left over from Czarist days there were portable wallboards to relate the positions to 3,000 more people. Virtually every session was attended by an overflow crowd.

The third cycle of play was more of the same as the first two. Botvinnik lost his first game but won three others, and this only increased his lead. Meanwhile Reshevsky lost two games, so his victory over the tournament leader also cost him ground. And Euwe finally won a game, but his troubles continued.

BOTVINNIK-EUWE: *1 P-Q4, P-Q4; 2 N-KB3, N-KB3; 3 P-B4, P-K3; 4 N-B3, P-B3; 5 P-K3, QN-Q2; 6 B-Q3, PxP; 7 BxBP, P-QN4; 8 B-Q3, P-QR3; 9 P-K4, P-B4; 10 P-K5, PxP; 11 NxNP, PxN; 12 PxN, Q-N3; 13 PxP, BxP; 14 O-O, N-B4; 15 B-KB4, B-N2; 16 R-K1, R-Q1?; 17 R-QB1, R-Q4; 18 B-K5, BxB; 19 RxB, RxR; 20 NxR, NxB; 21 QxN, P-B3; 22 Q-KN3!!, PxN; 23 Q-N7, R-B1; 24 R-B7, QxR; 25 QxQ, B-Q4; 26 QxKP, P-Q6; 27 Q-K3, B-B5; 28 P-QN3, R-B2; 29 P-B3, R-Q2; 30 Q-Q2, P-K4; 31 PxB, PxP; 32 K-B2, K-B2; 33 K-K3, K-K3; 34 Q-N4, R-QB2; 35 K-Q2, R-B3; 36 P-QR4 Resigns.*

The Dutch pride themselves as great opening theoreticians, but here we have seen their failure when faced with Soviet theory. Black should have played 14 . . . O-O, and later he could have held the balance with 16 . . . NxB; 17 QxN, BxN; 18 QxB, O-O. Mikhail Moiseivich's brilliant twenty-second move won the Q because 24 . . . Q-Q3 would be met by 25 RxB, P-Q6; 26 R-R7, Q-Q1; 27 QxRP.

In this cycle Keres made his big push. First he outwitted Euwe in a short Siesta Variation of the Ruy Lopez and then swindled Reshevsky. The American was a P ahead in the second session of play:

And he played the natural *47 R–N5?*, although he could have drawn immediately with 47 RxP!, PxR; 48 P–N7, R–K1; 49 QxPch. Black devilishly played *47 . . . B–K2!!*, and White's R had nowhere to go after *48 RxPch, B–B3; 49 K–B3, Q–R6.* Black's advantage of the Exchange scored the point in sixty-three moves.

This left Keres 1½ points behind Botvinnik in the last round of the cycle, April 20. Again Keres obtained an inferior position with White: *1 P–Q4, P–K3; 2 P–K4, P–Q4; 3 N–Q2, P–QB4; 4 PxQP, KPxP; 5 KN–B3, P–QR3; 6 PxP, BxP; 7 N–N3, B–R2; 8 B–KN5, N–KB3; 9 KN–Q4, O–O; 10 B–K2, Q–Q3; 11 O–O, N–K5; 12 B–K3, QN–B3; 13 NxN* and now *13 . . . BxB!* was strong. Keres had his choice between a dubious attack and the equal ending of 14 QxP!, NxP! (14 . . . QxQ; 15 N–K7ch) 15 QxQ (15 RxN?, QxN), N–K5ch; 16 K–R1, NxQ. He played *14 PxB?, PxN; 15 B–Q3, N–B3; 16 Q–K1,* and soon had an inferior game after *16 . . . N–N5!; 17 Q–R4, P–KB4; 18 R–B4, N–K4; 19 Q–N3, R–R2!; 20 QR–KB1, QR–KB2.*

In the middlegame complications Black won a pawn. The ending was very difficult because Black had to win with his KNP:

Here White can draw if he plays 53 R–Q5!. For example, 53 . . . R–B6ch; 54 K–B2, K–N5 (54 . . . R–QR6; 55 R–R5); 55 R–Q6, R–B7ch; 56 K–B1, K–N6; 57 RxP, P–N5; 58

R–KN6!, R–B8ch; 59 K–K2, K–R6; 60 K–B2! Black cannot control the queening square.

However, Keres played *53 R–Q3?* and after *53 . . . R–B5; 54 R–R3, P–R4; 55 K–R3, R–QN5* he was steadily pushed back. Black eventually won the QRP and advanced it with the support of his K.

Botvinnik now lead with 9 points compared with Keres at 6½, Reshevsky at 6, Smyslov with 5½, and Euwe with 3. The fourth cycle of five rounds would determine whether Botvinnik could be stopped.

And once again the steady play of Mikhail Moiseivich came through. At the fatal moment others would tremble away from the brink. For example, Reshevsky on May 3:

White (Reshevsky) has played an enterprising attack against Botvinnik's French:

1 P–Q4, P–K3; 2 P–K4, P–Q4; 3 N–QB3, B–N5; 4 P–K5, P–QB4; 5 P–QR3, BxNch; 6 PxB, Q–B2; 7 Q–N4, P–B4; 8 Q–N3, PxP; 9 PxP, N–K2; 10 B–Q2, O–O; 11 B–Q3, P–QN3; 12 N–K2, B–R3; 13 N–B4, Q–Q2; 14 BxB, NxB; 15 Q–Q3, N–N1; 16 P–KR4!, QN–B3; 17 R–R3, QR–B1; 18 R–N3, K–R1; 19 P–R5, R–KB2; 20 P–R6!, P–N3; 21 R–B1, KR–B1; 22 N–K2, N–QN1; 23 K–B1, R–B5; 24 K–N1, QN–B3; 25 B–N5, N–KN1; 26 R–K1, Q–KB2; 27 P–QB3, N–R4; 28 N–B4, R–B3.

How does White break through? Ilya Grigorevich?

I. G.: It would appear he should play B–B6ch at some point so that he can profit – rather, enrich his chances – from the opening of the K-file.

GROZNITSKY: Exactly. But this requires timing. The correct method was 29 R(3)–K3, N–B5; 30 R(3)–K2 so that on 30 . . . NxQRP White decisively opens the game with 31 B–B6ch. If Black delays with 30 . . . R–K1, White can continue with 31 Q–N3.

However, the American immediately played 29 B–B6ch? and was surprised to find 29 . . . NxB; 30 PxN, N–B5! This in-between move prevents the doubling of Rooks on the K-file. Following 31 Q–N1, QxP; 32 P–R4, P–KN4!; 33 N–Q3, P–B5 Black won easily.

Nor was Reshevsky the only player out of form. Keres lost badly to Smyslov on the 25th and then found this position against Reshevsky on the 27th.

Keres (White) has won a P in the opening: 1 P–K4, P–K4; 2 N–KB3, N–QB3; 3 B–N5, P–QR3; 4 B–R4, N–B3; 5 O–O, NxP; 6 P–Q4, P–QN4; 7 B–N3, P–Q4; 8 PxP, B–K3; 9 Q–K2, N–B4; 10 R–Q1, NxB; 11 RPxN, Q–B1; 12 B–N5, P–R3; 13 B–R4, B–QB4; 14 N–B3, P–N4!?; 15 B–N3, Q–N2; 16 NxQP, O–O–O. But the position is very delicate for him in view of . . . P–KN5 and . . . N–Q5.

His best was 17 N–K3 to consolidate. After 17 N–B6?, P–KN5; 18 N–K1, N–Q5; 19 Q–B1 (19 Q–K4, B–B4!),

P–KR4; 20 *B–B4, P–R5;* 21 *B–K3, P–R6;* Black had fine compensation for the P. Black's initiative grew with 22 *R–Q2, PxP;* 23 *QxKNP, N–B6ch;* 24 *NxN, BxB!;* 25 *RxRch, RxR;* 26 *N–K1, B–Q5;* 27 *N–Q3, B–KB4;* 28 *R–K1, P–R4;* 29 *N–K4, K–N1;* 30 *P–N4, P–R5!*

Here White had to try 31 N(3)–B5 so that on 31 . . . Q–B3 he has 32 P–QB3, BxKP; 33 N–KN3 with drawing chances and on 31 . . . KBxN; 32 PxB!, BxN; 33 QxB, again with drawing chances.

But Keres played a careless blunder: *31 P–QB3?* and lost soon after *31 . . . BxN;* 32 *RxB, BxQBP:* 33 *R–K3, QxQch;* 34 *KxQ, RxN!;* 35 *RxR, BxP(7).*

Naturally, when Keres faced Botvinnik on May 4, he was in no shape to put up a stern battle. Mikhail Moiseivich won a nice N-ending in fifty-nine moves and completed the fourth cycle with a lead of 3½ points: Botvinnik, 12; Reshevsky and Smyslov, 8½; Keres 7½; Euwe 3½.

The anticlimax came on May 10, when Botvinnik accepted a draw from Dr. Euwe on the fourteenth move of a Queen's Gambit Declined. This clinched first place and the World Championship for the 37-year-old Muscovite. As Vidmar's 6-year-old daughter Eileen presented a handful of tulips to the new Champion, he was seen smiling for the first time since the event began.

The remaining games were, naturally, less exciting than their predecessors. However, Smyslov, using his new variation of the Gruenfeld, moved into second place with a fine win from Euwe.

EUWE–SMYSLOV: 1 *P–Q4, N–KB3;* 2 *P–QB4, P–KN3;* 3 *N–QB3, P–Q4;* 4 *N–B3, B–N2;* 5 *Q–N3, PxP;* 6 *QxBP, O–O;* 7 *P–K4, B–N5;* 8 *B–K3, KN–Q2;* 9 *Q–N3, N–N3;* 10 *P–QR4, P–QR4;* 11 *P–Q5, BxKN!;* 12 *PxB, Q–Q3!;* 13 *N–N5, Q–N5ch;* 14 *QxQ, PxQ;* 15 *NxP, RxP;* 16 *R–QN1?, N(3)–Q2;* 17 *N–N5, R–B1;* 18 *B–K2?, P–N6!;* 19 *N–R3?, BxP;* 20 *RxB, RxN;* 21 *K–Q2, N–R3;* 22 *KR–QN1, N(3)–B4;* 23 *B–Q4, P–K4!;* 24 *PxP e.p., NxP(3);* 25 *B–K3, N(2)–B4;* 26 *BxN, NxB;* 27 *K–B3, R–R5;* 28 *K–*

SCORETABLE

	Botvinnik	Smyslov	Reshevsky	Keres	Euwe	Total
1. Botvinnik	XXXXX	½½1½½	1½011	11110	1½1½½	14–6
2. Smyslov	½½0½½	XXXXX	½½1½½	00½1½	11011	11–9
3–4. Reshevsky	0½100	½½0½½	XXXXX	1½01½	1½½11	10½–9½
3–4. Keres	0001	11½0½	0½10½	XXXXX	1½111	10½–9½
5. Euwe	0½0½½	00100	0½½00	0½000	XXXXX	4–16

Q2, K–N2; 29 K–K3, R–Q1; 30 R–QB1, P–N3; 31 B–B4,
R(Q)–QR1; 32 B–Q5, R–R7!; 33 R(1)–QN1, R(1)–R5;
34 K–Q2, R–Q5ch; 35 K–K2, N–R5; 36 RxR, PxR; 37
R–QR1, N–B6ch; 38 K–K3, R–Q8! *Resigns.*

Position after 15 . . . RxP

And on the very last day, May 16, Botvinnik lost to Keres
in a sprightly French Defense. It was a concession to Keres,
who had lost his four earlier games with Botvinnik. Those
games, more than anything else, determined the victor at
Hague–Moscow. Had Keres split those points at 2–2, he
might have been Champion.

And on this foundation, my students, was built the
mighty Soviet hegemony on this ancient game that exists
today. Before we dismiss class today, did you have a question Boris Ewfemevich?

B. E.: Yes, Comrade Professor. Concerning the Soviet
hegemony: What about Bobby Fischer?

GROZNITSKY: Who?

VIII

Chess 1, Politics 0

Chess had survived the Dark Ages. It was preserved through the Inquisition. And there was no doubt it would outlast the Cold War, too. On September 3, 1961, the largest truly international tournament of individuals since 1949 began in Bled, Yugoslavia.

There had been grandmaster events throughout the 1950s but rarely with both American and Soviet representatives. The exceptions were largely limited to those tournaments in competition for FIDE titles such as the World Individual, Women's, Junior, Team, and Student Team championships. As these constituted only a fraction of the normal tournament schedule, the international exchange of chess ideas shriveled. Even contacts between Eastern and Western European masters were few during the period.

Milan Vidmar celebrated his 76th birthday in 1961, his next-to-last. Thirty years earlier he had used his considerable national reputation and international friendships to arrange the first great tournament in the Balkans. That was Bled 1931, a colossal success for Alekhine, who ran off with the top prize, 5½ points ahead of a field that included Bogolyubov, Nimzovich, Flohr, Isaac Kashdan, and Gosta Stoltz. Among Alekhine's fifteen victories were several classics; including his nineteen-move win over Nimzovich and the twenty-four-move victory against Pirc with the Black pieces. It was more an exhibition than a tournament, Vidmar recalled.

What better way to recapture the spirit of prewar competition, thought Vidmar, than by holding an Alekhine Memorial Tournament in the same Slovenian resort near the point where Austrian, Italian, and Yugoslav borders meet? Not only would there be two Americans and four Russians invited, Vidmar planned, but also ambassadors from every major chess nation—Yugoslavia, of course, and West Germany, Czechoslovakia, Hungary, Holland, Argentina, and so on.

Not every country of strength was represented, but there was no shortage of genius. Mikhail Tal, the 25-year-old flamboyant Latvian who had just surrendered the World Championship back to Botvinnik three months before, said during the tournament that there was no single giant in the game as there had been during the reigns of Alekhine and Capablanca. No, Tal said, there were now ten players of equal rank. Six of the names on his list—Keres, Tigran Petrosian, Ewfim Geller, and Tal of the U.S.S.R., R. J. Fischer of the U.S., and Svetozar Gligorich of Yugoslavia—were entered at Bled. Botvinnik, the primus inter pares himself, had promised to play but changed his mind after the wearying return match with Tal.

In addition, there were the war-horses of the 1950s such as Miguel Najdorf of Argentina, who had never been quite good enough to crack the inner circle of superplayers; Petar Trifunovich from the Adriatic coastal city of Dubrovnik, who had assumed Schlechter's mantle as the leading "drawing master"; and Ludek Pachman, the many-time Czech champion who was known as the world's leading opening theoretician.

And there were also the discoveries of the latter half of the 1950s—Arthur Bisguier of America, Jan Hein Donner of Holland, Fridrik Olafsson of Iceland, Borislav Ivkov of Yugoslavia, and the world's newest grandmaster, 24-year-old Lajos Portisch of Hungary. To fill out the tournament there were a handful of Yugoslavs, including 19-year-old Bruno Parma, who arrived by train just a few days after winning the World Junior Championship in Holland.

In essence, the Bled combatants were an entire new generation that, with a few additions, would divide up the tournament prizes and glory well into the 1970s. Most of all, Bled was Bobby Fischer's first supersuccess.

Winning the U. S. Championship at the age of 14 is one thing. Qualifying for a Candidates tournament, the last hurdle before the World Championship, at 15 is another. But nearly winning the strongest large tournament since AVRO 1938 was quite another.

Fischer was already an experienced veteran at 18: a tall, gangly teenager who had suddenly become clothes-conscious, who was slow to mix socially with the other grandmasters, and who had already determined that he was the greatest player who ever lived and just had to prove it to the rest of the world. Bobby led off the tournament on the evening of the 3rd of September with a slashing, tactical draw with Gligorich. Fischer played the King's Indian Defense against the player who had become "Mr. King's Indian" because of his many sparkling successes on both sides of the position. On the verge of securing a crushing positional edge, the Yugoslav found all the right moves, but Fischer discovered saving resources one after another.

Another first-round disappointment for the Yugoslav fans—perhaps the most intense chess-lovers in the world—was the narrow escape by Paul Keres from the grasp of the unexpectedly talented Parma. A Pawn behind, the Russian veteran ran away in the ending. A smattering of draws and sharp victories by Pachman over Aleksandr Matanovich and Geller over Portisch finished off the first day, but the finest game wasn't completed until the first rest day in the following week.

This was Tal's endgame squeeze of Ivkov in sixty-eight moves. The Yugoslav, who had won the World Junior Championship ten years before, chose a drawish opening with White (*1 P–Q4, N–KB3; 2 P–QB4, P–KN3; 3 N–QB3, B–N2; 4 P–K4, P–Q3; 5 N–B3, O–O; 6 B–K2, P–K4; 7 PxP, PxP; 8 QxQ, RxQ; 9 N–Q5, R–Q2!?; 10 NxNch, BxN*). Now he thought for an hour and 35 minutes before choosing 11 P–B5!?, a very sharp plan involving the wrecking of Black's Queenside pawns with B–QN5xN.

After thirty moves of exchanges Black had taken advantage of several minor errors to reach this:

If Black's K ran to the Queenside behind the blocking of his R, White would have had time to capture the QP. Tal first established a bridgehead on the Kingside with *31 . . . K–R4!; 32 P–R3, R–Q5!*.

White must either advance another weak P or withdraw his K. There followed *33 K–B2, K–R5; 34 K–N2, R–Q6; 35 K–B2, P–KR4; 36 K–N2*, and now Black was ready for the liquidation beginning with *36 . . . RxRP; 37 RxP, R–N6; 38 R–R2, RxNP; 39 RxP, R–N7ch; 40 K–B1, R–B7*.

Black visualized an ending in which he could trade off his KRP for White's three Kingside P's and then win with the two Bishop Pawns separated by two files. This was accomplished with *41 RxP, RxP; 42 K–B2, KxP; 43 R–KN7, P–R5; 44 R–N5, R–R4; 45 R–R5, R–R7ch; 46 K–K3* and now *46 . . . K–N7!!*.

On 47 RxBP Black will just queen his passed Pawn after 47 . . . P–R6; 48 R–N5ch, K–B8. And on 47 R–N5ch, K–B8;

48 R–R5 Black could win with 48 . . . P–B4!; 49 RxRP, R–B6ch; 50 K–Q2, RxP followed by capturing the last White P.

Ivkov actually played *47 RxRP, R–R6ch; 48 K–K2* (48 K–Q4, K–N6 scoops up the Pawns), *RxP; 49 R–R5!, RxP; 50 R–N5ch.* But even with Black's K cut off on the KR-file, his two Pawns were sufficient. Mikhail Tal was once again leading a tournament.

Tal had rarely failed to win a tournament up to that time. Few Westerners had ever heard of him before 1957, when suddenly he overcame a miserable start to win the semi-finals of the Soviet Championship, then the Championship itself, then the Interzonal tournament in Portoroz, Yugoslavia, a year later, then the Candidates tournament a year after that. Before wresting the world title from Botvinnik in June 1960, Tal had also added victories in the 1958 Soviet Championship and the strong Zurich 1959 event. Only at the 1959 international event held in his native Riga was Tal surpassed in the scoretable—by Boris Spassky, who had been hailed as Russia's strongest young master before Tal's rise in the late 1950s.

Tal's trademark in this period was the whirlwind mating attack, a tactical display that had disappeared from master chess for a generation or more. Tal would occasionally be humbled by the more solid masters such as Keres and Smyslov. For example, Keres won three of the four games with Tal at the 1959 Candidates tournament. But the "Sorcerer of Riga," as he was called, won the event by allowing only three draws in the sixteen games he played with Fischer, Gligorich, Olafsson, and Pal Benko.

It was at that time that Tal began to sign Fischer's autograph as well as his own, explaining with a smile that his 4–0 result with Bobby in the 1959 event made the American his slave. But in the second round at Bled 1961 Tal made a disastrous error as early as the sixth move.

FISCHER–TAL: *1 P–K4, P–QB4; 2 N–KB3, N–QB3; 3 P–Q4, PxP; 4 NxP, P–K3; 5 N–QB3, Q–B2; 6 P–KN3, N–B3?; 7 KN–N5!, Q–N1; 8 B–KB4, N–K4; 9 B–K2!,*

B–B4; 10 BxN!, QxB; 11 P–B4, Q–N1; 12 P–K5, P–QR3; 13 PxN, PxN; 14 PxP, R–N1; 15 N–K4, B–K2; 16 Q–Q4, R–R5; 17 N–B6ch, BxN; 18 QxB, Q–B2; 19 O–O–O!, RxRP; 20 K–N1, R–R3; 21 BxP, R–N3; 22 B–Q3, P–K4; 23 PxP!, RxQ; 24 PxR, Q–B4; 25 BxP, Q–KN4; 26 BxR, QxBP; 27 KR–B1, QxP; 28 BxPch, K–Q1; 29 B–K6, Q–R3; 30 BxP, BxB; 31 R–B7, QxP; 32 R(1)xBch, K–K1; 33 QR–K7ch, K–Q1; 34 R–Q7ch, K–B1; 35 R–B7ch, K–Q1; 36 KR–Q7ch, K–K1; 37 R–Q1, P–N4; 38 R–QN7, Q–R4; 39 P–KN4, Q–R6; 40 P–N5, Q–KB6; 41 R–K1ch, K–B1; 42 RxP, K–N2; 43 R–N6, Q–KN6; 44 R–Q1, Q–B2; 45 R(1)–Q6, Q–B1; 46 P–N3, K–R2; 47 R–QR6 Resigns.

"Finally he has not eluded mc," said Fischer.
"You cannot argue with Einstein's Theory," said Tal.
A second sensation of the second round was Petrosian–Parma:

Again the World Junior Champion was outplaying a top grandmaster. Parma (Black) could have taken a big edge in the ending with the simple 22 ... QxPch; 23 QxQ, NxQ; 24 BxQNP, R–Q7! but preferred the tricky 22 ... RxB!?.

After Petrosian recaptured, Black could have played 23 ... NxPch; 24 PxN, Q–R3ch; 25 K–N2, QxR with advantage since 26 P–B4 is met by 26 ... N–N5! However, Parma tried 23 ... NxBP?, and after 24 R(4)–Q1, N–Q5; 25 QxN (25 RxN, QxR; 26 QxN, BxPch), NxB; 26 R–B1 he com-

pounded his error by entering an ending with *26 . . . Q–N3?*
27 QxQ, RPxQ. White scored the point with *28 QR–Q1,
N–B4; 29 K–N1, R–B2?; 30 R–Q8ch, K–R2; 31 P–N4!,
NxKP; 32 NxN, BxN; 33 R–B4 Resigns.*

The third round saw another sensation – Bisguier taking
advantage of a Keres blunder to win in thirty-five moves.
Despite the promise of the youngsters, the leaders after
three rounds were 36-year-old Geller, 51-year-old Najdorf,
51-year-old Trifunovich, and Bisguier, who at 32 was the
only one below the tournament average of 33. Tal moved
into a second-place tie with Fischer, Petrosian, and Klaus
Darga of West Germany with a phenomenal attack against
Olafsson.

With White Tal opened with *1 P–K4, P–QB4; 2 N–KB3,
N–QB3; 3 P–Q4, PxP; 4 NxP, P–K3; 5 N–QB3, Q–B2; 6
B–K3, P–QR3; 7 P–QR3, N–B3; 8 P–B4, P–Q3; 9 Q–B3,
B–K2; 10 B–Q3, O–O; 11 O–O, B–Q2; 12 QR–K1, P–QN4;
13 Q–N3, K–R1; 14 NxN, BxN; 15 P–K5, N–N1; 16 Q–R3,
N–R3; 17 P–B5!?.* Black's defensive plan of . . . K–R1 and
. . . N–N1 had been popularized by Najdorf in similar posi-
tions.

Tal rose to the occasion with *17 . . . NxP; 18 RxN!?, PxR;
19 BxBP, P–N3; 20 B–Q4!,* and now:

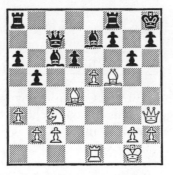

The complications arising out of 20 . . . Q–Q1! are im-
mense, but Black saves himself miraculously in each line.
For example, on 21 P–K6ch, B–B3 (21 . . . P–B3; 22BxNP);
22 Q–R4!, PxP; 23 RxP White would win after 23 . . .

BxBch; 24 QxBch, K–N1; 25 RxQP or 23 . . . K–N2; 24
RxB!, RxR; 25 B–K4! But he loses after 23 . . . B–K4!!.

On the other hand, 21 PxPch, B–B3; 22 Q–R4! would be
OK after 22 . . . BxBch; 23 QxBch, K–N1; 24 B–K4, R–K1;
25 R–Q1 or 22 . . . K–N2; 23 B–Q7!!, BxB; 24 N–Q5, BxBch;
25 QxBch, P–B3; 26 R–K7ch but would run out of steam
after 22 . . . B–KN2!!

Deluged with complex variations, the Icelander played
20 . . . K–N1? 21 P–K6, B–N4 and lost material after *22
PxPch, RxP; 23 BxP!, R–N2; 24 Q–K6ch, K–R1; 25 B–K8!!*
Tal won on the thirty-eighth move.

The fourth round saw a decline in fighting spirit, with
only Fischer's Queen sacrifice against Olafsson to remember, and at the outset of the fifth round Najdorf's score of
three wins and one draw led the field. The Polish-Argen-
tinian was in no mood to quarrel with his old friend
Trifunovich, so they drew in eleven moves. Horrified by
the shortness of the game, Vidmar stopped all the other
games and made a speech to the players and spectators
denouncing such grandmaster draws. Only later in the day
did someone unkindly recall that Vidmar had once drawn
in eight moves and that he held a negative record of offering an opponent fifteen times during a Yugoslav Championship game.

The Parma–Fischer game was also a draw, but it made up
for Najdorf's "rest day" when the Yugoslav developed a
crushing advantage:

Fischer experimented with his "Poisoned Pawn" variation in the Sicilian Defense and had taken too many liberties on the Queenside. Suddenly Parma sent the American reeling with *21 R–N3!, K–R1; 22 RxB!, KxR; 23 R–B3* with a threat of 24 R–N3ch and 25 Q–R6.

Fischer saw that 23 . . . P–R3; 24 R–N3ch, K–R2 was no defense because of 25 B–N6ch!, K–N2; 26 B–R7ch!, KxB; 27 R–KR3. And 23 . . . R–KR1 would be met by 24 N–K6ch! So he played *23 . . . R–KN1; 24 R–N3ch, K–B1!; 25 Q–R6ch, K–K2* and hoped.

Parma found *26 QxRP!* but after *26 . . . PxN* (26 . . . RxR; 27 QxPch, K–Q1; 28 N–K6ch! wins) he missed 27 BxP!!, which would have won shortly. He played *27 QxPch*.

Fischer responded *27 . . . K–Q1; 28 RxRch, K–B2; 29 N–B4, Q–R6! 30 N–Q5ch, K–N1; 31 P–KR4, N–K6*, and once again Parma missed a clear win with 32 QxB!! – e.g. 32 . . . BxR; 33 Q–B7ch, or 32 . . . Q–B8ch; 33 K–R2, N–B8ch; 34 K–R3. White played *32 RxRch, KxR; 33 NxN, QxN 34 B–B3* and Black found a perpetual check with *34 . . . Q–B8ch; 35 K–R2, Q–B5ch.*

Meanwhile Keres joined the plus scores:

PACHMAN–KERES: *1 P–QB4, P–K4; 2 N–QB3, N–KB3; 3 N–B3, N–B3; 4 P–Q4, PxP; 5 NxP, B–B4!?; 6 NxN, NPxN; 7 P–KN3, P–KR4?! 8 B–N2, P–R5; 9 O–O, PxP; 10 RPxP, Q–K2; 11 B–B4, B–N2; 12 P–QR3?, N–R4!; 13 Q–Q2, NxB; 14 QxN, B–Q3; 15 Q–Q2, O–O–O; 16 P–QN4, B–K4; 17 QR–B1, P–KB4; 18 P–B4, B–B3; 19 P–K4, P–KN4!; 20 P–K5, B–N2; 21 Q–KB2, PxP; 22 PxP, QR–N1; 23 P–N5, B–B1!; 24 PxP, BxBP; 25 N–Q5, Q–R2; 26 Resigns.*

The sixth round brought television cameras to the tournament hall, and they were rewarded with two of the best-played games so far—Fischer's devastating refutation of Geller's opening novelty and Keres's destruction of Portisch's French Defense. Geller, a jovial Ukrainian, played the opening quickly and appeared in good spirits as Fischer weakened his Kingside Pawn protection. The innovation cost Fischer a good part of an hour. But suddenly he cleared away the center Pawns and began to hammer at Black's unmoved King. Geller took longer and longer for his moves, while Fischer's Queen penetrated the Queenside. The American's twentieth move was a surprise, choosing to allow Geller to strip Fischer's King of Pawns. But Geller with just seconds left and eighteen moves to go discovered he was losing a Rook and a piece. Thunderous applause for the Brooklyn star followed Geller's resignation.

Petrosian also came in for an ovation from the fans:

Having refuted Pachman's opening—always a surprise— he now played *18 R–K4, R–Q1; 19 QxBch!!*, after which *19 . . . KxQ; 20 B–K5ch, K–N4; 21 B–N7!* forced mate. Well after the applause died down someone pointed out that 18 R–K4? was inferior to the immediate 18 QxBch!!, KxQ; 19 B–K5ch, K–N4; 20 B–N7!.

The following day, September 11, was scheduled for adjourned games, and it turned out to be a disaster for Aleksandr Matanovich, the Belgrade grandmaster who later revolutionized chess literature with the nonverbal *Chess Informant* magazine. Matanovich had three adjourned games on his "Black Monday" and lost all three.

So with one-third of the tournament over the leaders were Fischer, Najdorf, Petrosian, and the resurgent Tal at 4½–1½, followed by Gligorich, Keres, and Trifunovich with 4 points. A dull seventh round knocked Petrosian back a step as he blundered in a bad position against Portisch.

Fischer nearly followed the Armenian in the eighth round when Matanovich outplayed him on the Black side of the Ruy Lopez. As usual, the Russians followed Fischer's troubles closely:

After 47 QxPch, K–K1 Black was safe enough to threaten the crushing 48 . . . Q–K7ch. Bobby found an ingenious defense: *47 Q–B6ch!, K–K1; 48 Q–K5ch!, QxQ; 49 BxQ, B–B4; 50 K–Q3!,* so that if Black took the BP, Fischer would have neutralized his greatest danger with 51 K–K4. Matanovich answered *50 . . . P–N4; 51 K–K4, P–N5; 52 B–N3, P–R4* so that he could meet 53 K–B5 with 53 . . . B–K2. Instead, Fischer ran in the other direction with *53 P–R5!, K–Q2; 54 K–Q5, B–R2; 55 K–K4.* Now with his Bishop out of position, Black played *55 . . . K–B1,* intending *56 . . . B–N1,* but after *56 K–B5!, B–N1; 57 K–N5!!* Fischer forced a draw since on *57 . . . BxB; 58 KxP, BxP; 59 KxP* White eats the last Pawn.

Petrosian engineered a positional masterpiece to push Najdorf out of first place. "Look at me. I am laughing. I'm making pleasantries," Najdorf said after the game. "And probably I am not going to be able to sleep tonight."

Tal and Fischer were alone at the top with 6½–2½ after the next round. The day was distinguished only by two joke games. First, Ivkov completely discredited Petrosian's opening: *1 P–K4, P–QB4; 2 N–KB3, P–Q3; 3 P–Q4, PxP; 4 NxP, N–KB3; 5 N–QB3, P–QR3; 6 B–KN5, QN–Q2; 7 B–QB4, Q–R4; 8 Q–Q2, P–K3; 9 O–O–O, P–N4; 10 B–N3, B–N2; 11 KR–K1, N–B4?; 12 P–K5!, PxP; 13 BxP!, PxB; 14 NxKP!, QN–Q2; 15 BxN, NxB.* But then he accepted Petrosian's draw offer because he didn't see a clear continuation and only had fifteen minutes left for twenty-five moves. Actually, 16 RxP, K–B2; 17 Q–B4! with a threat of 18 R–Q7ch is crushing.

Nearly as painful was Trifunovich's failure to punish Geller when the Ukrainian sacrificed his Queen with *1 P–K4, P–K4; 2 N–KB3, N–KB3; 3 P–Q4, PxP; 4 P–K5, N–K5; 5 QxP, P–Q4 6 PxP e.p., NxQP; 7 N–B3, N–B3; 8 Q–KB4, P–KN3; 9 B–Q2, Q–K2ch; 10 B–K2, B–K3; 11 N–KN5, B–R3! 12 O–O–O?!, P–B3; 13 NxB, BxQ; 14 NxB.* Somehow White worked up enough compensation to draw in thirty-six moves.

Fischer moved ahead in round 10 by flattening Mario Bertok, one of the local "rabbits." Tal drew quietly with Petrosian. After a sightseeing tour of the nearby Julian Alps on the free day of the 19th, the American found a bit of luck against Milan Germek, another rabbit. A Pawn behind in a constricted position, Fischer took advantage of his opponent's time pressure to squeeze out a draw.

It was a double setback for Tal, who let Gligorich off the hook:

Overlooking Black's reply, Tal played *31 Q-Q2* with the idea of B-K3. Gligorich shot back *31 . . . R-N7!!* and after *32 QxR, P-B5ch; 33 K-R1, Q-B7; 34 R-KN1, B-N5!* Tal had nothing better than *35 R-N2, Q-K8ch; 36 R-N1, Q-B7* with a draw. On 35 P-R7, BxB; 36 QxB, QxQ; 37 P-R8(Q), QxKPch Black also has a perpetual check. And 35 B-K3, B-B6ch; 36 BxB, QxQ; 37 P-R7 is handled by 37 . . . Q-R7 and 38 . . . B-R3.

The twelfth round maintained Fischer's half-point lead over Tal as Bobby ground down Trifunovich in seventy-three moves while Tal did the same to the bearded Donner in fifty-six.

Tal's rambunctious Kingside advance could have been exploited earlier when the Dutchman had opportunities to use the Queen-file effectively. But inaccurate play by White allowed Tal now to leap into complications with *27 . . . NxP!!*

White is clearly not prepared for 28 PxN, BxNP; 29 Q-moves, BxR and 30 . . . P-K5 or 30 . . . Q-N6. The real choice is between 28 N-K4 and 28 R-Q6. On 28 N-K4, Q-N3; 29 R-Q6, N-R3; 30 N-B5, R-K1; 31 BxP White has met the tactical challenge. But Black could improve with 28 . . . Q–R4!; 29 R–Q6, Q–R7ch; 30 K–B1, B–B1!; 31 PxN, P–B6 with a winning attack.

So Donner played *28 R–Q6* with the idea of *28 . . . Q–K2; 29 RxB, QxR; 30 PxN.* No better was 30 B–R3, Q–Q3!; 31 BxN, Q–Q5ch; 32 Q–B2, QxN; 33 B–K6ch, K–R2; 34 Q–R4ch, B–R3; 35 Q–K7ch, K–N3, escaping the perpetual check.

But he hadn't reckoned on *30 . . . P–K5!*, e.g. 31 BxP, R–K1! (31 . . . BxN??; 32 B–Q5!) wins a piece, or 31 QxP, Q–B3; 32 N–Q1, P–B6; 33 B–B1, Q–Q3 with too much pressure. Instead, Donner played *31 NxP* and lost back material after *31 . . . B–Q5ch!; 32 K–B1* (32 K–R2, Q–R3ch; 33 B–R3, P–B6; 34 Q–B1, Q–R2), *P–B6!; 33 BxP, QxNP; 34 N–B6ch, RxN; 35 Q–K8ch, K–R2; 36 Q–K7ch, Q–N2.* One more error in the ending sealed Donner's fate.

Tal was still the great trickster both at the board and away. When he went for long relaxing walks around the lake near the tournament site, he kept a fully polished pair of shoes outside his hotel door so that his opponents would think he was preparing openings for them.

But Fischer was the main subject of tournament talk. Later in the day of the twelfth round, when some players gathered at the luxurious Hotel Teplice, Keres took the young American to task for his boast that he would defeat all four "Russians" in the tournament.

Not possible, Keres said, according to the endgame composer, Harold Lommer, who was reporting on the tournament. "To date you have beaten a Ukrainian and a Latvian. That leaves me, an Estonian, and Petrosian, an Armenian," said the diplomatic Keres.

Fischer replied: "Never mind what states you come from, you're all Russians to me."

Round 13 on the 23rd was an exceptionally tense round, with every game lasting at least thirty moves and four hours and a half. Fischer livened up a drawish King's Indian against Pachman in this manner:

Black may have good winning chances after the simple retreat, 16 . . . Q–Q1 followed by a subsequent . . . N–Q5 and . . . P–B3. But Fischer was eager for more, and he captured the Tal spirit and a pawn: *16 . . . PxP!?, 17 NxP, PxP; 18 B–Q5ch, K–R2* and after *19 NxR*, Black had to find the right followup to his Rook sacrifice.

The position was highly unclear, and some players later suggested 19 . . . N–Q5 with the idea of 20 B–K3, R–Q1 and 21 . . . RxB or 20 K–R1, RxP. Black chose a different method of attack: *19 . . . N–K2; 20 B–K3, P–R7ch; 21 K–R1, B–R6; 22 N–B7, N–B4*, with threats of 23 . . . NxB or 23 . . . P–K5.

But Pachman rallied with *23 N–K6!* intending to capture a second R with check. After *23 . . . R–B3; 24 NxB* Black played *24 . . . NxB; 25 PxN, RxRch; 26 QxR, BxQ; 27 RxB, KxN* and Pachman announced a perpetual check with *28 R–B7ch*. A bad blow to the American's chances.

Meanwhile:

TAL–PARMA: *1 P–K4, P–QB4; 2 N–KB3, N–QB3; 3 P–Q4, PxP; 4 NxP, P–KN3; 5 P–QB4, N–B3; 6 N–QB3, NxN; 7 QxN, P–Q3; 8 B–K2, B–N2; 9 B–K3, O–O; 10 Q–Q2, B–K3; 11 QR–B1, Q–R4; 12 P–QN3, KR–B1?; 13 O–O, P–QR3; 14 P–B4, P–QN4; 15 P–KB5!, B–Q2; 16 PxP, RPxP; 17 P–B5!, B–K3; 18 B–B3!, PxP!; 19 P–K5, N–N5; 20 BxR, BxKP?!; 21 B–Q5!, NxB; 22 BxB, R–Q1; 23 Q–KB2, N–B4; 24 Q–K2!, B–Q5ch; 25 K–R1, PxB; 26*

QxPch, K–N2; 27 N–K4, Q–B2; 28 N–N5, R–KB1? 29 QxN!, Resigns.

Two-thirds of the way home and there were only two leaders, Fischer and Tal at 9½–3½ a full point ahead of Gligorich, Keres, and Petrosian. The next day didn't change the picture because Fischer couldn't win a crushing position against Milo Udovcich and Tal played a quiet draw with Darga.

Fischer had a phenomenal score against the grandmasters but had failed to beat Udovcic, Germek, and Pachman — all tailenders in this event and all of whom fell to Tal. Surprisingly, this was the first tournament in which Fischer could regularly beat the highest rated contestants, but he failed to dominate the field because of his lack of success with the rabbits.

"Fortunately" Bobby's next opponent was Portisch, a newly confirmed grandmaster. He was ground down in forty-seven moves. Tal kept pace by beating Bisguier, who had previously downed Keres and Najdorf and would outplay Geller two rounds later. Gligorich was now just half a point behind the leaders, with Petrosian and Keres just behind him.

The sixteenth round saw Tal in first place for the first time in the tournament. The Latvian used his favorite Modern Benoni Defense to crunch Germek, while Fischer had to contend with Keres. Again Fischer's board was ringed with grandmasters. Bobby innovated against Keres's Caro–Kann and enjoyed the initiative well into the middlegame, when the Estonian sacrificed a Pawn. Fischer gave it back so that he could enter a Q-and-B vs. Q-and-N ending in which he had a Pawn on QN7. But Black had enough perpetual check possibilities to draw. Fischer wasn't going to defeat all four Russians.

Tal gained another point the following day with an exotic opening:

TAL–PACHMAN: *1 P–K4, P–QB3; 2 P–Q4, P–Q4; 3 P–K5, B–B4; 4 P–KR4, P–KR3; 5 P–KN4!?, B–Q2; 6 P–R5!, P–QB4; 7 P–QB3, P–K3; 8 P–KB4, Q–N3; 9 N–B3, QN–B3; 10 N–R3, PxP; 11 PxP, O–O–O; 12 N–B2, K–N1; 13 B–Q3, KN–K2; 14 R–QN1, N–R4; 15 B–Q2, R–B1; 16 P–QN4, N–B5; 17 P–N5!, NxB; 18 NxN, P–N3; 19 N–N3!, BxP; 20 N–B5, RxN; 21 PxR, Q–R4ch; 22 Q–Q2, QxQch; 23 KxQ, BxB; 24 KxB, N–B3; 25 PxP, PxP; 26 N–Q4, NxN; 27 KxN, K–B2; 28 P–B5, NPxP; 29 PxP, K–B3; 30 PxP, BxPch; 31 K–Q3, P–N3; 32 QR–KB1, P–KR4; 33 R–B7, P–R4; 34 R–R4, R–R3; 35 R–B6, R–R1; 36 R–B5, R–KN1; 37 KRxP, R–N6ch; 38 K–K2, P–Q5; 39 R–B3, R–N7ch; 40 K–Q3, RxP; 41 R–B7 Resigns.*

Even prettier was Ivkov's brilliancy against Portisch:

IVKOV–PORTISCH: *1 P–K4, P–K3; 2 P–Q4, P–Q4; 3 N–QB3, B–N5; 4 P–K5, P–QB4; 5 P–QR3, BxNch; 6 PxB, Q–B2; 7 Q–N4, P–B4; 8 Q–N3, N–K2; 9 QxP, R–N1; 10 QxRP, PxP; 11 K–Q1?!, B–Q2; 12 Q–R5ch, K–Q1?; 13 N–K2!, B–R5?; 14 N–B4!, QxKP; 15 Q–B7, B–Q2; 16 B–Q3, Q–Q3; 17 R–K1, P–K4; 18 P–QR4!, B–K1; 19 Q–K6, QxQ; 20 NxQch, K–Q2; 21 N–B5ch, K–B1; 22 RxP, QN–B3; 23 R–K2, RxP; 24 BxPch, K–Q1; 25 NxPch, K–B2; 26 B–B4ch!, N–K4; 27 RxN, NxB; 28 R–K7ch!, K–B3; 29 R–B7ch, K–N3; 30 R–N1ch, K–R3; 31 R–B6ch!! Resigns.*

The exciting chase, first Tal behind Fischer, then with positions reversed, only served to draw comparisons between the two young men. They both had incredible memories and calculating ability. Tal later recalled that he lost his adolescent interest in mathematics because his schoolteacher would not accept the answers he gave on tests because the young schoolboy claimed to do all the calculation in his head, which the teacher said was impossible. Fischer, like Tal, could remember thousands of games at random. After winning his quarter-finals Candidates match from Mark Taimanov of the Soviet Union in 1971, he showed Taimanov all the moves of a 1958 friendly game that Fischer had played with Evgeni Vasyukov in Moscow, when Bobby was 15. Total recall.

Still, it didn't seem to be helping him in the concluding rounds at Bled, since Tal led by a point with two games left. On the 30th Tal quickly drew with Portisch and then spent the next four hours agonizing over Fischer's game with Petrosian. First it appeared that the Armenian's Caro–Kann had equalized easily. On the twenty-third move Petrosian made a small slip and four moves later made another. All of a sudden Fischer had a Queenside majority and the advantage of Bishop against Knight in a tricky endgame. Fischer went after Black's Queenside Pawns, while Petrosian gobbled up the Kingside. On the thirty-fifth move Petrosian walked into a murderous discovered check and resigned in face of mate. "The applause for Fischer that followed was indescribable," reported Lommer, "and it was long minutes before order could be restored for the other games to be continued."

The tournament was up for grabs with one sudden jolt. Fischer was still a half-point behind, but he faced Ivkov, while Tal was up against the Argentine Evergreen, Najdorf. The other significant pairing was Petrosian–Gligorich, with third prize hanging in the balance. This was a disappointing game for Yugoslav fans as they watched "Gliga" gamble two Pawns for scant compensation and then fail to take advantage of Petrosian's weak twentieth move. Petrosian, Gligorich, and Keres (who crushed Donner in twenty-three moves) finished in a tie for third place with $12\frac{1}{2}$–$6\frac{1}{2}$.

Fischer and Tal both gained the upper hand in the endings that resulted from their games. But Tal's technique was superb.

Tal had a big edge with the White pieces but had no clear winning plan. First he played 27 Q–N3! intending 28 B–Q5 or 28 BxN and 29 Q–N6. Najdorf traded into an inferior ending: 27 . . . QxQ; 28 PxQ (threatening 29 BxN followed by 30 R–Q1 and 31 R–R1) N–Q1; 29 P–QN4!, K–B2; 30 R–Q5, K–K1; 31 P–N5, PxP; 32 RxNP, R–B2; 33 R–N6, K–Q2.

White could not take the NP because of . . . K–B2. So he tried 34 B–Q5, R–B5; 35 P–KN3, and Black made things easy with 35 . . . R–QR5 when 35 . . . R–B3; 36 P–QB4, K–B2; 37 P–B5 is still hard. Tal finished off with 36 BxP!, R–R8ch; 37 K–N2, K–B2; 38 R–R6, R–N8; 39 B–Q5, RxP; 40 R–R7ch, N–N2 41 K–B3, and Black was in a complete bind. The game concluded with 41 . . . K–N1; 42 R–R6, K–B2; 43 R–R8, N–B4; 44 R–R7ch, N–N2; 45 P–R4 (White has gained a move) K–N1; 46 R–R6, K–B2; 47 R–R8, R–N4; 48 P–B4, R–N6ch; 49 K–N4 Resigns. White's king will win the Kingside Pawns.

On the adjoining board, Fischer watched the Russian seal control on first place. Fischer could win, lose, or draw in the complex defensive position he had against Ivkov, but he would still finish second. The American gave his opponent excellent chances, and in time pressure, Ivkov misplayed into an ending in which both sides had a Knight and two Queenside pawns, but Fischer held a passed KBP.

While Tal was administering the final coup to Najdorf, Fischer played on. Just before Fischer could mobilize his

SCORETABLE

		T	F	Pe	K	Gl	Ge	Tr	Par	Bi	M	Da	Do	N	O	Po	I	Pa	Be	Ge	U	Total
1.	Tal	X	0	½	½	½	½	½	1	1	1	½	1	1	1	½	1	1	1	1	1	14½-4½
2.	Fischer	1	X	1	½	½	1	1	½	1	½	½	½	½	1	1	½	½	1	½	½	13½-5½
3–5.	Petrosian	½	0	X	½	1	½	½	1	½	½	½	½	1	1	0	½	1	1	1	1	12½-6½
3–5.	Keres	½	½	½	X	½	½	½	½	0	½	½	1	½	1	1	1	1	½	1	1	12½-6½
3–5.	Gligorich	½	½	0	½	X	½	½	½	1	1	½	½	½	½	½	1	1	1	1	1	12½-6½
6–7.	Geller	½	0	½	½	½	X	½	1	0	½	½	½	½	0	1	1	½	1	1	½	10½-8½
6–7.	Trifunovich	½	0	½	½	½	½	X	½	½	½	½	½	½	½	½	½	1	½	1	1	10½-8½
8.	Parma	0	½	0	½	½	0	½	X	½	½	½	½	½	1	½	1	½	½	1	1	10-9
9–10.	Bisguier	0	0	½	1	0	1	½	½	X	0	½	0	1	0	½	1	½	½	1	1	9½-9½
9–10.	Matanovich	0	½	½	½	0	½	½	½	1	X	½	½	0	1	½	½	0	1	1	½	9½-9½
11–13.	Darga	½	½	½	½	½	½	½	½	½	½	X	½	½	0	½	0	½	1	0	1	9-10
11–13.	Donner	0	½	½	0	½	½	½	½	1	½	½	X	1	0	½	1	½	0	0	1	9-10
11–13.	Najdorf	0	½	0	½	½	½	½	½	0	1	½	0	X	1	½	0	½	1	1	½	9-10
14.	Olafsson	0	0	0	0	½	1	½	0	1	0	1	1	0	X	1	½	½	½	½	½	8½-10½
15–16.	Portisch	½	0	1	0	½	0	½	½	½	½	½	½	½	0	X	0	½	½	½	1	8-11
15–16.	Ivkov	0	½	½	0	0	0	½	0	0	½	1	0	1	½	1	X	1	½	½	½	8-11
17.	Pachman	0	½	0	0	0	½	0	½	½	1	½	½	½	½	½	0	X	½	½	½	7-12
18.	Bertok	0	0	0	½	0	0	½	½	½	0	0	1	0	½	½	½	½	X	½	1	6½-12½
19.	Germek	0	½	0	0	0	0	0	0	0	0	1	1	0	½	½	½	½	½	X	½	5½-13½
20.	Udovcich	0	½	0	0	0	½	0	0	0	½	0	0	½	½	0	½	½	0	½	X	4-15

Pawn in support by his King, Ivkov contrived to give up his Knight for two Pawns. He was about to take the last Black Pawn when Fischer extended his hand for the draw.

The player who plays best in a tournament never wins first prize, Tartakover once said. He wins the second prize and finishes behind the player with the most luck. Like most of Tartakover's aphorisms there was just enough truth to bolster the wit. Fischer had come as close to fulfilling his ambitions without actually winning the Bled event. He didn't lose a game, he scored $3\frac{1}{2}$–$\frac{1}{2}$ against the four Russians who had humbled him before, and he finished just a point behind Tal.

Svetozar Gligorich said simply about the result: "Bobby is going to be World Champion."

IX

The Age of Fischer

Chess tournaments are not easy races to predict. Even with a small field of contestants, each of them numerically evaluated by rating and past results, there are as many surprises as in a football season or a golf tournament.

Even less easy to forecast is the location, date, entries and playing conditions of the next great tournament to be held. But as Bobby Fischer was crowned World Champion on September 1, 1972, a close observer could make some good guesses.

The next tournament of significance, you could say, would probably be in the United States, where the chess fever in the summer of '72 filled a vast entertainment vacuum. It would probably be organized by newcomers, that is, by "new money" like James D. Slater, the British financier who had rescued the Fischer–Spassky match with a timely contribution of $120,000. And the invited players would include several would-be successors of Fischer, each of them young, ambitious, and controversial.

231

And those would be exceptionally good guesses. When the event known as "Church's Fried Chicken, Inc. First International Chess Tournament" opened on November 18 in the Mission Room of the San Antonio, Texas, convention center, the Fischer influence was clear although the champion was absent.

Fischer had already begun another of his prolonged self-exiles from competition. Boris Spassky, who was also invited, was said to be "unavailable" by Soviet chess officials. It was no secret, however, that Spassky was being punished for failing to play on the U.S.S.R. team in the Chess Olympics held in Skopje, Yugoslavia, just three weeks after the World Championship match.

The "New money" came from George W. "Bill" Church, Jr., the son of the founder of a fast-food fried chicken empire. Church's Fried Chicken began as one small store in downtown San Antonio in 1952, grew slowly to eight in the south Texas city when the younger Church took over the company in 1962, and by 1972 had blossomed to an international chain of 400 stores, "Grandmasters of Good Food."

The money itself totaled nearly $10,000 in prizes with a $4,000 first. Although this is considerably better than most international events, it was no breakthrough. The last large American tournament of such prestige—New York 1924—dispensed more than $5,000 in prizes at a time when the dollar was worth considerably more. In fact, until the Reykjavik sweepstakes, the richest prize fund by comparison was the 1921 world championship match between Lasker and Capablanca for $20,000.

To make up for the missing Fischer and Spassky, Church and a tournament staff that included the highly respected Harry Golombek of England and George Koltanowski of San Francisco invited a good variety of masters. From the older generation there was Paul Keres, 56, and Svetozar Gligorich, 49, both veterans beginning to slow down in strength. Although virtually every top grandmaster was a teenage champion, the peak years for most players is from

30 to 45. From this middle group the San Antonio tournament had Bent Larsen, 37, Tigran Petrosian, 43, and Lajos Portisch, 35, all in their prime and all still hopeful of becoming World Champion.

Hungriest of all were the youngsters—23-year-old Walter Browne, then representing Australia, 28-year-old Vlastimil Hort of Czechoslovakia, 22-year-old Julio Kaplan of Puerto Rico, 20-year-old Henrique Mecking of Brazil, 26-year-old Duncan Suttles of Canada, and 21-year-old Anatoly Karpov of the U.S.S.R.

Finally, there were five "local" players: Donald Byrne (invited at the last minute when Lubomir Kavalek canceled out), Larry Evans, Anthony Saidy, and Ken Smith of the U.S., and the Mexican champion, Mario Campos-Lopez.

In all, there were ten grandmasters, four international masters, and two without international titles. The average rating of 2,538 made it the strongest large event held outside the Soviet Union in a decade. The rating system, devised by Wisconsin professor Arpad Elo, was introduced into FIDE tournaments as a basis for evaluating players and granting titles two years before. This added a new element to the competition. Ordinarily, for example, Campos-Lopez, a civil engineer and amateur chessplayer, and Smith, a Dallas contractor and chess magazine publisher, would have little chance of accomplishing something in such a tournament because the top prizes would almost certainly go to the grandmasters. But, under the new FIDE rules, they could take a giant step toward the international master title if they made the "IM norm"—in this case, six points. Similarly Suttles, Saidy, Kaplan, and Byrne could not count on brushing past Portisch, Petrosian, Larsen, *et al.* for the top prize. But in San Antonio they could make one of the two results necessary for the grandmaster title if they won one more game than they lost for a score of 8–7.

The first round began at 4 P.M., November 19, at the convention center, two blocks from the Mission San Antonio de Valero, the famous Alamo. Although the city is one of the steadiest growing in the South, San Antonio preserves a large sample of Spanish, French, and Texas Republic heritage in the downtown area, where there are several eighteenth-century missions, cathedrals, and residences.

Characteristically, the first session was interrupted by complaints from Browne about a special row of overhead lights. Instead of the usual problem of dimly lit tournament areas, Browne said it was too bright. Off went $3,000 in lighting. But Evans said it was OK. Back on came the lighting. Finally, another objection—from Mecking—kept it off.

Lighting and first-round jitters may account for some of the excesses that day. Kaplan fought from a bad opening against Mecking and almost equalized in a time scramble. Inexplicably, he wasted all but a few seconds on a blunder and forfeited on the thirty-first move. Saidy also blundered, but he was losing a Bishops-of-opposite-color middlegame to Karpov when the blow fell. However, Portisch's disaster was the worst.

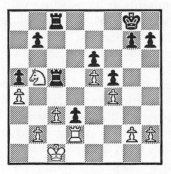

Having won Campos–Lopez's Exchange, the Hungarian could consolidate easily beginning with 29 . . . R–Q4 and 30 . . . R–B5. All of a sudden the sound of dance music from a band in a nearby hall began to pierce the tournament quiet. Portisch, who rivals Browne, not to mention Fischer, in his need for optimum playing conditions, chose 29 . . . R–B5??, overlooking 30 N–Q6 and had to concede a draw to a hooked fish.

Gligorich, who positionally crushed Suttles, joined Karpov, Mecking, Keres, and Larsen in the lead as the round ended. Keres eliminated one of his competitors just by advancing his QP the next day.

KERES-MECKING: *1 P-Q4, N-KB3; 2 P-QB4, P-B4; 3 P-K3, P-K3; 4 N-KB3, P-Q4; 5 N-B3, N-B3; 6 P-QR3, PxBP; 7 BxP, PxP; 8 PxP, B-K2; 9 O-O, O-O; 10 B-B4, P-QN3; 11 Q-Q3, B-N2; 12 QR-Q1, R-B1; 13 B-R2, N-N1?!; 14 KR-K1, N-Q4; 15 B-N1, P-N3; 16 B-R6, NxN; 17 PxN, R-K1; 18 P-B4, Q-Q3; 19 R-K3, B-KB3; 20 P-Q5!, PxP; 21 PxP, N-Q2; 22 B-R2, N-B4?; 23 Q-Q2, RxR; 24 QxR, N-R5?; 25 R-K1, Q-Q1; 26 P-Q6, N-B6; 27 BxPch!, K-R1 28 P-Q7 Resigns.*

Karpov kept up the pace by confusing Browne in the opening with *1 P-QB4, P-QB4; 2 P-QN3!?*. Instead of setting up a Pawn formation with . . . P-Q3 and . . . P-K4, or with . . . P-K3 and . . . P-Q4, Browne played the natural *2 . . . N-KB3; 3 B-N2, P-KN3*, allowing *4 BxN!*. White had a clear advantage in the center after *4 . . . PxB; 5 N-QB3, B-N2; 6 P-N3, N-B3; 7 B-N2, P-B4; 8 P-K3, O-O; 9 KN-K2, P-QR3; 10 QR-B1!, P-QN4; 11 P-Q3, B-N2; 12 O-O, P-Q3; 13 Q-Q2* and established zugzwang on the forty-first move.

Meanwhile Gligorich trapped Donald Byrne's QR on its original square by playing N-QN8!, and Larsen successfully took several risks against Evans.

White's attack, which had looked so promising ten moves before, ran out of steam. Instead of consolidating, Evans played 32 R–K5?! and after 32 . . . BxR; 33 RxB, N–Q6ch; 34 K–N3, NxR; 35 BPxN it appeared that White may have lucked out with a perpetual check.

Despite the apparent dangers Larsen coolly played 35 . . . B–N2!, and White ran out of checks after 36 Q–R8ch, K–K2; 37 Q–B6ch, K–Q2; 38 QxPch, K–B2; 39 Q–B7ch, QxQ; 40 PxQ, B–Q4; and Black won.

When Keres skillfully outplayed Saidy on the Black side of a deadly even position, the oldest man in the event took the lead in the third round. He was perhaps the strongest player who never became World Champion. Keres had never even played in a title match, although he finished second in four consecutive Candidates tournaments. Every new World Championship cycle brought a surprise reversal. Had he drawn quietly in his two games with Smyslov in the 1953 event, he would have tied for first. Three years later he was a half-point behind Smyslov in another Candidates tournament when he blundered away a won position to Dr. Miroslav Filip of Czechoslovakia in the penultimate round. Three years after that he crushed Tal 3–1 but could not defeat the lesser grandmasters as easily as the Latvian. Finally, in 1962 in another penultimate round when he could have nearly clinched the tournament, he lost to the unheralded Pal Benko. Despite this, Keres said that good and bad luck equalized each other eventually: "It all comes out the same in the end, and the final score is always just."

Also in the fourth round Karpov and Larsen drew with one another and Browne returned to form:

BROWNE–KAPLAN: 1 P–K4, P–QB4; 2 N–KB3, P–Q3; 3 P–Q4, PxP; 4 NxP, N–QB3; 5 N–QB3, P–K3; 6 P–KN3, P–QR3; 7 B–N2, B–Q2; 8 O–O, R–B1?; 9 R–K1, N–B3; 10 NxN!, BxN; 11 N–Q5!, BxN; 12 PxB, P–K4; 13 P–KB4, Q–B2; 14 Q–K2, N–Q2; 15 B–R3!, P–B3; 16 B–K3, P–KN3; 17 B–K6, B–N2; 18 QR–B1, Q–B5; 19

Q–N4, R–B2?; 20 P–N3!, Q–B6; 21 BxNch, RxB; 22 Q–
K6ch, K–Q1; 23 B–N6ch, K–B1; 24 R–K4 Resigns.

And as Suttles was scoring his first win (over Smith),
so was another late starter, former World Champion
(1963–1969) Petrosian.

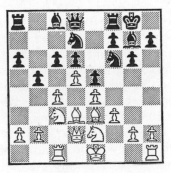

The Armenian has White against "Mr. King's Indian,"
Gligorich. White has geared his pieces to handle the opening of Queenside lines that would follow 11 . . . NPxP;
12 BxP, P–B4. But Gligorich mistakenly reasoned that this
meant White was unprepared for the usual Kingside play
in this variation. So he played 11 . . . P–N5?, 12 N–Q1,
P–B4 and met 13 P–N4 with 13 . . . P–KR4. Normally, this
diversion would give Black at least equal chances on the
King's wing, but here Petrosian redeveloped with 14 N–B2,
PxP; 15 PxP, N–R2; 16 P–KR4.

In a difficult position there is nothing worse than trying
to force the issue. But that is what Gliga did with 16 . . .
P–B4?; 17 NPxP, PxP; 18 PxP, P–K5. White accepted a
second pawn — 19 BxKP, N–K4; 20 N–N3, N–KB3; 21 O–O —
and soon had seized the attack. He won in thirty-five moves.

While Keres drew a careful Benoni Defense with Browne
in the following round, Larsen and Karpov moved up to
join him with relatively easy victories over Campos-Lopez

and Kaplan. In this round Smith "sprang" his favorite opening plan, the Morra Gambit in the Sicilian Defense. Renamed the "Smith–Morra Gambit" and extensively analyzed in Smith's *Chess Digest* magazine, the line looks reasonable, but Smith didn't provide the reason. Against Byrne after *1 P–K4, P–QB4; 2 P–Q4, PxP; 3 P–QB3, PxP; 4 NxP, N–QB3; 5 N–B3, P–Q3; 6 B–QB4, P–K3; 7 O–O, KN–K2!* Smith continued *8 B–KN5, P–QR3!; 9 Q–K2, P–R3; 10 B–R4, Q–R4; 11 B–KN3, N–N3; 12 Q–Q2, KN–K4; 13 NxN, PxN!* — and Black was already winning.

The same day Suttles won an excellent game from Evans in typical fashion. With Black he made eight Pawn moves in the first ten, didn't bring out his King Knight until the thirteenth move, and then sacrificed it on the fourteenth. Evans had taken care to bring his King to safety on the Queenside only to find that Black's wait-and-see strategy allowed him to bombard the Queenside while keeping his own King in the center. Also, Saidy was devastating Mecking until the Brazilian offered a draw. In the preceding time-trouble battle Mecking had been vainly trying to win despite Saidy's superior chances. So, when Mecking made his offer while Saidy was in the process of sealing his forty-first move, the American grabbed it.

In the fifth round two events overshadowed Karpov's grinding victory over Suttles and Gligorich's downing of Portisch, the latter being the latest in the Yugoslav's many attempts to refute the Gruenfeld Defense.

The first incident involved the enfants terrible Browne and Mecking. In addition to the refused invitations mentioned before, the tournament committee received one from Robert Huebner of West Germany. Huebner, who is quite controversial in his own right, told friends that he wasn't going to Texas because of the other players. He could take Browne's antics. And he could probably put up with Mecking, he said, but not with both of them together.

Browne was already known for a loose, semigambling style of play punctuated with outbursts of emotion and complaints. Mecking, an international master at 14 and a millionaire by Brazilian standards before 21, had not matured socially to match his talent and wealth.

When both players plunged into time trouble by the thirtieth move, Mecking began moving his pieces with one hand and hitting the clock button with another. While this saved valuable seconds and is not against the laws of the game, it is proscribed in most "rapid-transit," or speed, tournaments. Browne howled to no avail. As Browne's position deteriorated, both sides accelerated their nervous gestures, Browne twisting and turning in his chair, Mecking bobbing up and down. When the game was to be adjourned and Browne's position was certified as hopeless, he refused to help Mecking fill in the missing time-pressure moves on his scoresheet.

The other affair involved tournament leaders Keres and Larsen. The Dane was, perhaps, the most talented player in the world when given the task of injecting new ideas into old positions. Regularly he accepted bad Pawns and weak pieces in order to complicate the position. True, in one out of four or five games he was defeated by a weaker master, a rabbit. But he usually won the three or four other games, putting him ahead of conservative colleagues who accepted early draws.

The endgame Larsen reached with Keres offered slim chances of a win if there had been Knights on the board, even slimmer with Rooks, but virtually none with Queens on. "One must play for a win," Keres often said. "But only with *reasonable* risk."

Nine out of ten grandmasters, as Fischer would say, would accept a draw offer here. But Larsen played 59 *K–B4?, Q–R7ch; 60 K–N5??* in a desperate attempt to win. The reply was simple but effective: *60 . . . Q–N6!*.

Now White had to contend with a threat of . . . PxP. He had to move his Queen, but to a square that still prevented a check on K4 and a capture on KB6. The only idea was *61 Q–K3, PxP; 62 Q–B4, QxP; 63 QxP, Q–K6ch; 64 Q–B4, Q–K7!; 65 Q–N3, Q–N4ch; 66 K–B4, Q–B4ch; 67 K–K3, QxP,* and on the ninety-first move White conceded.

A blunder, you say. But what happened the next round? Byrne moved into a normal position in the Dragon Sicilian Variation, which he invented. Instead of a careful waiting move he found a loss of the Exchange which ended the game and put Karpov back in the lead. Hort took a big edge out of the opening against Portisch but matched one slight error, losing the initiative, on the twentieth turn, with a gross piece-losing blunder on the twenty-fifth. "My hand should be cut off for making this move," said the amiable, atheletic Hort.

Worst of all was Kaplan–Suttles, a battle between the two likeliest grandmaster prospects—an Argentine-born, red-haired mathematics student and an American-born Canadian mathematics student.

In an up-and-down positional duel Kaplan (pronounced Ka-plahn) refused a draw offered and played *32 P–QB4?*,

PxP; 33 BxP?, banking on 33 . . . NxP; 34 B–Q5, NxR; 35 BxR with a draw likely. However, *33 . . . NxP; 34 B–Q5?* was met by *34 . . . R–B8ch!* winning a Rook.

After six rounds: Karpov and Keres, 5½–½; Gligorich, 4½–1½; Petrosian, 4–2; Larsen, Mecking, and Suttles, 3½–2½.

In the seventh round Browne lost to Hort by following theoretical continuations in Alekhine's Defense and reaching a lost position after sixteen moves. The other games were quiet draws or one-sided matchups. Karpov and Keres kept the lead a full point over Gligorich.

This margin widened to two points as Karpov systematically walked over the Yugoslav's Ruy Lopez and Keres won the Brilliancy Prize against Byrne.

In five moves White has levitated one Rook to KB4 via QR4 and the other from K1 to K5. Now, following the simple retreat *27 R–B3!*, Black had great difficulties in protecting his Kingside Pawns from capture and from corruption after P–KR4–5.

Byrne banked on the Queenside with *27 . . . P–N5; 28 N–K2, P–R5!?* so that on 29 PxP he wins with . . . N–B5. There followed *29 QxP, P–R6; 30 PxP, PxP.* The passed Pawn cannot easily be restrained, e.g. 31 Q–Q2, R–B7 or 31 P–N4, P–R7; 32 R–R3, R–B7, or 31 N–B4, P–R7; 32 NxP, P–R8(Q)ch; 33 K–N2, QxR!

Keres responded *31 R–N5!!*, which threatened Rook captures on KB7 or KN6. On 31 . . . P–K3, for example, White plays 32 R–B6 and captures on KN6 the following move. Or 31 . . . R–B8ch; 32 K–N2!, Q–B7 (covering KN6) 33 NxR.

Byrne might as well die a rich man, so he played *31 . . . P–R7; 32 RxP!, P–R8(Q)ch*, and after *33 K–N2 resigned* in face of immediate mate.

Keres's colleague in first place was a mystery to most westerners. Unlike the other tournament youths, Anatoly "Tolya" Karpov tended to fade into the background. He was exceptionally quiet, almost shy compared with the gregarious Browne and irascible Mecking. His chess was strong, of course, but lacked the bizarre, provocative nature that was distinctly Suttles' or the solid aggression of Hort. "Style?" Karpov said. "I have no style." He was simply extremely impressive without quite impressing.

Karpov was born in the southern Urals in 1951 and learned the moves from his father when he was 4. He had hardly begun school when he was playing in tournaments. At 11 he was a candidate-master, the equivalent of U.S. master. Four years later, after his family had moved to Tula, about 100 miles south of Moscow, Karpov was a Soviet master, and four years after that a grandmaster.

His first international challenge was the 1969 world Junior Championship in Stockholm. The Soviet entrants in these biennial events are always rated as favorites, but somehow no Russian had succeeded in winning since Boris Spassky did it in 1955.

With his trainer, grandmaster Semyon Furman, at his side, Karpov began the preliminaries in Stockholm very uncertainly. He was on the verge of elimination when Werner Hug of Switzerland missed a mate in four moves against him. And Karpov held a hopeless endgame against Eugenio Torre in which the Russian had rook and bishop against the Filipino's rook, bishop and two connected pawns. But both Hug and Torre misplayed, and Karpov sailed into the finals. Not looking back, Karpov won his first eight games in the finals and finished three points ahead of his nearest rivals.

And he hadn't looked back since. He tied for first in both the 1971 Moscow and the 1971–1972 Hastings tournaments. Moscow, especially, was a major success, for it was hailed as the strongest international tournament in the Soviet Union in fifteen years.

Somehow this slightly built, almost frail economics student from Leningrad State University was leading another tournament with his typical policy of playing long, exacting battles that exhaust everyone else. Most of all, Karpov could play to win in the style of his first hero, Capablanca. That is, by taking no risks and avoiding a loss at all costs. From San Antonio until the final Candidates match of 1974, he played in more than 100 games with masters and grandmasters. He lost six.

And one of these losses came in the ninth round against Portisch:

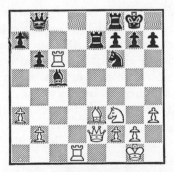

Portisch's advanced Rook on QB6 is endangered, and the natural protection (22 N–Q4, Q–K4!) tends to favor Black. So White sacrifices soundly: *22 RxN!, PxR; 23 N–Q4*, intending to drop a Knight on KB5 or QB6.

Karpov doesn't have to be prodded, and he played *23 ... BxN; 24 RxB, Q–K4!*. Black is ready to consolidate with 25 ... R–K3 and 26 ... R–QB1. Portisch found *25 Q–B3* with threats of 26 R–N4ch or 26 R–Q5 followed by 27 B–Q4.

At this critical moment, Karpov makes an uncharacteristic blunder which later proves to cost him nearly $1,700. With 25 ... P–B4; 26 R–Q5, QxP!; 27 B–Q4 Black can survive with 27 ... Q–N8ch and 28 ... P–B3. But Karpov tried

25 . . . K–R1?? instead and resigned on the spot following *26 R–Q5* because now 26 . . . QxP; 27 B–Q4, Q–N8ch; 28 K–R2 allowed a crushing 29 BxPch.

Meanwhile Larsen continued a pattern of winning with White one round – and losing with Black the next. This time he victimized Hort in a Knight-vs.-bad-Bishop ending. Browne was upset by Campos-Lopez, Gligorich swindled Kaplan into a draw, and Smith got a second chance to play his gambit. This time after *1 P–K4, P–QB4; 2 P–Q4, PxP; 3 P–QB3, PxP; 4 NxP, N–QB3; 5 N–B3, P–Q3; 6 B–QB4* Evans played 6 . . . *P–QR3; 7 O–O, N–B3; 8 B–KN5, P–K3 9 Q–K2, P–R3.* In just a few moves White's initiative was ended: *10 B–R4, P–KN4!; 11 B–KN3, N–KR4!; 12 KR–Q1?, NxB; 13 RPxN, P–N5; 14 N–K1, N–K4; 15 B–N3, P–KR4!* and Black won in forty moves.

After the tenth round Karpov had rejoined Keres at the top of the tournament with eight points, followed by Larsen, Petrosian, and Portisch 1½ back and Gligorich and Suttles at 6. In the following round Byrne played the "worst game" of his life against Browne, Suttles saved a hopeless ending the Exchange down against Larsen and Smith scored his first win with Kaplan being the victim. The leadership was shaken up as three themes began to emerge: Karpov began to play safe with draws, Keres began to falter, and Petrosian and Portisch started to win.

The key game saw Keres miscalculate a tricky position. With 21 . . . R–K1! here, the Estonian forces 22 Q–Q5 (22 B–N2 hangs a Bishop to 22 . . . N–K7ch and 23 . . . R–K4) QxQ; 23 BxQ, R–Q1; 24 R–K1, P–N3 and a sure draw.

What he overlooked was that by playing *21 . . . N–K7ch* instead, after *22 K–N2, NxP; 23 RPxN, QxB* Portisch had the crushing *24 Q–B7!*. Black was then paralyzed by threats of 24 Q–B8ch and 24 B–Q5. The game ended with *24 . . . P–KR3; 25 B–Q5, K–R2; 26 Q–N8ch, K–N3; 27 B–B7ch!, K–N4; 28 QxPch* (28 Q–R7! was faster) *K–B4; 29 B–R5, K–K3; 30 B–N4ch, P–B4; 31 BxPch, KxB; 32 Q–B7ch Resigns.*

December 4 was the date of the twelfth round, another key session. Suttles virtually clinched the grandmaster norm by beating Campos-Lopez for a score of 7½–4½. Keres let Smith escape a Rook ending with a draw, and Gligorich saved a ridiculous game against Saidy in which the American won a piece on the twentieth move of an early endgame and then played weakly enough to lose on the fifty-third turn.

Karpov continued to keep the lead by drawing, but when he again split the point in round 13, Petrosian and Portisch moved up to within a half-point of the youngster by winning. Portisch's was a tidy ending against the fading Saidy, but the Armenian won a bizarre game from Larsen.

After several attempts to break out of his "prison of draws," as he put it, Petrosian took Larsen's opening (1 P–Q4, P–K3; 2 N–KB3, P–KB4; 3 P–KN3, N–KB3; 4 B–N2, P–QN4!?) apart. Gligorich, who had been talking to Petrosian while Larsen was considering his fourth move was stunned speechless by . . . P–QN4. After twenty-seven moves:

Black is helpless against the savage 28 B–N6!, e.g. 28 . . . Q–K2; 29 Q–B2 wins the Exchange with the threat of B–R7ch and N–N6ch. But "Petrosian never advances when he can retreat," as one U.S. grandmaster remarked, and White played 28 B–N2?. After 28 . . . N–Q2; 29 RxP, P–B4; 30 PxP, N–N3; 31 R–R5, NxP Black appeared to have solved most of the immediate crises.

But Petrosian's 32 R–N3!, R–Q1 33 RxB! forced the issue into an ending which must favor White's several minor pieces and Rooks. On 32 . . . R–N1 White would have played RxB anyway since the Exchange sacrifice is even sounder than the Queen sacrifice.

In rapidly deepening time trouble the game continued: 33 . . . N–K6; 34 Q–K2, R–Q8ch; 35 QxR, NxQ; 36 RxRP, N–K6; 37 R(6)–R7, N–B4; 38 P–N4!, Q–Q1!. Black's last hope was a penetrating advance of his Queen. This would be foiled by 39 B–B3, for example 39 . . . Q–Q7; 40 PxN threatening mate in three and not permitting a perpetual check.

Once again Petrosian let his opponent off the hook with 39 P–R3??, allowing 39 . . . Q–Q7 with the idea of perpetual check after 40 N–N6?, Q–K8ch; 41 K–R2, Q–N6ch. And, naturally, Larsen returned the compliment by choosing 31 . . . Q–Q8ch??; 32 K–R2, Q–Q5, after which 41 N–N6 forced a very favorable ending for White with 41 . . . N–K6; 42 RxPch.

The final act came on the fifty-second move:

Larsen, who had muffed his easy win against Suttles earlier in the day when this adjourned game was resumed, now played *52 . . . N–N4??* when the simple *52 . . . N–K4; 53 K–K3, NxP!* is a drawn King-and-Pawn ending. He overlooked that *53 B–B5, K–B3; 54 K–K3!* was playable because the B is indirectly protected by the pregnant NP. After *54 . . . N–K3; 55 BxN, KxB; 56 K–K4, K–B3; 57 K–Q5* White won with his Knight Pawn in a few moves.

Every session of such drama deserves a breath of relief, and this was provided by the Smith-Morra Gambit:

SMITH–MECKING: *1 P–K4, P–QB4; 2 P–Q4, PxP; 3 P–QB3, PxP; 4 NxP, N–QB3; 5 N–B3, P–Q3; 6 B–QB4, P–QR3; 7 O–O, N–B3; 8 P–QR3?, P–K3; 9 Q–K2, P–R3; 10 R–Q1, P–K4; 11 N–Q5, B–K2; 12 B–K3, NxN!; 13 PxN, N–N1; 14 NxP??, PxN; 15 P–B4, PxP; 16 P–Q6, PxB; 17 QxP, N–B3; 18 B–Q5, O–O; 19 BxN, B–N4! 20 Resigns.*

With two rounds left any one of seven players could share the $4,000 first prize: Karpov with 9½ points; Petrosian and Portisch at 9; Gligorich and Keres at 8½; or Larsen and Suttles at 8. Karpov drew a short game in the fourteenth round with Keres, while Larsen was going into contortions to squeeze a point of Gligorich. The Yugoslav, who was under medication for bronchitis during most of the tournament, lightened a difficult endgame by making two moves in a row. It seems that while Gliga was away from the board, Larsen got up before making his intended twentyninth move, Bishop to Bishop two. Gligorich returned to an empty table, saw nothing on the board to change his intention to play his Rook one square up from the Rook-file, and did so. Only when Larsen returned to the scene and figured out why Black had gotten an extra move in, was the position corrected. Still, only a draw.

This was another good day for Tigran Petrosian, who sailed through his Mexican opponent with maneuvers even Suttles might blush at:

CAMPOS-LOPEZ-PETROSIAN: *1 P-K4, P-K3; 2 P-Q4,
P-Q4; 3 N-QB3, B-N5; 4 P-K5, P-QN3; 5 N-B3, B-B1!;
6 B-K2, N-K2; 7 O-O, N-N3; 8 R-K1, B-K2; 9 P-KN3,
P-QB4; 10 P-KR4?!, P-KR3; 11 B-Q3, N-B1!?; 12 P-R4,
P-R3; 13 P-QR5?, P-B5; 14 B-B1, P-QN4; 15 B-Q2,
N-B3; 16 B-R3, P-N5; 17 N-K2, NxRP; 18 P-R5, N-B3;
19 N-R2, Q-N3; 20 B-K3, P-R4; 21 P-N3, B-R3; 22
N-QB1, B-QN4; 23 P-B4, P-R5; 24 PxRP, RxP; 25
RxR, BxR; 26 N-B3, N-QR2!; 27 P-B5, N-N4; 28 R-B1,
N-B6; 29 Q-K1, BxP; 30 P-B6, PxP; 31 PxP, B-Q3;
32 Q-Q2, B-K5; 33 N-K5 Resigns.*

Petrosian and Portisch were models of impassivity but
with a difference. While Petrosian was always the good-
natured, almost lighthearted traveler away from the board,
Portisch was always serious. Petrosian was never upset
by noise the way the Hungarian was, probably because of
his hearing aid. After a long tenth round win over Mecking,
the Armenian was unruffled but his opponent was fuming
about alleged improprieties. Petrosian bobbed his legs up
and down, Mecking said. And he stirred his coffee with a
rattle. And he rolled a coin across the table. And he kept
nudging the table. "After two protests I told the judge the
only way to keep him quiet was to tie his hands and feet."

But the charges—especially because they were coming
from Mecking—were ignored by Tigran, who just turned
off his hearing aid and watched the Brazilian wunderkind
forfeit on the eighty-seventh move.

Petrosian's tournament plan was simple: you only need
so many points to win a tournament. There was no reason to
overexert yourself. He was always a tough opponent but
somehow lacked the fighting spirit of a Tal, a Fischer, or a
Viktor Korchnoi.* "I never had any ambitions and I never

---

* Mikhail Tal tells a pair of stories of this difference in fighting style. In
1965 Korchnoi was approached by reporters after he had won the Asztalos
Memorial Tournament in Ghyula, Hungary. Korchnoi's score was an incredible fourteen wins and one draw. The tournament winner traditionally
tells the press what a wonderful tournament it was, how worthy his op-

will," he said at San Antonio. "That is my happiness and my unhappiness."

It was Karpov and Petrosian at 10 points when the last round began, followed by Portisch a half-point behind, and the two elder statesmen, Keres and Gligorich, just beyond that. There was still a mathematical chance that if Larsen won his last round he would leap ahead of Hort and Suttles, with whom he was tied, and into third place. This chance was the basis for most of the tension as the tournament drew to a close on Sunday, December 10.

Most last rounds, however, are dull because the majority of the players have little chance of bettering their score and prize money enough to risk an all-out attack. Byrne, who had a creditable 6½ points, was in no fighting mood and neither was Hort, who had Black. They drew in twenty moves. Shorter was Kaplan–Keres: fifteen moves.

And shortest of all were the games of the two tournament leaders, Karpov and Petrosian. According to one eye-witness, "Petrosian offered Suttles a draw, Suttles coughed, and Petrosian accepted his handshake before Suttles knew what he was agreeing to." This was after ten moves, one more than Karpov and Mecking finished. After making his draw offer to Suttles, Petrosian walked to Karpov's board, whispered something to him, and almost immediately the two of the youngest players in the tournament had agreed on a draw.

This was all witnessed by none other than Bobby Fischer, who was in San Antonio for a three-day convention of his faith, the Worldwide Church of God. Fischer arrived with

---

ponents are, etc. But Korchnoi complained bitterly about that one draw. How could I let him draw this position, he said angrily, to no one in particular.

Six years later Korchnoi faced Petrosian in the tenth game of their semifinals Candidates match. Petrosian led 1–0 with eight draws and only needed to avoid losing. He sealed his forty-first move, a winning move, and then . . . offered a draw. Korchnoi refused. When the game was resumed, Kochnoi saw the sealed move, recognized its strength, and said, "Well, draw or I'll resign." Petrosian said "Draw."

Korchnoi wasn't satisfied by draws even when victory was not essential. Petrosian accepted draws even when he was winning.

the charismatic leader of the booming church, Garner Ted Armstrong. As the two Russians signed scoresheets and walked over to survey Portisch's game, Fischer, watching the games through binoculars, made his only comment: "They're chicken."

Petrosian had achieved his tournament plan and would tie for first place with Karpov. But Portisch could also tie for the biggest prize. Mathematics played a role here. If Portisch won, the Russians would share $7,000 with him, or $2,333 a piece. But if Portisch drew or lost, Petrosian and Karpov would have $3,000 each. From Portisch's point of view it looked this way: a loss gave a tie for fourth place, or $650, a draw was worth $850, but a win was nearly $1,500 more. He had to play for the win. Fortunately for the Hungarian, his opponent was Larsen, who had his own prize money to think about. If Larsen drew, he would tie for sixth with a mere $400. But a victory would give him a share of fourth place, or $600, while a loss meant about $250 and a tie for eighth place. It was in his interest, too, to fight in the last round.

PORTISCH–LARSEN: *1 P–Q4, P–K3; 2 P–QB4, P–QB4; 3 P–Q5, PxP; 4 PxP, P–Q3; 5 N–QB3, P–KN3; 6 N–B3, B–N2; 7 B–B4, N–KB3; 8 Q–R4ch!?, B–Q2; 9 Q–N3, Q–B2; 10 P–K4, O–O; 11 B–K2.*

Black's development is somewhat confused as a result of
8 Q-R4ch since his QB is misplaced on the best developing square for the QN. There are several ideas for Black
(11 . . . P-QR3 and 12 . . . B-N5, 11 . . . R-K1), but the
sharpest, and probably the best attempt at refutation of
White's opening, is 11 . . . P-QN4!, e.g. 12 NxP, BxN; 13
BxB, NxKP or 12 BxP, NxKP!; 13 NxN, Q-R4ch or 13 . . .
R-K1.

11	. . .	N-R4?!
12	B-K3	N-R3
13	N-Q2!	P-B4

This is a consequence of 11 . . . N-R4 since Black would
not allow 14 BxN without some active play in exchange for
the ruined Pawn structure and since Larsen would rebel
against playing 13 . . . N-B3.

14	PxP	PxP!
15	BxKN	P-B5
16	O-O!	PxB
17	PxP	N-N5?

Black has two Bishops and some interesting chances on
the Kingside because of the temporary misplacement of
White's pieces. With 17 . . . B-B4!?, for example, Black
retains the possibilities of . . . Q-K2-KR5, . . . N-N5-Q6
and . . . B-Q6. On 18 P-K4 White gives up a good center
square for his pieces. Black should then play 18 . . . B-Q2
intending . . . P-QN4 or . . . N-N5.

18	N(3)-K4!	P-R4
19	N-N5!	. . .

White has a very strong game on the Kingside now, and
he rushes to add the heaviest piece to the attack.

19	...	P–R5
20	Q–B4	P–R3
21	N–K6	BxN
22	PxB	P–Q4
23	B–B7ch	K–R1
24	Q–R4	Q–K4!

Otherwise White would win simply with N–B3, Q–R5, and N–R4–N6ch. Larsen offers an Exchange sacrifice to break the attack: 25 P–K7, QxKPch; 26 K–R1, QxN; 27 PxR(Q)ch, RxQ with survival chances.

25	N–B3!	QxKPch
26	K–R1	N–Q6

Again, Black cannot handle the Knight intrusion with tries such as 26 ... N–B3; 27 QR–K1 or 26 ... Q–K5; 27 QxQ, PxQ; 28 N–R4.

27	QR–K1!	...

A very fine winning move. The Exchange can be returned quickly when White plays Q–R5 with the dual threat of P–K7 and N–R4. Portisch made the move quickly, knowing as a strong grandmaster does that such a sacrifice must be sound.

SCORETABLE

	Kar	Pe	Po	G	Ke	H	Su	L	M	By	Br	E	Kap	C	Sa	Sm	Total
1–3. Karpov	X	½	0	1	½	½	1	½	½	1	1	½	½	1	1	1	10½–4½
1–3. Petrosian	½	X	½	1	½	½	½	1	1	½	½	½	½	1	1	1	10½–4½
1–3. Portisch	1	½	X	0	1	1	½	1	½	½	½	½	1	½	1	1	10½–4½
4. Gligorich	0	0	1	X	½	½	1	½	½	1	1	½	½	1	1	1	10–5
5. Keres	½	½	0	½	X	1	½	1	1	1	½	0	½	1	1	½	9½–5½
6–7. Hort	½	½	0	½	0	X	½	0	1	½	1	½	1	1	1	1	9–6
6–7. Suttles	0	½	½	0	½	½	X	½	½	½	½	1	1	1	1	1	9–6
8–9. Larsen	½	0	0	½	0	1	½	X	0	1	0	1	1	1	1	1	8½–6½
8–9. Mecking	½	0	½	½	0	0	½	1	X	½	1	½	1	1	½	1	8½–6½
10. Byrne	0	½	½	0	0	½	½	0	½	X	0	1	½	1	1	1	7–8
11–12. Browne	0	½	½	0	½	0	½	1	0	1	X	½	1	0	0	1	6½–8½
11–12. Evans	½	½	½	½	1	½	0	0	½	0	½	X	0	½	½	1	6½–8½
13. Kaplan	½	½	0	½	½	0	0	0	0	½	0	1	X	1	½	0	5–10
14–15. Campos	0	0	½	0	0	0	0	0	0	0	1	½	0	X	1	½	3½–11½
14–15. Saidy	0	0	0	0	0	0	0	0	½	0	1	½	½	0	X	1	3½–11½
16. Smith	0	0	0	0	½	0	0	0	0	0	0	0	1	½	0	X	2–13

27 ...	NxR
28 RxN	Q–Q6

Here Portisch took his time to calculate a forced win. On 29 P–K7?, RxB or 29 N–K5?, BxN; 30 QxPch, Q–R2; 31 QxQch, KxQ; 32 RxB, P–B5; 33 RxP, KR–Q1! Black is able to turn the tables.

29 Q–R5!	P–R6
30 P–QN3	B–B6
31 P–K7	K–N2

White forces a Queen capture on 31 . . . RxB; 32 QxR, BxR 33 N–K5. Larsen can put this off for only a few moves.

32 PxR(Q)ch	RxQ
33 BxP!	BxR
34 Q-K5ch	R–B3
35 Q–K7ch	Resigns

The race was over and ended in a photo-finish three-way tie. For Petrosian it was another trophy, for Portisch another credential, and for Karpov another big step toward the World Championship. For the rest it would be just a wait until the next great tournament.

Index of Players

(*Games and Fragments*)

Index of Openings